ETHICS FOR A SHRINKING WORLD

Also by Gerard Elfstrom

MILITARY ETHICS   (*with N. Fotion*)

Ethics for a Shrinking World

Gerard Elfstrom
Assistant Professor of Philosophy
Auburn University, Alabama

St. Martin's Press   New York

First published in the United States of America in 1990

Printed in Hong Kong

ISBN 0–312–03204–8

Library of Congress Cataloging-in-Publication Data
Elfstrom, G. (Gerard)
Ethics for a shrinking world/Gerard Elfstrom.
p.   cm.
Bibliography: p.
Includes index.
ISBN 0–312–03204–8: $39.95 (est.)
1. International relations—Moral and ethical aspects.   I. Title.
JX1255.E44   1990
172′4—dc20   89–33433
                                                        CIP

Contents

v

Introduction

Well-intentioned failure often provides the best occasion for moral reflection and the most fertile source of moral insight. This work was inspired by such a failure, that of the American President, Jimmy Carter. He wished to establish a foreign policy based on even-handed concern for the moral rights of all humanity. For the citizen, the prospect of a great power setting aside its customary hypocrisy and attempting a policy of genuine moral sensitivity was cause for elation. For the philosopher, the theoretical difficulties of this goal offered intriguing possibilities for reflection. How, for example, can one nation justify intervention in the domestic affairs of another? What is the difference between strictly domestic problems, such as corruption in government, and issues which demand international attention, such as genocide? Or are there any genuine principles of international distributive justice?

These and other issues gave theoretical exercise, but Carter's program came to grief for other reasons. It floundered on the barrier of domestic politics and also on practical difficulties which arose, for instance, when concerns of national security collided with those of human rights, as occurred in the Philippines and South Korea. However, the most basic problems were those of how to go about institutionalizing moral sensitivity and making it a continually effective influence on policy.

Carter's idea, as so many others in his tenure, sprang full blown from his brow. In good engineer's fashion, he analyzed the issue, worked out his response, then attempted to impose it on an unwilling and bewildered constituency. At this stage his plans quickly bogged down. This pattern is a widely recognized feature of Carter's style as President. But what is not so well appreciated is that philosophers and theoreticians often reproduce his engineer's approach. They believe it sufficient to examine problems in a vacuum, pronounce one course of action or another correct, and then castigate those who fail to heed their prescriptions. The mistake lies in a failure to examine the context in which action must occur. Standards of conduct which are feasible in an established society with common values and effective means of enforcement cannot be directly applied to the international arena. Ethical analysis of international relations must take its special conditions into account if it is to avoid futility and irrelevancy.

1

The international conditions which confirm the difficulty of this project also underscore its necessity. The breakdown of European colonial empires and the increasing impotence of the great powers to mold international affairs have resulted in an unruly world which contains a large number of small, youthful nations with little experience in self-government and less in international affairs. These nations, often poor and frequently squabbling, are the scene of enormous human suffering resulting from natural causes, human incompetence, or old-fashioned greed and viciousness. The great powers themselves contribute in various ways to human anguish, not least by maintaining the threat of nuclear war. Their enormous power and wide ranging interests seem to have dulled their moral sensitivity rather than the reverse. Immense resources have allowed them to ignore the thinking of others and the genuine condition of the world, as well as the real limitations of their own power – luxuries which other nations cannot afford. Yet part of the thesis of this work is that these same conditions not only allow morally responsible action but provide grounds for the hope that a genuine moral culture can be achieved, one with shared principles and institutions which would nurture greater moral rigor and more widespread responsibility. The challenge and the opportunity which the current situation provides are the touchstones of the ideas developed here.

Moral problems which arise on the international level can be usefully sorted as concerning the use of violence in international affairs, the limitations of sovereignty of individual governments, and the moral significance of national borders. In view of this, a lengthy chapter is devoted to a sampling of the problems of each sort. Given the concern of this work for the concrete situation in which moral action occurs, the concluding chapter is devoted to an examination of what factors currently undermine international moral sensitivity, how these can be overcome, and how we may work to shape institutions so that a more ambitious ethic can be expected in the future.

The first order of business, however, must be an examination of the characteristics and problems of the ethics of international relations, laying out the normative principles which will guide the analyses of this work, and illustrating the ways in which they must be applied to concrete issues. This is the project of Chapter 1.

1 Issues and Challenges

The world is closing in. Famine, genocide, oppression and terrorism are as near as the evening news, and jet transport makes them physically close as well. The current travels in both directions. Comfortable Westerners can easily devise ways to make money in far corners – or destroy them in a twinkling. The forces that bring the world closer also magnify the potential for doing good and doing ill. In the past it was easy to remain ignorant of distant suffering and even easier to remain indifferent to it. Yet, though the earth now touches more closely, old ideas of moral responsibility and moral accountability remain.

It is widely recognized that pictures, whether in magazines or on television, are better able to touch human feeling than any number of words. Pictures of starving children or dazed refugees make human suffering clear and immediate, and are capable of prompting vague feelings of a moral responsibility to act.[1] But people, whether ordinary citizens, politicians or theoreticians, are generally uncertain of how to respond to the twinges and starts of conscience prompted by the latest electronic marvels. Is it the responsibility of individuals to give assistance in these cases of human need, of governments, of both? Should assistance extend to welcoming refugees into one's homeland? But don't citizens have the prior obligation to attend to the needy already among them? And what about violations of human rights by governments or individuals? Who has a responsibility to remedy those? Or should the sovereignty of foreign governments always be inviolate? Many claim that these twinges should be ignored, that moral responsibilities end at national borders, and that there is no place for moral constraint in the international arena.

The task of this work is to begin to lay such doubts and uncertainties to rest by showing what an ethics of international relations should look like and by exploring the conditions under which it is feasible. Challenges come from two directions, from skeptics who doubt that any such ethics is possible and from those moralists who insist on an ethics founded only on the strictest standards of moral accountability.[2] The danger of the skeptics is obvious, but the stringent moralists pose a more subtle threat, that of undercutting the feasibility and credibility of international ethics by ignoring its special constraints. Too often moralists proceed as

3

though the problems of human life are met in a Kantian kingdom of selfless, rational deliberators. The world and its actors are not like that, and a morality which is to make a difference must take note of the contrast. This point applies *both* to the ethics of personal relations and to the ethics of international relations. However, the lapse is less important on the personal level. In part this is because individual actors have greater control over their personal decisions than when they function as part of an institution. Also, human societies contain structures and pressures which both define and encourage morally responsible conduct but which are absent on the international level. The Kantian perspective, while flawed, works better and is more plausible when focused on problems of individual life. It is less satisfactory when the focus is on individuals operating within institutions or on relations between the institutions themselves.

Oddly, these two challenges are rooted in a common misconception. They fail to recognize that the way in which moral issues arise on the international level, and the way in which they must be met, differ from problems of individual relations. Because the ethics of personal relations is the source of preconceptions of what a genuine ethics must be like, people are disoriented when they face moral difficulties which diverge from this model. Both skeptics and moralists suffer from this disorientation, with the former insisting that the differences of the two levels rule out any ethics at all, while the latter respond that an international ethics must be exactly like personal ethics.

Skeptics are fond of arguing that the international arena closely resembles a Hobbesian state of nature.[3] They are quick to draw the conclusion that in such conditions none but the foolhardy would subject themselves to moral restraint. Moralists all too often agree with this inference and are then obliged to attack the premise. That is, they must devise heroic arguments in the attempt to show that, appearance to the contrary, the international arena is an essentially civil place. The root of their heroics is the view, shared with skeptics, that all morality must closely resemble the paradigm set by the moral relations of individual human beings.

These misconceptions are best allayed by careful examination of the ways in which an ethics of international relations must diverge from ethics on the personal level. These differences require changes in thinking about the way in which ethics should function. Once they are understood, however, a serviceable and humane ethics of international relations is entirely feasible. It is not sufficient to make an assessment of how leaders ought to act on the basis of abstract analysis of moral principles. The context of moral action determines what agents can, and cannot, reasonably be expected to do. Since leaders cannot be obliged to do what circumstances forbid, this understanding of context must be part of the overall normative analysis. For this reason analysis must also focus on the conditions shaping international relations. A clear-headed understanding of these conditions will reveal how the international arena allows the operation of an ethics, but one which, oddly perhaps, must be less precise and more dependent on individual initiative and solitary reflection than personal ethics. International affairs are not as essentially Hobbesian as some believe, but neither do they resemble a well-ordered society.

SPECIAL FEATURES AND CHALLENGES OF THE ETHICS OF INTERNATIONAL RELATIONS

Both philosophers and ordinary people are accustomed to thinking of moral problems in terms of face-to-face relations between individuals, where responsibilities are clearly defined and enforced by cultural sanctions.[4] On the level of international relations all of these elements change. There are differences in the kinds of relationships, the nature of the agency involved, and the context in which moral activity must occur. While the combination of these is not sufficient to make the ethics of international relations essentially different from that of personal relations, it does require some adjustment of moral thinking and moral sensitivity.

On the level of personal relations, for example, the traditional focus of attention is the directly intended and foreseen consequences of individual action. The usual assumption is that the moral agent need not be greatly concerned about people with whom he or she has no direct, personal contact. The reason for this is clear. The range of consequences of the acts of even quite skilled and clever persons is usually quite limited. So long as they take care to treat others they encounter decently, people can be fairly sure that their moral accounts are in order. Furthermore, in advanced industrialized societies at least, they can be confident that institutions exist, both governmental and social, to assist people who are in substantial need and are unable to look after themselves. Where these needs are unmet, the ordinary person is likely to assume that the responsibility to set things right lies elsewhere and is not the burden of the private individual. There are exceptions to this general view, of course. Private individuals do sometimes feel obligated to take action to remedy social ills or to exercise due care, lest by inadvertence they cause harm to some unknown person. These exceptions, however, are comparatively minor and do not alter people's view of their normal moral responsibilities.

   In contrast, the activities of institutions, whether governments or business corporations, reverberate much louder and farther. Directly intended consequences are very important and give scope to all manner of mischief. But given the great power of these institutions and the complexity of their interaction with the world, what is unforeseen and unintended is quite likely to wash far beyond the institution itself and substantially affect the well-being of large numbers of persons. An automobile company, for example, may require platinum for the emissions control equipment on its cars and be willing to pay high prices for it. But, in establishing its lines of supply, it may be propping up a despotic regime. Or a powerful nation may undertake to construct military bases in a region of strategic importance, astride major shipping lanes perhaps. In seeking this end, though, it forces its attentions on an unwilling government and upsets the delicate political balance of the region.

   In large institutions such as governments the head is likely to be far from the body. Those who make decisions, and are accountable for them, may be poorly placed to grasp the full spectrum of effects of their policies. It is possible, of course, that decision-makers cannot reasonably be held accountable for distant and intricate effects. They may well have difficulty simply keeping track of the institutions they are pledged to manage. Concern for indirect and unintended effects rippling out beyond the institution itself may be too much to ask. They are quite likely to be limitless, and it is often humanly impossible either to become aware of them or react effectively to them. It may also be impossible to determine just which of these myriad consequences should be of moral concern and which can be safely ignored.

   In view of these complexities it is plausible to believe that whatever human suffering is caused in this unforeseen fashion is a regrettable aspect of human life but one for which it is unreasonable to assign moral responsibility. This result is not fatal for an ethics of international relations, but it would yield a lot of territory to the skeptic. A workable ethics may be able to accommodate this outcome, but it certainly should not be accepted without considerable soul-searching. It is worth having a look to see whether the application of an international ethics can avoid it.

But the challenge of inadvertence raises another. Individuals who are selected for positions of authority normally have a clear sense of the responsibilities they owe the institution and the goals they are pledged to seek. These are often explicit in legal statute or corporate code. Business leaders, for example, are normally made to understand that they have a duty to seek profits or growth. The responsibilities of leaders of governments are more complex and wide-ranging, but certainly include looking after national security and seeing to the material needs of their citizens. These duties and responsibilities are commonly taken as a moral trust. Both leaders and their constituents know what these obligations are and agree that their positions are being well filled if these goals are actively and successfully pursued. Responsibilities of this sort are none too different from the clearly understood responsibilities of individual persons. Each life holds a variety of known obligations to definite individuals, such as parent to child or worker to worker. People understand and accept these and feel secure in their moral rectitude when they comply with them.

Often enough, people will find conflicts among the duties of their ordinary lives. People recognize them as moral dilemmas and feel the tug in both directions. If an ethics of international relations is to be taken seriously, there will often be conflicts between the explicit and obvious institutionally defined duties of leaders and the claims of a much more amorphous and ill-defined sort posed by those in other nations – outside their normal constituency.

In these instances it will be easy to ignore the plight of outsiders, and leaders will often be tempted to do so. Given the structure of values and priorities of the institution, decision-makers are unlikely to be held accountable for such remote effects. Where this is so, and where they are not well positioned to become aware of them, it is not difficult to understand why leaders should fail to take them into account. This is particularly likely to be the case when these concerns clash with values they are explicitly committed to uphold, for instance when disposing of waste in the cheapest and easiest manner causes health-threatening pollution or where a politically popular tax reduction is likely to result in the loss of much-needed aid for a struggling nation.

But there are deeper and more troubling reasons for ignoring such claims, reasons which will strike at the very root of the possibility of an ethics of international relations. Institutional leaders, it may be said, are not free to pick and choose their moral standards the way private persons are. As participants in an institutional structure, they are bound to uphold the duties established for them within it. They would be abrogating their trust as leaders if they were to commit themselves unilaterally to other standards of conduct. Institutions themselves cannot be held responsible for any and all human needs or consequences for others.

The challenge is to explain how adopting such extra-institutional responsibility can be justified and how leaders may be allowed to do so. If this can be accomplished, there must be guidelines which determine what is to count as legitimate overriding of institutional responsibility and how far this sensitivity to external turmoil should range. Without answers to these questions, it is difficult to imagine that any purported ethics of international relations could be taken seriously.

This task is particularly delicate since people on both the institutional and personal levels will be more sensitive to difficulties and feel greater responsibility where they have explicit responsibilities and there is institutional machinery for tending to specific problems. The moral sensitivity of ordinary persons responds awkwardly when faced with cases of need with no defined duties or habits of response. At such times individuals are forced to rely on their own sensitivity and act, perhaps at some cost to themselves, where no one will blame them for remaining quiescent. Situations like this are all too easy to ignore. They are often identified as instances of charity or supererogation on the personal level, but analogues are found on the institutional level as well, and are at once of greater consequence for human life and easier to overlook. It is not sufficient, in an applied ethics, simply to point the way of rectitude. Roadblocks in the way and means of getting round them also require attention. When conditions change, or new ranges of moral accountability open, traditional conceptions of the mode and scope of moral accountability must give way. Yet the sanction of moral intuition and accepted practice will fall within traditional bounds. The attempt to recalibrate moral sensitivity cannot fail to include a response to this challenge.

Another part of the problem is that moral agency on the level of personal relations is thought to be embodied in the autonomous human individual. People are comfortable with the thought of individual persons holding moral agency, but they are much less at ease in thinking of human institutions as moral agents.[5] Yet on the international level institutions are the most powerful and consequential actors. If they cannot intelligibly be counted as moral agents in some sense of the term, then the scope of international ethics will contract to triviality. The challenge is both to comprehend how such agency can be apportioned to institutions and to understand what the range of agency within them will be.

As entities, institutions are quite different from human individuals, and this difference accounts for much of the reluctance to count them as moral agents. There are a number of opinions as to why it makes sense to think of individual human beings as possessed of moral agency and therefore of moral accountability, but the various positions converge on several common elements. Individuals, it is said, are conscious, have the ability to choose their actions freely, are able to engage in reasoned reflection, and can choose the principles which guide their conduct. It is often argued that institutions can have none of these abilities. They are certainly not conscious and cannot act or reason in the way persons can. In fact, whatever action or reasoning they can be said to achieve is really that of individual persons. They themselves can only do so in derivative fashion, by means of the human individuals operating on their behalf. But even if they are able to reason and act in some sense, they do not necessarily qualify as agents. A computerized robot can be said to make reasoned decisions and direct its actions to accord with them. It is not an agent, however, because the acts it performs are determined by the formalized instructions in its brain. Because it is programmed, it is not free. Institutions are also programmed in a sense, for their charters, legal guidelines and functions determine what they can and cannot do. And institutions cannot change these instructions in the way an individual can by, say, being converted or born again. Such changes can, again, be made only by individuals acting on their behalf.

Even if these issues could be resolved and institutions were thought to possess the qualities necessary for moral agency, another problem awaits. When a human being is determined to be a moral agent, it is easy to see where the agency resides. *That person as a whole* is morally responsible. The individual thinks and acts as a unit and is morally accountable as such. But to claim that an institution is morally accountable in its entirety is unilluminating. It does not function as a single bodily structure in the manner of an organic person. If the distribution of agency cannot be adequately explained, there is little point in ascribing it to institutions. The ethics of international relations must thus meet the twin challenge of formulating a workable conception of the agency of institutions and also of explaining the exact manner in which such agency must be apportioned.

While the above problems may appear sufficiently daunting, the most important and widely discussed challenge to an ethics of international relations arises from the context in which moral action on the international level must occur. In the context of personal relations, moral action takes place within a social setting where there is broad agreement on moral standards to be followed and institutional apparatus of some sort for enforcing them. Within societies, peer pressure alone is often an effective means of enforcement. In some societies, such as the Japanese, simple ostracization of individuals is an effective instrument of coercion. For the most serious moral standards organized societies have other more direct and physical means of enforcement, including police, courts and penal institutions. However, the most effective and pervasive instrument of social moral conformity has not yet been mentioned. It is that individuals are bred to internalize moral scruples and find them re-enforced at every turn. Societies have highly effective means of inculcating and enforcing standards of moral conduct. Hence they are able to punish the wayward and reward exemplary behavior, as well as provide a stable structure of expectations and re-enforcements for morally responsible action.

No such elaborate constraints exist on the level of international relations. The international arena is not a society of the sort required for nurturing consistent and effective moral action. Indeed, it is often presumed by skeptics that the conditions of international relations model the situation which would make effective moral conduct either irrational or impossible. Just as the conditions of the Hobbesian state of nature prevent moral constraint on the personal level, so similar conditions on the international level negate restraint there.

On the international level, for example, there is no completely effective means of enforcing standards. Particular nations can exert pressure of various kinds on miscreants, but, short of physical violence, there are few genuinely effective measures to be taken. Even when nations are agreed on punitive measures, unity among them generally becomes frayed by self-interest or erosion of enthusiasm. Nations are readily tempted to mix concerns of politics, ideology and economics into their actions. Without some centralized authority to set standards and enforce them in consistent fashion, there is precious little bite to international standards. In spite of initial high hopes, the United Nations has not proven an effective instrument of such enforcement. It is presently hopelessly fragmented, politicized and swayed by international rivalries. It can be no more effective than sovereign nations wish it to be, and there is little prospect that any substantial portion of its membership is willing to grant it such powers. Miscreants are thus unhindered, and nations who accept risks for the sake of moral rectitude often find themselves isolated and exposed.

There has been substantial debate among theoreticians about whether there is a common international standard of morality.[6] Those who argue in favor of such a standard often point to the ideals of the United Nations' Universal Declaration of Human Rights. They note that nations wish to become members of the UN and all who do must pledge to accept the standards of the Declaration. It is true that debate within the UN is often framed in the language of the Universal Declaration and that it has had sufficient bite to force nations into hypocrisy on occasion. But there is little reason to believe that these goals constitute an effective international morality. A great deal of political and ideological diversity remains in the world. Governmental systems and cultural perspectives remain highly varied. Though nations nominally adopt the ideals of the Declaration, it is not always apparent that its values have any genuine significance for them. Even where this is not true, placing these ideals in the context of different cultures gives them varying meanings and significance. It should not be presumed that the right to work mentioned in the Declaration means the same thing in societies as diverse as the United States, the USSR and Togo, for instance. In part this is due to the very general and abstract nature of the ideals themselves. In other part, there is no common agreement on applying these ideals to particular cases, no understanding of how to determine what conduct and policies constitute compliance with the right to work and what constitute violations of it. Yet if the ideals are not effective in shaping judgements about actual cases, they must have little significance at all.

Presently the nations of the world have neither the sense nor the experience of being members of a common social unity. There is no feeling of belonging, no nurturing of common values and perspectives. There is no effective means of controlling miscreants, or, more significantly perhaps, of giving recognition and honor to those who are exemplary.

Most importantly the nations of the world are in a permanent state of virtual war with one another, as Hobbes understood the term. For Hobbes, individuals are in a state of war when they are disposed to fight and there is no authority with sufficient power to stop them. Since individuals are thus in permanent peril of life and limb, extreme measures are justified in the effort to seek security. None could expect to survive for long if burdened with moral scruples. Moral restraint in such circumstances is both futile and irrational. Hobbes himself noted that the nations of the world are in a similar condition of virtual war.[7] They clearly are often disposed to fight, and there is clearly no one to stop them. Furthermore, particularly in a nuclear era, complacency or error can be quickly and decisively fatal.

The challenge for international ethics is to determine whether an effective morality can be established under conditions of this sort. Personal morality functions within a social context, and it is this background which provides the model for thinking about moral action. It is easy to see why skeptics, noticing this difference, conclude that no morality is possible in the international arena, while stringent moralists, accepting the same inference, insist that the international arena really does constitute a society, all appearance to the contrary. An ethics of international relations must demonstrate what sort of morality is possible under these conditions. If it is unable to do so, the entire project becomes moot.

NORMATIVE THEORY

The basic normative position of this work is a version of utilitarianism, none too different in its essentials from the ideas of R. M. Hare and R. B. Brandt.[8] Utilitarianism offers flexibility and sensitivity to actual circumstance not found in competing theories, principally the rights-based theories devised by John Rawls, Alan Gewirth, Ronald Dworkin, Henry Shue, D. A. J. Richards or Charles Beitz.[9] Most importantly, a utilitarian theory can be formulated which will capture the strengths of competing theories while avoiding their weaknesses.

Like the work of Brandt and Hare, the fundamental principle of moral endeavor in this work is that of maximizing the rational preferences of individuals. It follows Hare in distinguishing two levels of moral thinking, the critical and the intuitive. Critical moral thinking involves the use of logic and facts (i.e. facts about the preferences of human individuals) both to settle particularly difficult moral issues and to devise standards of moral conduct which will guide the conduct of most people most of the time. That is, critical moral thinking wide be devoted in part to formulating fixed guides to conduct which are to be internalized as moral norms. There is utilitarian value in having these as guides to action in stressful situations, co-ordinating the actions of differing persons and providing some fixed points for educating the young or guiding the intellectually unsophisticated. When people apply these standards in uncritical fashion to particular cases, they are said, in Hare's term, to think intuitively. On occasion these moral standards must be overridden. This is because they are designed to apply to most cases, most of the time. When special cases arise or conditions change, the standards will not apply, so critical thinking must be done. When this happens, the usual standards must be overridden by appeal to the fundamental principle of attempting to satisfy the greatest number of preferences of the greatest number of people.

The ultimate moral concern must always be particular human persons. All proposed action must be measured against the standard of the welfare of the individual person. As will be argued later, even if governments of nation-states are moral agents in some sense and therefore have moral responsibilities, their fates are not of moral concern as such. They matter only in so far as what happens to them affects individual human beings.

The ethics of international relations makes special demands on this general utilitarian perspective. Meeting them requires that it be fleshed out in several directions. Most fundamentally, utilitarian schemes require information about the intelligent preferences of relevantly affected individuals in contexts in which decisions are made. On the level of personal relations, these contexts are fairly well-defined. They involve decisions about specific actions which will relevantly affect some limited number of persons, whose preferences can be known and considered. The context loosens somewhat in rule utilitarian versions. Rules must be long-term, apply to a broad range of cases, and affect a large array of people, not all of whom will be known when the decisions are made.

On the international level the context stretches and frays even more. Often the judgements to be made will not concern specific situations but will be decisions of policy which will direct a wide array of actions for some indeterminate period of time. Even where decisions are fairly specific, agents will be unsure of exactly who will be affected by their policies or what preferences they will have. The effects of decisions will range across widely varying cultures and ideologies, which may generate preferences in ways nearly unintelligible and often quite unforeseen to far-off decision makers. Because policies and programs operate over time, the conditions and persons affected will change, and so will relevant preferences. Further uncertainty is produced by the considerable cultural diversity of the world and the remoteness of the consequences of decisions from the immediate awareness of policy-makers. Finally, policy-makers do not have the option of treating all persons alike. The obligations of their offices include special responsibilities to their constituents. The notion of the free and unencumbered autonomous agent is an unfortunate abstraction which is part of the mythology of Western European moral philosophy. Even private individuals have special relationships and special responsibilities to other particular persons. Human life would certainly be much poorer without them. There is something grotesque about the idea of parents attempting to show the same level of personal involvement and concern to all children as to their own. Much of what is rich and satisfying in human life would be lost in such an effort, and it is certainly not a requirement of utilitarianism that the attempt be made. The conflict of the institutional policy-maker is only one facet of the more general conflict between particular obligations and generalized human responsibility.

In view of these difficulties, the operating assumption of this work is that people in general desire the means to sustain life and desire security from harm by others. It will assume further they they are likely to place the highest priority on these desires. These can be called 'basic wants'. Note that for the most part they are easily measured and relatively easily met, as a modest amount of beans and rice will preserve bodily life. In actual cases the detail of satisfying basic wants will vary. Sometimes people will not value them as highly as is usual. Adventurers, for example, appear to value excitement and discovery more than bodily security. Nevertheless, it is reasonable to suppose that these assumptions will hold true for most people most of the time.

Arrayed against basic wants are what can be called 'secondary wants'. People soon tire of beans and rice and crave more exotic fare. But, at this stage, tastes vary widely and often unpredictably. Satisfaction of the desire for food beyond the simple requirement of nourishment is conditioned by individual taste, social value, or current fashion. Furthermore, where the amount of food necessary to sustain life is easily measured and relatively modest, secondary food cravings often reach distinctly immodest proportions. But secondary wants involve far more than cravings for luxury. They include values like companionship, self-respect and fulfillment, or cultural enrichment. These are not matters of supplying foodstuffs but depend on the working of a social context, something not easily supplied by outsiders.

In general terms the position of this work is that all have a strong obligation to work to satisfy basic wants wherever they are found, but a much weaker obligation to look after the secondary wants of each and every human being. This priority is based on several assumptions: that people generally place the highest value on life and the means of life, that these are necessary for other values to be enjoyed, that satisfying them will be relatively uncomplicated and inexpensive. In other words, basic wants stand apart from the general array of preferences as particularly important. Because secondary cravings vary widely from culture to culture and from person to person, because it will often be quite difficult to satisfy them, and because supplying them may depend on the continued operation of cultural and social contexts which are not easily engineered by outsiders, these wants will generally have secondary importance. It is thus reasonable to assume that in the majority of instances of conflict between the claims posed by the secondary wants of outsiders and the special responsibility of leaders to their own citizens, the latter will have greatest weight. For one thing, special responsibilities are often directed toward securing the life and well-being of one's constituents. For another, these special responsibilities have considerable value by preserving the social contexts necessary for enjoying secondary preferences. Of course, all of these assumptions are true only in a general way and may not apply in specific instances. But since politics and planning must be general and long-range, some such broad assumptions must be relied upon.

Matters are complicated by the fact that international ethics must be practised in a world where there are no generally agreed-upon standards of conduct and no effective means of enforcement. Where enforcement is lacking, for example, it is unrealistic to expect that each and every case of wrongful human suffering receive a vigorous rebuke or that each and every miscreant be brought to justice. Present circumstances simply do not allow moral scruples to cut so fine. Furthermore, would-be moral agents will often face action against the background of a hostile or indifferent world. At such times, when personal or national well-being is at risk, they have good reason for giving their own security substantial weight. Once more, this is simply a feature of present circumstance. As the concluding chapter illustrates, there is an obligation to strive for a world where an international moral culture is firmly established, but it is foolish to act as though it exists already.

Global diversity of moral belief and cultural practice creates other complications. There are lots of practices in differing parts of the world which appear wrong to Western European sensibility. The practice in some Islamic nations of cutting off the right hand of thieves, the Soviet view that civil liberties are justified only in so far as they benefit the state, or the practice of institutionalized bribery found in some societies are examples. From the perspective of the present moral position, several factors must be taken into account in determining how to respond to these cases. For one thing, what counts is the preferences of individual human beings. In the examples at hand, the preferences of those most deeply involved will be shaped by their own moral culture. In the culture of the Labrador Eskimo it is believed that those who die violently will reside in the most desirable places in heaven (near the Aurora Borealis) and will pass their time in pleasurable activity ('playing football with a walrus head'). Those who die simply from disease or old age, on the other hand, will spend their after-life in much less desirable circumstances.[10] Therefore, to be killed violently or to kill others is not necessarily to be harmed or to inflict harm, but may instead be beneficial.

In the most basic sense of 'harm', people are only being harmed if they undergo experiences which they wish to avoid. If the masochist enjoys pain and seeks it, then, other things being equal, he or she is not being harmed by this singular choice of entertainment. However, in another sense, sometimes people seek a particular experience, not because they value it for itself, but because they believe it will result in some further benefit which they desire. The Labrador Eskimos value violent death for the vigorous and pleasant after-life which they believe it will bring and not because they esteem death in itself. Other cultures have the quite reasonable belief that people will spend eternity in the physical and mental condition they enjoyed when they died, so it is much better to die when young and vigorous than when old and infirm. But if these latter groups and the Labrador Eskimos are mistaken in their beliefs about life after death, they are being harmed by their practices. They are being harmed because they would most likely not continue their ways if their ideas about results changed. So it is possible that the Labrador Eskimos are being harmed after all. Of course, accurate information about the true nature of life after death is nowhere to be found at the present time. The beliefs of the Labrador Eskimo have as much chance of being correct as the very different beliefs of others, and it stretches credibility to say they are being harmed as the result.

But not all instances will be like this. Sooner or later, practices will be encountered that seem clearly harmful, both in the sense that they are undesirable in themselves and are mistakenly thought to result in desired consequences. Perhaps the best examples here are where people rely on shamanistic medical practices and thoroughly reject the techniques of Western medicine. In such instances, the futility or harmfulnes of the traditional practices can be clearly demonstrated, along with the effectiveness of modern medical techniques. These results can be as thoroughly demonstrated as any of the beliefs of advanced industrialized societies. However, doing so requires acceptance of the techniques of proof and investigation of modern science, which need not be accepted by all cultures. In order to demonstrate conclusively that shamanistic practices are futile and harmful, much has to be assumed about the techniques of scientific proof and values which need not be accepted by all. So, once more, it is very difficult to claim baldly that harm is occurring in such cases.

However, all societies have conventions governing punishment, and these vary widely. The law of the *Koran*, followed in a number of Islamic nations, requires cutting off the right hand of thieves and the stoning of adulterers.[11] In China and other countries of the Far East, it was once common practice to punish all the members of a family of an individual who had committed a crime or had otherwise fallen into disfavor.[12] Since the point of punishment is to inflict harm, there is no question that individuals subjected to such practices are being harmed, in their own view as well as that of others. The issue is whether such harm is justified. Certainly, such practices are at odds with Western European views and, quite plausibly, with utilitarianism as well. Measures far less draconian than amputation, for example, would appear sufficient to deter theft. However, given Islamic views of the authority of the *Koran* and Chinese views of the relation of family and individual, these practices cannot be deemed either arbitrary or unreasonable, at least not for the members of the cultures that hold them. Given the structure of belief in such societies, it is

not impossible that such practices could be justified, even on utilitarian grounds. Even for a utilitarian who is outside a particular web
of cultural belief, it must be recognized that normally the preferences
of the members of such societies are for such practices to continue.

But another group of troubling cases remains. In both Japan and
India there have existed outcast classes who were thought distinctly
inferior to other members of society. India, of course, possessed an
elaborate caste system as well, though many cultures have had strati-
fied social classes. More recently, Blacks, Jews, and other distinct
groups, such as homosexuals, have been singled out for brutal treatment. In many of these cases it is possible to say that a cultural schema
existed which provided some justification for the abuses which took
place or are still taking place. Yet it seems clear that these are the
archetypical cases of which humanity should be intolerant.

In traditional caste societies, individuals in lower castes could
expect less satisfactory lives than if their lot differed. However,
so long as no one questioned the system, they probably did not
think of themselves as being harmed in any special way, or, if they
did, the harm was seen as being justified in terms of the cultural
perspective which underlay it. For their views to change, they would
have to alter their cultural perspective, but then they would become
different people and may suffer losses as the result of the transition,
along with the gains.[13] In such cases, outsiders would be ill-advised
to attempt to intervene. It is reasonable to assume they will be less
likely to magnify harm if they restrict their role to accommodating
such change as arises from within.

Cases of bigotry against Jews and Blacks differ. In the main
the difference is that their treatment includes being subjected to
vilification, torment and, in extreme cases, great physical hardship or
death. This is quite different and far more injurious than simply being
assigned a role in society, even a lowly one. Secondly, the difference
from caste systems is that these groups are not considered part of the
societies that vilify them, and they do not share in whatever cultural
perspective shapes the attitudes of society to them. Therefore they
are not likely to accept any cultural justification for the treatment
they receive. They will, in other words, be harmed and suffer greatly
as the result. Furthermore, since the harms will be directed against
them as outsiders, there will not be the aura of impartiality which
is found in traditional caste systems. A Hindu Brahman may well
acknowledge, for example, that, *karma* requiring, he or she might
have been born into a lesser caste, but Klansmen cannot allow the

thought that they *might* have been Black. In particularly egregious cases of bigotry, such as Hitler's Germany or contemporary South Africa, justifications for bias can easily be shown to rest on misinformation or fallacious reasoning such as the German racial theories of Aryanism or the policies concerning the 'homelands' of South Africa. Once such fabrications are exposed, there can be little appearance of justification for continued bigotry.

The diversity of the world thus necessitates great care and sensitivity for those attempting to decide how to respond to alien cultural practices that seem harmful or benighted. Sometimes, when preference and culture are considered, there will literally be no unjustified harm done, even though a given practice seems cruel or wrongful to outsiders. In other cases, practices can be shown to rest on demonstrably wrong, though honestly held, beliefs. When this is so, censure or argument can perhaps be justified but not overt intervention, since the wishes of those most closely involved are that the practices continue. Overt intervention, with *its* attendant harms and risks, is required only where practices are imposed on unwilling outside groups or they are appealed to falsely, as when covering up political repression. Concrete cases, as later chapters will show, readily allow distinctions between the genuine working of a cultural practice and its abuse for political or financial ends. That is, an examination of conditions in South Africa will expose the bigotry of the ruling class and the untenability of the arguments it presents. Analysis of the cultural background of the caste system in India will be a much more complex and difficult matter.

The utilitarian perspective of this work is certainly not relativist in the strict sense. That is, it is not the view that whatever practices or beliefs differing peoples may happen to have on moral subjects are correct for them. However, moral analysis must take account of what the circumstances will allow. Differing cultural or ideological perspectives need to be acknowledged and respected, even when they appear obviously mistaken. This does not amount to relativism. The ultimate moral principle, in this case that of satisfying the greatest number of relevant preferences, remains unaltered. It simply mandates differing responses as circumstances change. The intentional killing of innocent humans is normally unjustified in peacetime, for example, but may be required in war where all is at stake. Most fundamentally, however, the relative nature of the concept of 'harm' developed here will require differing judgements in varying contexts and cultures. There is certainly cross-cultural bite to the principle of utility, but the bite must result from careful examination of the situations at hand.

ALTERNATIVES TO UTILITARIANISM

Utilitarian theory is not without its critics. Indeed, it has become fashionable in certain quarters to hold it in contempt. It is likely, though, that the weaknesses of utilitarian theory and the strengths of its competitors are greatly overstated. The most recently developed alternative is virtue-based ethics. This approach, however, is only feasible for small groups of persons in close-knit communities with common values. It is simply inadequate to deal with the issues typical of international ethics.

The principal alternatives to utilitarian theory are the rights-based theories of various kinds which have been worked out in the past decade and a half. What is striking about these theories is the great efforts their creators have to make clearly to distinguish their positions from utilitarianism and to avoid, as Thomas Scanlon notes, falling back into the utilitarian fold.[14] Some of these share the feature of picking out a set of essential goods, claiming people have fundamental rights to them, and then building theories on these claims. Henry Shue picks out 'subsistence and security' in *Basic Rights*.[15] Alan Gewirth in *Reason and Morality* opts for 'freedom and well-being'.[16] In *A Theory of Justice* Rawls plumps for 'primary goods'.[17] These are not much different from the 'basic wants' mentioned earlier, a concept which will form the cornerstone of the applied practical utilitarian theory of this work.

Rights theorists will not be impressed by this similarity, though. They will argue that the essential feature of their approach is that people are 'entitled' in a fundamental way to these goods, whereas for the utilitarian these are simply preferences, or whatever. Also, they will argue that these rights should never be taken away from people, but mere wants may be overridden by other wants.

These claims have greatly impressed many people, so it is worth having a look at them. The second is simply false. Rights are overridden all the time or superseded by more basic rights. Sometimes rights clash, and choices must be made among them. It is not obvious that the basic wants of particular individuals would be overridden more often in utilitarian theories than rights would be denied in rights-based theories. Rights theorists are likely to claim in response that rights can only be overridden by other rights, whereas basic wants can, in theory, be outweighed by the most trivial or the most despicable whims. However, as has been argued previously, there are good utilitarian reasons for allowing basic wants to be overridden only by other basic wants. Once more, there will be no great difference between theories.

Rights theorists will not be won over by these considerations, for they will return to their initial emphasis on entitlement. They enjoy good sport by claiming that utilitarian theories view individuals as mere collections of preferences or sets of appetites. They believe human beings are much more dignified than this and so work out theories of 'personhood', 'respect', 'dignity' or 'autonomy' to serve as the basis for rights entitlements. These various theories exhibit great ingenuity and sophistication. But the question is, just what concrete difference does 'entitlement' make in formulating moral decisions? Previous discussions show that they add very little to what would be required by a sound utilitarian theory.

Some of the more acute rights theorists appear to recognize this difficulty and wish to ground the distinction between utilitarian theory and rights theory on procedural differences. Rawls argues in *A Theory of Justice* that contractors in the original position would opt for rights principles rather than utilitarian.[18] In *Taking Rights Seriously* Ronald Dworkin believes that his basic principle of equal concern and respect is significantly different from the utilitarian insistence on counting each as one and no one as more than one.[19] Both theorists are well aware of how close their ideas come to utilitarian theory and work hard to try to avoid the stigma. The view of this work is that their efforts fail and that neither Rawls nor Dworkin has developed a theory which is significantly different from the utilitarian.

But if utilitarianism and rights-based theories are similar, why choose the utilitarian? Utilitarianism has a bad name, and rights theories have strong rhetorical advantages. In recent history the language of rights has continually been used to press the claims of the oppressed and needy. Following the horrors of the Second World War, it was natural for the United Nations to formulate its highest goals and values in terms of rights. It has long been recognized that those who wish to press their claims in the strongest possible fashion will cloak them in the language of rights.

There are, nonetheless, several good reasons for returning to embattled yet perennial utilitarian theory. Utilitarianism has parsimony on its side for one thing. It need not rely on difficult ideas of autonomy, personhood, or human dignity. It can get essentially the same results without them. A related advantage is that utilitarian theories do not drift off on ideas like autonomy, freedom, or democracy without asking why anyone should care about them. It is useful for demythologizing obscure ideas. Does 'freedom' mean, for example, anything more than the ability to choose and act on one's choices? If not, why should anyone worry about it?

Another abstract and obscure concept important for rights theorists is that of autonomy. They construct various arguments founded on claims that people are autonomous and that autonomy should be respected. The difficulty is that people display varying levels of autonomy, and it is stretching things to claim that some people in some situations are autonomous at all. The degree of autonomy enjoyed by the common soldier in the heat of battle and the experienced physician is totally different. The physician has expertise, is used to making judgments and acting upon them, can gain some detachment from his or her situation, and enjoys the respect and deference of others. The physician comes close to exemplifying what philosophers have in mind when they talk about autonomous being. The common soldier enjoys none of these qualities. Most people are arranged between the physician and the soldier in their possession of them. When analyzing moral responsibility, it is unrealistic at best to argue blandly that human beings are autonomous and to proceed from there. Moral responsibility is better served if it is asked in concrete terms what people can be expected to do and what kinds of institutions can be constructed to support a sense of responsibility. Utilitarianism is more amenable to bringing moral concepts down to earth and giving them concrete meaning than are rights theories.

The other practical advantages of utilitarianism are more widely appreciated. It is very difficult for rights-based theories to explain what must be done when rights conflict or must be overridden. There is no room for compromise or negotiation when rights are at stake. Rights theorists are prone to think of this inflexibility as a benefit, a safeguard against the loss of rights. In real-world conflicts where opposing claims are at stake, however, conflict can easily harden into protracted, bitter struggle if there is common insistence on rights. Where opposing parties are convinced they have immutable rights, they are unlikely to compromise and likely to insist on their due to the bitter end. Utilitarian theories can accommodate these conflicts in ways very difficult for rights theories to match.

Utilitarian theories also enjoy the advantage of flexibility. When interests, persons and circumstances change, utilitarian theories can readily adapt, since preferences will then differ, and so must utilitarian judgements. Rights-based theories, however, must of necessity focus on certain fixed values. In so far as specific content is given to rights, such as freedom of speech or the enjoyment of human life, their concrete meaning will be tied to specific contexts. When conditions change, they are likely to be left high and dry, or to become so abstract and ethereal as to be of little but rhetorical use in resolving moral issues.

The most important practical advantage of a utilitarian approach, however, is that it is much better suited than alternatives to deal with issues of international ethics, given present conditions. Consider, as an example, the brutal war in the Persian Gulf. Iraq was clearly wrong to have initiated it, committed a variety of atrocities in conducting the war, and has violated international agreements by using poison gas as a weapon. Iran for its part actively recruited young children for the war and sent them out, literally, to be slaughtered. There was clearly great moral culpability on both sides. Yet talk of punishment, of violations of rights, of insisting on rights, seems out of place. Any concern for rights which would threaten to prolong wars or expand their scope is morally grotesque at best and positively immoral at worst. The best course for the world is to put aside talk of recrimination or punishment and attempt to end wars as quickly and cleanly as possible. In other words, the basic utilitarian concern for life and security is most clearly relevant. Attempts at greater moral fastidiousness are counter-productive at best.

If there were clear standards of conduct on these matters; if the world had achieved a consensus on how to apply them to particular cases, if institutions and machinery existed with clear authority and power to establish and enforce these standards; if, in other words, world conditions more closely resembled the circumstances of personal morality; then it would make sense to talk about rights or punishment in cases such as the Persian Gulf War. The difficulty is that these do not exist and are not likely to develop at any time in the near future. From a utilitarian perspective, it would be very good if they did exist, and a strong case can be made for the view that the world community has the duty to work to bring these conditions about. Since they do not exist at present, it is foolish to attempt to act as though they did.

APPLICATION

Developing a plausible and defensible normative theory of morality for international relations is only part of the battle. The special features of international relations outlined earlier are accompanied by special challenges of application. If these challenges cannot be met – if there is no feasible way to apply normative utilitarian theory to concrete problems and policy deliberations – the whole set of issues becomes moot. The ethics of international relations will remain the abstract pastime of scholars, and rightly so.

The indirect and unintended consequences of action pose a special problem for utilitarian theories. On the personal level, consequences of this sort are usually unimportant and are legitimately ignored in developing theories of moral accountability. On the level of giant human institutions, these consequences loom much larger. Standard utilitarian theory is thought to have a straightforward answer to issues of this sort. Consequences are consequences. It is the degree of suffering or satisfaction that counts, not the limitations of the actor. To an extent this must be correct. Consequences are what matter for utilitarian theories, but it is a mistake to believe that utilitarian theories, like any other moral theories, do not require a concept of moral agency (though this concept of moral agency will be less elaborate and perform less normative work than the theories of personhood or autonomy used by some rights theorists). If utilitarianism requires what no right-thinking moral agent can perform, that is a strike against it as a workable moral theory.

Happily, there is no reason why utilitarianism, any more than other theories, should require agents to be held morally accountable for that which is beyond their control. There can be no utilitarian benefit in this. Like any other theory, though, utilitarianism may sometimes require that agents extend the range of their control and that their sense of moral accountability expand along with the scope and impact of their actions. The ethics of international relations is a good case in point, but there are other examples as well, such as medical ethics. As the context in which medicine is dispensed changed and the abilities of medical practice changed, so that more could be done to preserve life, medical practitioners and the general public were forced to rethink their responsibilities and redefine their relationships. New techniques and successes brought responsibility for making decisions in cases that previously could only be left to fate. So re-evaluation was, morally, necessary.

It is true that at present institutional leaders, whether in business or government, normally pay little attention to the consequences of their policies for people and institutions beyond their own. But it is also true that, from the standpoint of prudence and effectiveness as well as morality, they ought to. These considerations apply to governments with particular force. If they wish their policies to be effective, and if they wish to keep from entangling themselves in snares of their own inadvertent devising, they need to become more aware, or more broadly aware, of what they are doing. Of course, governments have elaborate means of gaining information about other nations. In contrast to leaders of other institutions, such as corporate officers, governmental leaders have a much broader range of authority to take action and set policies. For them the pressures are not those of demonstrating growth at stockholders' meetings but of responding to the promptings of various domestic groups and interests. For some positions in government, such as head of state, the role carries, along with broad authority, the patina of leadership which can be used to mold public opinion. Others, in lesser positions, have varying options for attempting to raise issues of moral concern for public discussion.

Events in South Africa have presently forced moral issues into consciousness in the political arena as well as in corporate boardrooms. Governmental leaders have the power to raise such questions for public discussion and awareness, use the authority of their offices to build public support for morally responsible policies and propose legislation to establish governmental machinery for creating moral sensitivity. In the United States, for example, the latter concern has been nurtured by various pieces of legislation which require, among other things, the presentation of annual reports on the status of human rights in various nations, the tying of aid programs to respect for human rights, and establishment of bureaus to oversee such matters.[20] More of this sort of thing would be useful, but such measures alone will be ineffectual if there is no broad support for them. The key is ultimately individual concern and effort, whether distributed throughout the larger public or working through governmental leadership. Nonetheless, the above shows that moral sensitivity is possible and illustrates some of the means by which it can be made politically effective.

Utilitarian theory does not condemn the special relations and responsibilities which individuals develop toward one another. Certainly they add great richness to human life, and this alone is sufficient to give them utilitarian weight. But there are good reasons for believing that this scheme of apportioning clearly defined responsibilities to specific individuals results in the greatest satisfaction of preferences over the long term. The institution of government also plays its role in supporting human life. If evidence is needed, the chaos of Lebanon should suffice to demonstrate the importance of stable and effective government for providing the basic requirements of a decent human existence. There is thus good reason for having governments and apportioning special responsibilities to those who manage them. It is quite possible that the limitations of human sensitivity, imagination and initiative will always require this specificity. This question will be examined further in the concluding chapter. For now, it will be assumed that institutional leaders are justified in accepting clearly delineated responsibilities to a specific constituency and in devoting their primary attention and energies to fulfilling these duties. There is presently no utilitarian reason why individuals should attempt to take the whole world as their constituency and attempt to improve the lot of humanity *en masse*. Human limitations and practical considerations preclude this. Even the most dedicated and self-effacing saint can aid only a finite number of specific individuals. If all were held responsible for everyone, it is quite likely that no one would feel responsible for anyone. Stretching the human sense of responsibility too thin will eventually cause it to shred in tatters.

There will be occasions, however, when these responsibilities come into conflict with other considerations and times when they will be overridden. Certainly catastrophic threat to the basic wants of individuals in foreign lands is one instance where many specific responsibilities must give way. This occurs also on the personal level where parents' duties to nurture their children may be overridden by a pressing need to save the lives of others. Conflicts of this sort do not arise often on the personal level, at least not in prosperous, well-ordered societies, but they occur with much greater frequency on the chaotic level of international relations. On the global level there are always masses of people who are starving, endangered or mistreated and who have no effective institutions with the explicit responsibility for looking after them. Not infrequently their own governments will be the cause of their ills. Well-ordered societies have provision for assisting the unfortunate, but there is nothing equivalent on the international level. Groups such as CARE, the International Red Cross, and Amnesty International are tremendously important, but it would be better to have the world organized in such a way as to be able to do without them.

Where leaders face conflicts between meeting the basic wants of their own constituents and those of aliens, they are justified in placing their own nations first. In part this is because they have such special responsibilities, but it is also because of the utilitarian value of preserving the structure of governmental order. However, they are not entitled to place the lesser concerns of their own citizens ahead of the vital concerns of others in cases where these clash. Whatever their explicit responsibilities to their own citizens, their non-specific obligations to preserve life will have greatest weight in the event of conflict. Special responsibilities are justified both because of their importance in meeting basic wants and their value in providing a stable social structure necessary for supplying secondary wants. But, obviously, there will be times when the value these provide will be outweighed by the more substantial requirements of other persons. Thus, they do not have the moral option of following policies which will bring cheap produce to their own citizens at the expense of the lives and well-being of others. Neither, closer to hand, do they have the option of closing their borders to prevent starving or endangered aliens from seeking refuge, even though to act otherwise would cause hardships for their own citizens. There are no utilitarian grounds for ignoring or discounting the preferences of any person.

On utilitarian grounds there are a number of reasons why institutional leaders should have a general obligation to meet the basic wants of all humans, where ever they are found, to the extent that this effort does not seriously detract from their ability to manage their own nations. For one thing, as was argued earlier, making an effort to meet the basic wants of all does not require any huge expenditure of the material resources of nations, at least not of the prosperous ones. There is little doubt that the world could be minimally fed and cared for at a cost of only a small fraction of the wealth of the prosperous nations. Working to provide more adequate security for individual persons requires much less in the way of material expenditure, but pressing for increased personal security has other difficulties. Sometimes the greatest danger to the security and well-being of individuals comes from their own governments, who must be pressured in some way if the lot of their citizens is to improve. There are various means, such as economic and diplomatic pressure, which can be used to foster these ends. Sometimes great value will result simply from having a national leader speak out against abuses, from taking a clear stand. It requires little more than what Jimmy Carter hoped for during his tenure as President of the United States. There is a variety of reasons for the failure of his efforts. Material cost is not among them.

National political leaders have the ability to gain support for such efforts if they make the attempt. President John Kennedy had great success in fostering an internationalism of this sort during his tenure in office. Other politicians could achieve similar awareness today. Of course, there are many reasons why they do not do so, and these will be examined in the concluding chapter. But none of these is insurmountable. All can be met if there is sufficient determination by those in position to take action.

The issue of meeting the secondary wants of persons is different and more complex. Clearly there are strong utilitarian grounds for greater equality in the distribution of the world's resources than now obtains. However, there are difficult questions of exactly what is to be sought and how to go about it. For example, it is not obvious that the goal should be to make all the nations and all peoples of the world into mirror images of advanced industrial nations. By now most recognize that industrialization brings mixed blessings at best. Its benefits in terms of wealth and influence are balanced by costs for the environment, traditional culture and the richness of individual life.

Furthermore, it is not obvious that what were once called primitive societies are greatly improved by a shower of material benefits from the outside. Their cultures and lives are now understood to be rich and vibrant, perhaps superior in some ways to those of the industrialized nations around them. The experience of the Eskimo groups in northern Canada amply illustrates this difficulty. They have received substantial material support from the Canadian government but have been transformed from a hearty, ingenious, independent people to wards of the state, with the usual problems of indolence, alcohol abuse, and heart disease. Gaining more control over their lives within the context of Canadian society would require moving even further from their traditional cultures and adopting more of the perspective and ways of life of the larger society.[21] It is not clear exactly what counts as benefit for them. Similar difficulties have arisen among the Greenland Eskimos under the more distant and even more benevolent tenure of the Danes.[22]

Even if the model of industrialized societies is taken as the norm for all parts of the world, permanent equality cannot be achieved simply by a transfer of material wealth. Creating industrialized societies requires the social, institutional and educational structures which make them possible and preserve their existence. Material goods alone cannot achieve this. Education and structural change are required. This point is amply illustrated by the experience of Japan and West Germany following the Second World War. Their material resources and physical equipment were almost totally destroyed. While rebuilding required enormous financial resources, the key lay in the social resources of these nations. It is not at all clear, for example, that a new Marshall Plan for Central America would even begin to solve the problems there.[23] Providing social resources of this sort would require far less material expenditure but far greater intrusion into social mores than simple, ephemeral transfer of wealth.

Working to meet the secondary wants of all the peoples of the world is far more difficult than meeting basic wants. Cultural diversity and practical difficulties of application are much less tractable because the basic issues involve ways of life and not only material resources. When this is appreciated, it is far from obvious that a utilitarian, or any other, moral theory requires simple equalization of material resources. These problems will be examined at greater length in the chapter on international distributive justice.

At this point it is possible to address earlier questions about the range of indirect consequences that international agents should worry about. They are obligated to attempt to discover the likely consequences of their policies for meeting basic human wants. This is not difficult to do, provided the effort is made. Agents have responsibilities where the unlikely or remote consequences of their actions affect the basic wants of others, wherever they may be. Since basic wants are fundamental, the benefits derived from assigning special responsibilities will be of secondary importance when devoted to meeting secondary wants.

As before, the issues of effects of secondary wants are more difficult to judge. As the case of the Eskimos shows, it is difficult even to know whether policies intended to be helpful do not cause unforeseen harms. What is more, it is much more difficult to repair damage to self-respect or ways of life than simply provide food and shelter to stave off death. Nonetheless, it can often reasonably be known whether given policies are likely to undermine or disrupt the ways of life of distant peoples. It is more difficult to know whether these effects will be helpful or harmful, particularly if the model of advanced industrialized societies is abandoned as the paradigm of social development. The issues of what should be done once it is decided that harm has occurred are difficult and will be discussed in detail in later chapters.

It is worth noting that there is a substantial difference between the range of responsibilities of governments and those of private institutions, such as business corporations. The latter are artifacts designed to create wealth. The particular responsibilities of their managers derive from this central purpose. Furthermore, since they are private, they do not represent either the collected judgement or the interests of an entire people. Their interests are those of a small segment of the population.

The scope of governments' responsibility and influence is much wider. They represent entire populations and are often open to influence by them in turn. Being sovereign, they are not constrained by legal statute and narrowness of purpose in the way private corporations are. For these reasons, there may be some benefit if the scope of the moral concerns of government were to range much wider. Furthermore, while there is a clear distinction between government and citizenry on the domestic level, governments represent and support their citizens in the international arena. Governments serve as their international agents and protectors simply because private individuals normally do not have the means to act effectively on that level. This relationship implies that their goals will not be narrowly defined, such as seeking profits or growth, but will touch many areas of human life.

It is fashionable to claim that institutions are not, and cannot, be moral agents. It is easy to see why this belief is held. Institutions are very different from human beings, who are the paradigms of moral agency. There is considerable mystery about just what sorts of things institutions are. But they can be described simply, in ways that grasp the essentials. They are groups of human beings who are related to one another and outsiders in certain fixed ways, often established by law, mutual agreement or common practice. Their existence may be justified by accomplishing ends, such as the creation of profits or the establishment of public order. These fixed relations determine not only what various persons within the institutions may do and how they may do it, but also create roles for them. They make certain kinds of acts possible and others impossible. They enable persons, within the structure, to act in ways unavailable to them outside it and prevent certain kinds of acts which are available to them outside the structure.

It seems appropriate to speak of institutions as taking action, to criticize them for acting one way rather than another, and to claim they have acted rationally rather than irrationally, or the reverse. There is no doubt that the structure allows certain kinds of acts to be done. However, these acts, unlike the acts of single individuals, are either complex, co-ordinated undertakings of various persons or artificial acts which exist only within a framework of law or institutional practice. When it is said that they reason, then, again, the mode of reasoning is not like that of an individual person. It is rather the deliberations of a group or of those whose roles mandate that they function as deliberators. When institutions act or when they think, these operations must be understood as the co-ordinated thought or action of the individuals within them or of particular persons designated to perform these roles.

Thinking and acting in this manner is obviously different from the thought and action of particular individuals. Do these differences imply that institutions cannot be held morally accountable in the way individual persons can? Certainly institutions are held accountable, in ways other than moral, by the law or by stockholders or by stockbrokers. There is little reason why this accountability should not extend to moral concerns as well. The same qualities that enable them to be considered agents in other contexts supply their agency in morality.

It is often argued that institutions are precluded from moral accountability by the fact that they are organized for certain purposes or have fixed goals embodied in their charters. Yet it is commonly acknowledged by proponents of this argument that these do not allow illegal activity.[24] If this is so, there seems little reason why immoral activity cannot be precluded as well. Furthermore, unlike the instance of robots, the actors within these institutions are often able to press for changes in goals or charters and are free to make changes in the way the institution operates. Agents within institutions certainly are constrained by them but are frequently able to alter these constraints and rework the institution itself.

While institutions have the responsibilities of moral agents, they do not have any of the moral entitlements of individuals. For one thing, they cannot be helped or harmed in any morally significant sense. Institutions can be described as flourishing or languishing, or as having received a battering in the market-place, so they can be helped or harmed. However, because they are not unified centers of consciousness in the way persons are, because their freedom and rationality are derivative, coming from the people who compose them, their fates are not intrinsically of moral consequence, any more than the flourishing or destruction of a distant star or an amoeba would be. The individuals within them, of course, may be harmed in morally significant fashion, but not the institutions themselves. Neither do they have any broad-gauge entitlements to remain in existence. Furthermore, while they may be said to have preferences, in the same derivative fashion they may be said to reason or act, these preferences need not be taken into account in moral deliberations – simply because of their differences from human agents. They matter from a moral perspective only in so far as what happens to them ultimately has consequences for individual persons. If there is any sense at all in which they may be thought to have moral standing, it is in terms of their relation to particular individuals.

Institutions are thus moral agents, in a secondary or derivative sense. They are agents only through the agency of those human beings that compose them. The moral standing of these enclosed individuals is difficult. In this century, as vividly illustrated by Kafka, the common view has been that of individuals caught and helpless in a web of institutional power. In this nightmarish vision, individuals have their lives, actions, values and expectations shaped and channeled by the enfolding network. There is much truth in this. But this truth must not be allowed to mask the opposing truth that these institutions are shaped by acts of human will, and these acts of will may not only reshape and refocus institutions but break free from them altogether. In its normal course of operation, it is easy to view the institution as a self-operating machine, but this operation requires a multitude of individual acts of will. It is odd and illuminating that in the dictatorships of Haiti and the Philippines, the sudden flight of a dictatorial leader suddenly caused the populace to believe they were free. Because they believed this, they in fact become so, even though all the apparatus of the state, the thugs and courts and jails, remained intact and ready to operate as always. All remained the same, except that individual beliefs changed, and this made all the difference. For this reason the ethics of international relations must always be ultimately directed at the individual wills of single persons. It is easy to over-emphasize the ponderous influence of the structure and forget that the structure resides on the countless acts of individual persons. The structure and the person interact, shape and reshape one another, but individual belief, action and will are the foundation.

The human agency involved in these matters is complex and requires further attention. Individuals react to the environment around them and its pressures. Part of the traditional theory of moral agency has it that they are essentially free of such forces – that is, that they are capable of overcoming them and acting counter to their pressure. But common experience affirms that only the rare individual can be expected to rise above circumstances of certain sorts. International moral sensitivity requires institutional change, but the irony is that these changes can only be made by individuals who see their importance. In such matters it is ultimately the individual will that counts and is active, but its *agency* must be understood in the context of its reaction *to* and its reaction *upon* external pressures.

There is an important difference between personal agency and the the agency of individuals who function as part of institutions. For the latter, it is not merely a matter of deciding to become morally responsible, though that is the ultimate goal, but of instituting structural changes that will allow and nurture moral accountability. The Henry Fords of industry, the founders and patriarchs, who are in complete financial and administrative control, are able to act within their institution with some of the same freedom and responsibility that lesser individuals have in managing their private affairs. Others, whose authority ranges more narrowly, must exercise their agency in different fashion.

Within any institution an individual has a set range of authority and responsibility. Save for absolute dictators or corporate magnates, these prerogatives are rarely unfettered. The individual has responsibility for making decisions; but the way in which decisions are made, the criteria and policies which shape them, are set by the institution. Furthermore, the authority of one individual is complemented and limited by that of others. For a given act to occur, a whole array of decisions by differing persons must be made in ways that complement and re-enforce one another. In order for individual decisions to be made effective, they must be made in the correct way and in the correct relation to the choices of others elsewhere in the corporate structure. Because of this, individuals wishing to change the manner in which the institution operates cannot simply decide to do so, but must first act upon the institution itself; they must determine how to reshape it so that it operates differently. In this regard, an institution is no different from a computer or a lawnmower. When persons wish institutions to operate differently, they must change them. If their authority is limited or they are unable to gain support from others for making such changes, persons must decide whether the issues at hand are sufficiently important that they can no longer continue association with the institution.

Understanding the role of individuals within the institutional structure opens the way to recognizing how to apportion moral responsibility for the acts of the institution. Too much has been made of the difficulty of this task. The loss of individual responsibility and initiative within the structure is easily over-emphasized. No institution operates at random. No institution can survive for long that lapses into courses of action that are unforeseen and unintended. There are people within the institutional structure with fixed lines of authority for conducting action. Rarely will a single individual within the system be the complete agent of an institution's acts. An action or decision will be the result of a series of separate decisions.

It is because of this, because no one has total responsibility, that individuals are tempted to take refuge in the plea that they have no responsibility at all. But individuals within the chain of authority make a difference, and to this extent they are morally responsible and accountable. They do not have the degree of control of their situation and actions available to private individuals, but they are able to work within and upon the institution, or leave it altogether, and this accounts for their moral responsibility. Differing individuals have varying levels of authority and responsibility for what occurs, so their moral accountability must differ. This responsibility is greatest for executive decision-makers. On the other hand, because acts of the institution are complexes of the conduct of differing persons, many do not have a hand in making decisions but simply carry them out. In many ways their situation is the most poignant of all, for they may feel responsibility for their acts as individuals which they lack within the institutional setting.

It is also true that institutions, and the larger society, can take steps to develop a greater sense of moral accountability. They can encourage people to speak out when they discover abuses or provide forums for airing issues of concern.[25] The larger society can also play a role by supporting those who take unpopular stands or simply by providing a forum for them to air their complaints. Many institutions, of course, actively discourage a sense of moral accountability, and this is in part why only exceptional individuals are willing to protest about what they see as wrong. Only a few have a sufficiently keen sense of responsibility and integrity that they are willing to act in the face of discouragement. But such people demonstrate that it can be done, that there is nothing intrinsic to the nature of large institutions that prevents moral accountability altogether. Institutions are able to take steps to provide an environment where even ordinary, insecure and modest persons come to develop a sense of moral accountability and act on it.

All of the above discussion counts for little if the conditions of the international arena make morally responsible action impossible. It is difficult to dispute the main contentions of skeptics on this matter. Quite obviously there exists no effective authority to establish clear international standards of conduct or to enforce them. While nations pay lip service to the ideals of the United Nations' Universal Declaration of Human Rights, there is little evidence that these ideals have any substantial effect on international conduct. The ideals themselves are too lofty, too abstracted from particular cases, to have any significant bite. What is more, it is in the interests of many nations to prevent this useful sort of specificity from developing. There is no strong sense of world community. Nations remain culturally and politically fragmented.

To this extent the picture of world affairs presented by the skeptics is highly plausible. However, one key element of their position remains contentious. The nub of the idea of the Hobbesian state of nature is that it is a state of war, a continual struggle of life and death where each participant is driven to seek ever increasing amounts of power over others. If this feature of the Hobbesian picture is accepted, it is difficult to avoid the conclusion that no nation can afford to hamper itself with the constraints of morality.

It is quite true that nations are sometimes in mortal danger, but the level of conflict of the international arena in several ways resembles the picture of Locke more than Hobbes. Israel, for example, is quite clearly in a state of virtual war with its neighbors, and mortal hostility is apt to erupt at any moment. But Israel's position is far more precarious than, say, Denmark. It is difficult to portray the Danes as being in mortal danger or clearly threatened by anyone.

Sometimes nations *are* threatened, but most often they are not. When they are not, they are in a condition of peace. What is more, even where nations are threatened, or actually at war, the threat is rarely mortal. Iraq and Iran, for example, were recently engaged in bitter war, but it was highly unlikely that a victory for one party would have resulted in the death of the other or in great hardship for its people. Some wars, what Richard Brandt calls 'serious wars', are mortal but most are not.[26] These lesser conflicts are wars that nations can afford to lose. Because of this, even these wars do not justify abandoning moral scruple.

Even where the threat to nations is mortal, several factors prevent their situation from being as desperate as that of individuals. Individuals can be killed in an instant. A short lapse of attention or lowering of guard is sufficient to allow a mortal blow. Nations, however, are large, and – nuclear weapons aside – difficult to destroy quickly and easily. There is therefore more leeway for constraint and moral scruple. More importantly, when the death of nations is currently described, what is usually meant is the destruction of governments, and not the dissolution of the common life of the people. This is a far less consequential matter. It is not obvious, as will be argued in later chapters, that any government has an absolute moral entitlement to remain in existence. Where governments are lost, people and nation will often remain, and that is what is essential.

Even mortal wars, therefore, do not negate moral restraint. It is possible that usual moral standards will be overridden in those instances where some act or another really will make the difference between the survival of the nation and its destruction. These instances will be relatively few, even in serious wars, and certainly do not justify wanton cruelty or random destruction. Specific moral constraints may always be overridden in particular cases, but specific conditions must exist for this to occur. Furthermore, this overriding is always specific and does not justify the general abandonment of moral restraint. From a strictly utilitarian perspective, of course, there is no overriding of basic principle at all. The guiding rule must always be the greatest general welfare. However, utilitarianism does countenance the formulation of moral rules and general guides to the conduct of war and of life. These are justified by their overall and long-range consequences, but *these* may be overridden in certain cases by appeal to the more basic principle.

The existence of nuclear weaponry, for those nations that have or are threatened by it, does provide the requisite degree of insecurity. Such weapons do allow a nation to be destroyed in a twinkling. However, current experience shows that the existence of these weapons requires greater cooperation, greater restraint and greater understanding than was required in the pre-nuclear era. The

Hobbesian picture is in fact undone by the lessons of recent history. Where threat and danger are evenly distributed and uniformly fatal, more integrity is required to avoid the fatal slip and ease the desperation. In the salient case, the United States and Russia are edging, almost in spite of themselves, towards conditions of greater stability and understanding. In the absence of an equal and equally mortal threat, it is not unlikely that they would have gone to war years ago, and it is not unlikely that the war would have been initiated by the United States.[27]

So present conditions do not rule out moral responsibility, but, if it is to exist, it must be of a special kind with special constraints. While it will not be entirely different from the morality of personal relations, it will be significantly unlike it. This morality must operate outside social constraint and without commonly accepted standards. It must be a morality of solitary agents whether nations or individuals, acting on an *ad hoc* basis without the comfort of social sanction. It must, in other words, be a morality of individual nations, individual corporations, or persons acting on their own best judgement. While there certainly is cooperation and group endeavor on the international level, there is rarely a force to bind agents closely together. They occasionally coordinate their actions and share common interests, but there is little that forces them to function as a unit in any sustained fashion Societies are capable of bonding individuals together into groups and directing them to sustained action and shared purpose. This occurs in all manner of formal and informal ways, from the structures of the family to the conventions of friendship to the formally structured organizations allowed and nurtured by society. None of these exists on the international level. Agents there must function essentially as individuals, even though this solitariness can be mitigated occasionally by loose, informal and often transient modes of associating with others.

This solitary character extends to the moral scruples on which agents act. They must choose their standards for themselves and must recognize that much of the rest of the world may not accept them, may differ in the detail of their application, or may shine them through the prisms of different cultures. Agents must act without the security of acknowledged authorities and must acknowledge the reality of cultural, political and moral diversity. Thus, they must act from their own standards while attempting to avoid moral imperialism or arrogance. Uncertainty about ultimate standards, however, is less daunting than the uncertainty about details of application. The world has little experience in applying these standards to particular cases and making judgements about them. Even where there is common agreement about an abstract standard, such as 'Aggression is wrong', there is much less agreement about what counts as a particular case of aggression or how to interpret the agreed-upon facts of a given case. A not inconsiderable problem is getting accurate information about particular cases. Access to facts is likely to be controlled by governments that are hostile or have something to hide. Without a body of applicable case law, agents must make decisions almost exclusively on the basis of their own best judgements with little else to guide them.

Given present circumstance, moral action on the international level must be crude and minimal. It must be crude in the sense that uncertainties about standards and about application will not allow the development of sophisticated and elaborate moral codes covering every contingency or aiming at high levels of compliance. It must be minimal in the sense that it will be difficult to attempt action on more than the most blatant and widely acknowledged instances of wrongdoing. This ethics must also be crude and minimal in another way, when the options for taking action and pressuring miscreants are considered.

Social pressure and ostracization are often highly effective means of shaping the behavior and attitudes of individuals. This is so in part because the individual depends so heavily on the larger society, not only for the material necessities of life but for the psychological necessities of companionship, respect and knowledge. It is true in other part because the individual is conditioned from birth to adopt the values of the encompassing society and be sensitive to its pressures. Nation-states are considerably more independent than solitary individuals. While they often seek the good opinion of their peers, they do not need it in the visceral way that individuals do. They are not bred and nurtured by the world community and not psychologically dependent on it. While nations are far more interdependent economically than in the past, they remain much more independent than individuals. In any case, economic pressure on them is difficult to sustain, both because of the difficulty of coordinating the large numbers of agents necessary to make such pressure effective and also because there will always be those with something to gain by evading the sanctions. In fact, the more effective the sanctions are, the more lucrative such evasion is likely to be.

If all else fails, physical coercion can always be used to subdue and direct human individuals. Violence, or the threat of it, is much less effectual on the international level. The instruments of war are much more efficient at destruction than guidance, and their employment is likely to cost the user as dearly as the target. Wars and more limited violence, in any case, are much more difficult to control and are highly unpredictable and volatile in their use.

Thus, it is not easy to direct the behavior of miscreants at the international level. The means available to those who wish to exert pressure are only marginally effectual, are likely to be costly to the user, and are difficult to apply with consistency and for sustained periods. This implies once more that would-be moral agents cannot hope to respond to every instance of wrong-doing but can only respond to the most salient cases. They will not, that is, be able to seek universal compliance with moral standards or seek adherence to any complex array of moral scruples.

Using the normative principles mentioned earlier, the moral analyses of this project will proceed in several directions. Often the most basic problem of an ethics of international relations is simply to demonstrate that particular issues, such as weapons sales or aid to developing nations, are genuinely moral questions and should be treated as such. Allied to this is the effort to demonstrate to the agents involved both that their responsibilities include moral aspects and that they have genuine options for action which will make significant differences for people's lives. Skeptics would deny just this sort of agency. Stringent moralists would insist upon it, but fail to acknowledge the accommodation which must be made to comprehend this agency in the light of the distinct conditions of international relations. The analysis of this project will work to steer a course between these extremes.

Though there is no elaborated morality operating at the international level, there are a number of scattered intuitive assumptions of what is correct and proper. Among them are the views that national sovereignty is sacrosanct, that aggressive war is always morally wrong, that nations have a legitimate entitlement to the bounty of their material resources, that 'the will of the people' is the ultimate authority in matters of governmental legitimacy. Part of the work of this project must be to examine these, to determine to what extent they are well-grounded, require modification or should be abandoned altogether. Given the conditions of the international arena and the absence of the requirements necessary to support an intuitive moral system, it is necessary that most of the moral thinking to be done at the international level must be, in R. M. Hare's terms, of the critical sort, and that it should not be allowed to harden into intuitive presumptions. Even though this is the case, it will often be possible to develop general guidelines and list general conditions to be acknowledged for critical thinking to be undertaken.

But there will be cases where it can be demonstrated that some intuitions should be established or strengthened. Later analyses will show, for example, that it would be good for people to develop further their intuitive belief that they have some responsibility to aid suffering in other parts of the world. Or it can be shown that it would be good to develop intuitions differing from those held presently about what is justified by the requirements of national security.

There will also be questions, mainly developed in the concluding chapter but also present in other chapters, about what responsibilities agents may have to work to create the conditions where something approaching the morality of ordinary life can be made present on the international level. A genuine, fully developed, moral system must include substantially more than a handful of normative assumptions. It must encompass means of apportioning moral responsibility to agents, of demonstrating who relevant moral agents are, and of establishing and enforcing adherence to accepted norms. These are the features of the systems of personal morality which are commonly taken as defining any and all moral activity. This is mistaken. The present work is in agreement with the skeptics' belief that such conditions do not presently exist on the international level and, in opposition to the opinions of the stringent moralists, that anything approaching personal morality can be expected on the international level in the absence of the requisite conditions, for ethics has always been and must remain among the arts of the possible.

2 Violence in International Relations

It is difficult to say whether international violence is more prevalent at the present than at other times. A recent tally of world conflict shows more than forty wars of one type or another, involving more than forty nations, or nearly one quarter of the nations of the world.[1] Since the end of the Second World War, the toll of human life resulting from conflicts of this sort has run to the tens of millions, with more injury and destruction of property than can be counted.[2] In addition, small-scale assaults on innocent persons, so-called acts of terror, seem a daily occurrence. While the toll of human life lost in these attacks is comparatively small, far less than caused by automobiles, alcohol or the other ills of modern life, its psychological impact is substantial. The threat of terrorist assault appears to weigh more heavily than the acts themselves. This threat is minor, however, in comparison with the different and more permanent threat of nuclear warfare. Other periods of human history may equal the present in violence, but the great burden of contemporary life is the overwhelming nuclear threat and the way it spills out and charges actual conflict.

The great powers of the world are locked in an enduring and frequently bitter confrontation. This global confrontation has often enveloped other, lesser, confrontations and made them part of the larger struggle, surrogates for the violence the great powers do not dare to inflict on one another. The struggle of the great powers has resulted in a great amassing of arms and much posturing and maneuvering, but little overt confrontation. This tension nonetheless feeds itself into smaller conflicts, making them symbols of the larger contest. Often this tie results in the involvement of more, and more advanced, weaponry, or pushes the scope of conflict beyond its natural limit.

Powerful weapons, massed armies, complex and global conflict are features of the mass violence of nations. But this violence is interlinked with a violence of a different sort, discrete violence. Small groups of political extremists, the politically displaced and disaffected, or revolutionaries often lack the resources to match the violence of nations. Instead, they may resort to discrete acts which can be undertaken with few people and limited equipment – acts of bombing, kidnapping, hijacking, assassination, and sabotage. Small numbers and light armament offer mobility, flexibility and stealth. Yet such acts often receive attention and have repercussions far out of proportion to the resources they require. Discrete violence is often, loosely and inaccurately, labelled 'terrorism'. But only some of these acts have the goal of generating fear, and only some combatants see fear as an important means to their ends.

Discrete violence has become identified in the public mind of Western industrialized nations with these small, unstable, impecunious political groups. This, too, is a misunderstanding. Discrete violence is employed by the CIA and the KGB, not to mention Libya and Syria or other nations of the Mid East, as recent studies have shown.[3] Discrete violence is as much a tool of national governments as of disaffected and brutalized political groups. The major difference is that this mode of violence is available to small groups in a way that the instruments of mass violence possessed by nations are not.

Neither is discrete violence new on the world scene. Its roots are found in antiquity, and it has been a common feature of guerrilla war in modern times. The Irish Republican Army and the Provisional IRA have been practising it in Northern Ireland for years. Death squads and related groups have been active in Central and South America for decades. What has changed recently is the introduction of new techniques, those of attacking airport terminals or hijacking airliners, and new targets, Western Europeans and Americans. These changes have made discrete violence a center of attention in the West in a way that other techniques and other victims have not.

From a utilitarian perspective, the steps to a moral justification for relying on violence of any sort are simple. The use of violence must be directed toward the achievement of clear-cut goals, and the value of the goals to be achieved must outweigh the cost of the violent means of achieving them. Unfortunately this elegant simplicity dissolves into formidable complexity with the attempt to put these principles into practice as guides to political action. Part of the difficulty lies with the character of violence when considered as a means. It is only rational to choose means which are readily controlled, which carry some assurance of achieving their goal, and which are not likely to incur additional costs. What is more, a means which carries great costs is only justified if the results it achieves substantially outweigh those costs. As will be seen shortly, a substantial portion of the moral criticism of violence can be traced to its deficiencies and limitations as a means. Another part of the moral analysis of violence must include an examination of the sort of ends which are sufficiently important to outweigh the burden of using violent means to achieve them.

Because discrete violence differs in technique, motivation and human context from mass violence, the two will be examined separately with a view to determining both their character as means and the sort of ends which may justify their employment. But mass violence has two quite distinct modes of employment, that of all-out warfare and what analysts term 'projection of power'. These are sufficiently important and sufficiently different to merit separate treatment. Along with perceptions of increased violence have come renewed efforts to control or mitigate it. But, as will be seen, these carry their own moral costs and limitations. As before, the problems and techniques of controlling discrete violence differ substantially from those of mass violence and so must be treated separately.

VIOLENCE AS A MEANS

Resort to violence *always* involves a substantial cost, that of the destruction of the lives or the security of individual human beings. Indeed, whatever value it may have in utilitarian terms depends on the presence of this cost. That is to say, its value is as a coercive instrument for achieving ends, whether they be national liberation, correction of injustice or imperialist domination. Because of this, only the gravely irrational or the morally bankrupt engage in acts of violence for their own sake. But, it must be understood, this is not because violent activity is without intrinsic satisfactions for those who indulge in it. The public and sensitive writers are well aware of the pleasures which accompany violent activity.[4] A complete understanding of its use and control depends on grasping this. That is, the *attractiveness* of violence must be understood. The difficulty, of course, is that this attraction for the wielder of violent means must always be weighed against its cost to victims, and possibly to the user as well. It is difficult to imagine circumstances where any intrinsic satisfaction resulting from violence can match the pain, anguish or death inflicted on its victims.

Since whatever intrinsic value violence may possess for the wielder will normally be outweighed by its cost, its use must be justified by some extrinsic goal. One difficulty is that it is comparatively rare for the extrinsic goal of violence to be accomplished simultaneously with the violent act itself. Sometimes the two will coincide, as when violence is used to free captives or to kill a brutal and deadly leader. Most often, though, the ostensibly justifying goal of violence will, at best, be only indirectly furthered by the act itself, as when a bombing raid is undertaken in the attempt to force a government to end its support for terrorist groups, or when government officials are kidnapped to press for the release of political prisoners. This distinction between the immediate result of violence and its further consequences underscores the uncertainty of violence when used as a means. The immediate result of violence is, say, an airfield destroyed or a government official killed. But these results do not, in and of themselves, justify the act. An airfield is destroyed to pressure a government to end its support of terrorist groups, and it is this further consequence that ostensibly justifies the act, not the immediate outcome. But there is no direct causal link between the immediate result and the desired further consequence. All too often the connection between the two is only wishful thinking.

Because of the frequently tenuous connection between means employed and ends to be achieved, the resort to violence must be a calculated risk at best. The act can only be justified by the achievement of its goal, but if there is a substantial degree of doubt that the act will fail, this too must be considered. A risk factor which is sufficiently large will deflate the value of any goal. This applies with particular force to acts of violence, since their negative costs will normally be much more certain than any purportedly justifying benefit.

A further difficulty is that violence as a means is much more difficult to control and limit than other instruments. An ostensibly surgical air strike, for example, may meet with much greater and more effective resistance than anticipated, or the skill and efficiency of one's own forces may fall short of expectation. Simple accident, loss of the element of surprise, failure of equipment or personnel, may all greatly increase the human and material cost of an armed venture. What is envisioned as a modest and justifiable foray can easily become a nightmare. It is important to understand that this is an inherent feature of the resort to violence itself. The unexpected and accidental, or the unforeseeable, are constituents of all acts of violence, and their presence, given the volatile nature of the means employed, can easily upset all nice balancing of means against ends.

Then, too, violence invites a violent response, so the original act is met with another, which requires a third, and so on. Again, escalation of this sort is an elemental feature of the resort to violence and can readily scuttle justifying calculations.

But the above are essentially practical difficulties. They link with issues of moral justification because acts of violence are clearly unjustified where there is little likelihood that they will achieve their goals or if they involve substantial risks of erupting into greater destruction than their goals are able to justify. If violence can be efficient in achieving some goals, it is important to ask which of these goals can be *morally* justified.

Recall that the central features of acts of violence are that they destroy life or the means to life and that these costs always accompany acts of violence. Such operations are volatile in the sense that there is always the possibility that these costs will radically increase in unforeseen and uncontrollable fashion. As argued earlier, it is wise as a general policy only to trade life and the means of life against these basic wants and not against secondary desires. In the usual course, therefore, violent acts can only be justified to save human lives or restore the secure means of life. The crudeness of violence as an instrument of change, its suitability for destruction rather than constructively improving human life, make it ill fitted to nurture the secondary wants of human beings. The variety and complexity of such wants, their vulnerability to whim and fashion, as well as their dependence on a stable social context, all make it unlikely that they can be achieved to any appreciable degree by the resort to violence. Whatever utility violence has as a means will generally be limited to preserving human life or security. Of course, on occasion people may decide for themselves to risk their lives in pursuit of values other than the preservation of human life, values such as religious integrity, ethnic culture, political freedom or simple adventure. Should they elect to do so, it may be impossible to say their choice is unjustified, but neither are they justified in risking or threatening the lives of others in pursuit of these goals.

The above implies, for example, that life-threatening violence may not be used against a regime which violates certain of the civil rights of its citizens, such as those of freedom of speech or freedom of association, but nonetheless does not imperil their lives or means of life. There are many justifiable ways of fighting such regimes, but life-threatening means are not among them. This holds true even if it can be reasonably assumed that life-threatening violence is likely to be the only effective instrument for removing such regimes or forcing them to change their ways. A further consequence is that violent responses, even to acts of aggressive warfare, are unjustified if the aggression is not directed against human life but involves, say, slicing off an uninhabited piece of territory. This does not imply that such aggression is innocuous or should be ignored. It only implies that a violent response to it is unjustified.

On these grounds the British battle to wrest control of the Falkland Islands from Argentina in the spring of 1982 was morally unjustified. This is so even presuming that Argentina's initial seizure of the islands was morally wrong, that the British effort was completely successful, and that a number of worthy consequences resulted, the downfall of the Argentine military junta among them. The British attack was unjustified because the lives and personal security of the Falkland Islanders were not at peril. It is true that the Falklanders did not desire the new arrangement and that the government of Argentina was likely to be less enlightened than the one they previously enjoyed. Control by Argentina was undesirable, but this consequence was not of sufficient weight to justify the cost in life required to undo it. The actual toll in human life and the suffering that resulted from the British assault, the risk inherent in such ventures that the toll could easily have been much greater, and the risk that the conflict could have spread beyond all foreseen proportions, were not counterbalanced by the prospect of significant preservation of human life or well-being.

These conclusions do not imply that Margaret Thatcher or other members of her government should have been tried as war criminals or even that control of the Falklands should be returned to Argentina. The results of the battle were generally beneficial, and, as these things go, Thatcher's transgressions were small. But, more fundamentally, there are no clear-cut international guidelines for such activity and little precedent for thinking about issues of this sort in moral terms or more specifically in terms of the value of human life at stake. In fact it is unlikely that Thatcher thought of the Falklands as presenting a moral issue. If she did so, it is likely that she believed the prerogatives of sovereignty justified her action. Her personal guilt, in other words, is small, and her activities are comprehensible to the ordinary, well-intentioned individual. Nonetheless, they are unjustified in the senses that, if she had viewed the issue as a moral one, she should have come to a different conclusion and that, if international principles of conduct were established for such matters, the option she selected should have been ruled out.

In sum, because violence always involves a serious cost, and this cost is explosive and difficult to control, it is unjustified if other means are available – even if these other means are slower, require more determined effort, and are less inherently satisfying. But this reveals a substantial advantage of acts of violence. They achieve their effects quickly. Where human life is in *immediate* danger, resort to violence may be preferable to other, slower, and less decisive methods. Normally, then, violence will be most clearly justified only where there is immediate threat to human life, and insufficient time for other methods to work.

WARFARE

The resort to mass violence is the most intrusive symptom of the Hobbesian state of nature which exists in international affairs. On this level, violence often seems the most satisfying way of exerting one's will or of fending off the unwanted attentions of others. Violence is readily perceived as quick, satisfying and direct. National leaders understand all too well that the flourish of arms is an excellent means of welding national unity or diverting attention from pressing domestic turmoil. The resort to arms, where successful, is hugely popular. At the very least, it can be touted as a mark of decisiveness, the fortitude to come to grips with problems. What is more, it is action, movement. Masses like to see their leaders doing things, and violence is the most spectacular and riveting doing of all. Thus, means which, it would seem, should be reserved for the last resort often become the first resort, and it is all too easy to see why.

Of the factors that allow international violence to flourish and make it appear attractive to national leaders, two loom above the rest. Nation-states have a monopoly of the instruments of mass violence, and there is nobody with the authority or means to prevent them from using it. The latter condition defines what philosophers going back to Hobbes have understood as the state of nature, and the activity of nations has frequently appeared quite Hobbesian. But what is often overlooked is that there are no effectual internal *constraints*, within nations, working strongly against the resort to violent means. There is no strong, active and influential constituency within nations capable of forestalling the decision to resort to violence. In part this is because, when violence is directed outward, there are no groups within nations whose interests are directly harmed by it. And there are often important sectors, the military and arms makers in particular, who reap substantial benefits from it. Then too, the speed and secrecy, which is often claimed to be an essential ingredient of planning military operations, forestalls public debate and prevents the formation of effective opposition. Also, and not incidentally, there is a strong emotional urge for citizens of nations to draw together when confronted with physical and external threat.[5] When faced with violent crisis, it often seems that unity is essential and that doubting and questioning should be reserved for a time when the urgency has passed.

None of this would matter if national leaders did not frequently believe they had a great deal to gain by resorting to violence – or a great deal to lose by restraint. As pointed out above, there are large domestic gains to be had from the successful resort to violence. In addition, national leaders are often attracted to the idea of helping themselves to slices of other people's territory. Lacking an international authority to keep order, there is little but the force of arms to stop them. Moreover, leaders are notoriously susceptible to the urge to exert their will on those in other nations. The most direct and satisfying way of doing so is the resort to arms. Of course, nations frequently feel threatened by others. When they are, a natural first impulse is to amass weaponry or signal threats abroad in order to calm unsteady nerves at home.

Another, lesser, factor remains, but it is one that is too often overlooked. National leaders seem to enjoy having large armies and sophisticated armaments for their own sake, apart from any reasonable use to which they may be put. This may be the simple analogue on the international level of persons who enjoy collecting arms, tinkering with them, and finding occasions for displaying or using them. Researchers have shown that, particularly for new and insecure nations, armies are a potent symbol of nationhood, the manifest sign of coming of age and taking one's place in the world community.[6] Like other attractive and powerful instruments, armaments in place carry the temptation to be used.

However, empirical factors explaining nations' propensity for relying on arms do not amount to a moral justification for their use. People have a variety of, often conflicting, intuitions about the moral justification of warfare. Even within a single, broadly defined position, that of moral skepticism for instance, there is frequently an array of such intuitions.

Some skeptics appear to believe, following Machiavelli, that governments are essentially beyond moral constraint. Therefore, wars which result from governmental activity are neither morally right nor wrong. They are simply events, like floods or hurricances, which cannot be controlled or judged. Early portions of this work have examined this view and presented arguments to demonstrate that it is mistaken. But it may be the case that wars are exceptions to this. It is possible that governments can be held morally accountable in their usual operations, but, when caught up in war, they are merely swept along by events. The historical record shows that this claim is only partially true. In 1939, for example, it is unlikely that Poland could have done anything to escape being caught up in war. The United States, on the other hand, clearly had a choice in the matter. Sweden, to consider a different instance, was able to remain neutral throughout the war by means of a combination of determination, ingenuity and luck.

Apart from leeway in deciding whether to enter wars, nations have options for determining how they will be fought. They can decide whether or not to use blockades to starve opponents into submission. They can decide to bomb population centers or refrain from doing so. It is sometimes claimed that nations must use whatever means they believe necessary to prevail in war. But this again is a half-truth at best. Most importantly, combatants rarely have only one option that is likely to prove effective. Furthermore, the most horrifying and notorious atrocities of wars are usually cases where the choices were not forced on the perpetrators and which did not appear to give any distinct military advantage. Allied bombing of population centers during the Second World War, for instance, was both optional and, at best, of limited military value. There is little point in attempting moral judgements of the conduct of nations where they are caught in a tide of events. But it is not true that they are always swept away in this fashion. Where they have control and where they have choices, it makes sense to expect them to be morally accountable and to make moral assessment of their conduct.

Pacifists, of course, would argue generally that wars are morally wrong. But there are distinct varieties of this position. One is that it is always morally wrong intentionally to take the life of a human being. The utilitarian perspective of the present work cannot support that view. Sometimes lives will be saved and human welfare secured if life is taken. Killing Adolf Hitler or Idi Amin before their careers came to an end would doubtless have saved many lives and averted much human suffering. Similarly, Tanzania's invasion of Uganda to oust Idi Amin or India's war with Pakistan before the succession of Bangladesh, while costly in human life, surely avoided much human death and misery. Those who choose to avoid taking life where doing so is likely to save the lives of others must come to terms with their role, however indirect, in *those* deaths. There is no way, in situations of this sort, of avoiding being responsible for some deaths.

There is another pacifist intuition, distinct from the above, which has more bite, at least from the utilitarian perspective. With the rise of modern mass armies, it may be argued, and technical advances which have greatly increased the range and destructiveness of current weaponry, it is nearly impossible to contain and manage the use of deadly force. For this reason, wars are almost certain to squander more human life than they preserve. There clearly are some wars of which this is true, and it is quite probably true of most of them. It applies to the British effort in the Falklands and to the recent war in the Persian Gulf. While Iraq was criminally wrong in attacking Iran in 1980, Iran was wrong to respond with the force and on the scale it did, and both were morally wrong in continuing a war which cost approximately a million human lives.[7] But other cases are more difficult and more complicated, and it is not obvious that the argument applies to them.

Part of the problem is that it is very difficult to establish any precise estimate of how many lives may have been saved by a given war, how much suffering averted – or to what extent threats to life and the means to life have been neutralized. The Second World War provides an instructive example and a difficult one. The number of deaths in battle ran to tens of millions and was compounded several-fold by deaths from disease, starvation and the general dislocation of war.[8] If there had been no resistance to the German armies at all, it is quite probable that this number would have been greatly reduced. The suffering resulting from the violent dislocation of the war may well have decreased substantially. Even this is not certain. Hitler's regime was as murderous as the world is likely to see and did not appear to be significantly less so where it encountered little violent resistance. But what is reasonably certain is that, if the German armies had prevailed, large stretches of the world would have been at the mercy of a cruel, ruthless and capricious tyranny. Even where people were not killed or deprived of the means of life, they would have been under the continual threat of violent oppression. The Allied victory averted that outcome and was therefore worth a great deal. It is reasonable to presume that people, when faced with the choice between the risk of violent death and the certainty of living in circumstances where their lives and well-being, and those of their families, are permanently at threat, would be willing to make the immediate gamble of their lives. In fact, it is reasonable to suppose that this is how people actually do weigh these matters, in so far as they weigh them at all. Talk of liberty, freedom or democracy are mere abstractions with little concrete meaning for most people. The attraction of these words comes with their aura of positive associations rather than precise content.

Yet the above analysis carries two assumptions which rest uneasily with one another. One is that the number of deaths which actually resulted from the Second World War was somehow preordained. This is mistaken. There are measures which could have been taken by the Allied forces to reduce this toll. For one thing, greater attention could have been given to the needs of refugees. There is evidence, for example, that many thousands of Jewish lives could have been saved if the United States had acted decisively early in the war to provide them with haven, or if the Allies had demonstrated greater interest and concern during the course of the conflict.[9] There is also reason to believe that the Allied insistence on unconditional surrender and their refusal to negotiate with the Germans prolonged the war and increased its toll. The human cost of the war could have been significantly lower if there had been greater concern for it.

Another assumption of the above analysis is that the alternative to fighting the war was that of giving no resistance to German advances. This presupposes a world much closer to the ideal than the one we have. Neither the United States nor Britain was faced with a choice between war or no war. They were forced to decide whether to enter an ongoing and violent conflict. It is not obvious that their participation increased the human cost of the war. But it is clear that their efforts made the difference of the outcome and prevented the considerable cost of a German victory.

So active participation in the Second World War by the various Allies was probably justified. The utilitarian stance does not allow the luxury of certainty in cases of this sort. Moralists indebted to Kant will be unhappy with this, insisting that rights and duties should be known clearly, that there should be an unambiguous answer to every moral problem. But in the actual world this certainty can be achieved only by relying on ethereal and attractive concepts like rights and liberty whose content is not defined with precision and which therefore are of little use as concrete guides to action. Under certain circumstances the requisite specificity can be obtained, but only by being established within a cohesive community which has authority to establish and interpret norms. No such community exists at the present on the level of international relations. The closest candidate is the United Nations. But its Universal Declaration of Human Rights is hopelessly infected with vagueness and abstraction. The United Nations itself is deeply politicized and lacks the authority and power to establish precise norms or provide some measure of enforcement. The utilitarian standard of concern for human life has the decided advantage of being clear and possessing strong intuitive appeal. In addition, in so far as decision- makers explicitly address themselves to maintaining life and security and weigh this concern in their decisions, lives in fact are likely to be saved and protected.

The Second World War is a difficult case. There are others that are considerably easier. The incursion of India into what is now Bangladesh in December of 1971 to halt the ravages of Pakistani troops no doubt saved lives. The number of such clearly justified wars is no doubt small. But the fact that they exist at all is highly important.

If the Indian incursion into Bangladesh is clearly justified, another of the common intuitions about war is in peril, one which is both widespread and deep-seated. It is the view that wars of aggression are always morally wrong – the greatest wrong which nations can commit, in one commentator's view.[10] Although there is some obscurity concerning just what constitutes 'aggression', the Indian attack on Pakistani troops was aggression in the sense that it was clearly initiated without provocation and the Pakistani armies posed no immediate threat to India. Yet the attack saved lives and ended repression much more quickly and more effectively than other methods India was likely to have available. In fact it is unlikely that any other measures would have been successful. Aggression in this case was therefore justified, as it was in the case of Tanzania's incursion into Uganda.

The intuition that aggression is always wrong is thus mistaken. Some acts of aggression are justified and may even be morally obligatory. An excellent illustration of this is provided by the former United States Senator George McGovern, a persistent critic of US involvement in Vietnam. In 1978 he argued that it was the duty of the international community to dispatch a force to Cambodia to halt the murderous activity of the Pol Pot regime.[11] His plea was unsuccessful, of course. It was largely undone by the complexities of international politics and also by grave doubts concerning the feasibility of such an effort. However, its spirit was correct and important.

A close companion of the above intuition is the belief that wars of *resistance* to aggression are always justified. Previous discussion shows this to be mistaken as well. Pakistani leaders were not morally justified in directing troops to resist the onslaught of the Indian army. Britain was not justified in resorting to force to rectify Argentina's wrongful seizure of the Falklands.

However, cases of justified aggression are few in number and far outweighed by the instances of wrongful aggression. Given the disarray of international affairs and the attractions of violence for nations, aggression is far more likely to be misused than not. Like a recovering alcoholic swearing off drink, it may be necessary for nations to take the pledge and swear off aggressive war. Certainly this view is given credence by a look at the developments of world history which have caused nations to arrive at a consensus supporting this intuition. It may be important to maintain the rhetorical force of the term so that it can be used as a tool for excoriating wrongful aggression.

There is much to be said in favor of this view, but there are also some important considerations which may be raised against it. For one thing there is no evidence that this intuition has actually served to deter wrongful acts of aggression. Nations that are determined to misuse the instruments of mass violence do so, and search for pretexts later. If the world were such that it was effectively possible to get *all* nations to swear off aggressive acts and there were sufficient communal unity and cohesion to exert pressure on backsliders – if, in other words, the conditions of the international arena more closely resembled those of the lives of individuals – such universal temperance would be feasible. But, as things stand, responsible nations will continue to restrain themselves, and those that are not will not. This is not to say that 'aggression' should become a term of commendation. Rather, it might be better if a new term were coined, something like 'humanitarian intervention', to provide a rhetorical tool to be used to garner support for justified aggression. And it would be good to possess such a tool, since it would aid morally responsible nations to work to combat abuses and might begin to establish conditions which can lead to greater moral accountability.

It is possible that the above argument has cast its net too broadly. There may be certain categories of response to aggression that are always justified, such as those of self-defense. It is possible too that attacks which are directed at destroying a nation are always wrong. These possibilities link to another common intuition concerning the justification for warfare, the belief that wars of self-defense are always morally justified. This intuition has a great deal of plausibility, and its plausibility depends in part on the intuition resident in the ethics of personal affairs that individual self-defense is always morally sound. Indeed, the moral force of national defense may be stronger, not only because of the greater numbers of people, but because it involves protecting those who are too weak to defend themselves and preserving the common life of the nation.

The difficulty with this view, as will be elaborated in the following chapter, is in determining just what is protected when a nation is defended. If the reference is to the lives and well-being of ordinary citizens, then wars of national self-defense are justified if any are. But if the reference is to a portion of the territory of a nation, then resort to war to defend territorial boundaries is not as obviously justified and may in fact be unjustified. Where attacks are narrowly directed against a particular government or the officials of government, wars of self-defense may sometimes be unjustified as well, particularly where the government is corrupt and oppressive, as was the government of Idi Amin. Where attacks are directed not only against citizens, but also against their institutions and common life, wars of self-defense have the strongest justification of all. The paradigm case here may be the Yom Kippur War of October 1973, where it was apparent that the existence of Israel as a nation, along with the lives and welfare of its citizens, was at stake. However, it is important to recognize that not all cases of what is commonly construed as national self-defense are like this. In fact, most are probably not, and where they are not, many will be unjustified.

As the present discussion illustrates, the traditional set of intuitions about the justification of war are rough guidelines at best. Moreover, there may be little value in wishing to establish intuitions at this level. Governments are equipped with the resources to examine such issues fully and carefully. They do not require an unreflective set of guides to conduct in the way individuals do. What is more, intuitions on this level can be counter-productive, as when they are turned into slogans or instruments of propaganda and so serve to quiet dissent or prevent the public airing of issues. The usual intuitions about war may serve as useful starting points for thought and discussion on such matters but should not replace them. They are useful, that is, as rules of thumb, or as rough indications that certain courses of action should be avoided while others are more likely to be defensible. But they should not be allowed to harden into unthinking guidelines.

The goals of war discussed thus far are only the remote outcomes of war, the hoped-for results of hostile activity. But these should not be confused with the immediate results of war, the consequences which military combat is capable of bringing about directly. The assessment of warfare as an instrument requires an understanding of these immediate results and a grasp of their suitability for bringing about remote, but justifying, consequences.

The list of possible immediate consequences is both short and unprepossessing. It includes: halting or reversing the movement of a hostile army, destroying a hostile army, the invasion and occupation of a nation, the capture of military forces or government officials, or the destruction of the physical means of warfare – the weapons, factories, bridges and roads – of a hostile nation. This is what wars can directly accomplish. The central question is whether these direct results are likely to be effective in bringing about remote but justifying consequences.

Examination of this array of direct consequences of warfare demonstrates that it is capable of being reasonably effective for the defense of a nation, by preventing hostile armies from doing their work. In some cases aggressive war may serve a useful function. A pre-emptive attack may serve to neutralize a threat. An armed invasion may halt oppression or remove a tyrannical government. There is a tendency, when seeking to justify warfare, to reach for the most elevated and glittering rhetoric. Thus it is proclaimed that wars are fought 'to make the world safe for democracy' or 'to provide world stability' or 'to nurture human freedom and dignity'.[12] These goals are too abstract and ethereal to be clearly linked to the destructive acts of war. They may be useful for stirring up populations and garnering support for conflict, but they are too vague and too remote from the destructive acts themselves to be able to justify war.

Wars can only destroy. But sometimes destruction is necessary, to prevent further destruction. It is important to keep clearly in mind that nothing grand can be achieved by war. Sometimes a tyrant can be overthrown and freedom gained, but this freedom is only the limited and particular freedom from oppression of that particular tyrant. Freedom in the larger and grander sense of self-determination and individual flourishing cannot be attained by this means. The instrument of war can only remove some of the conditions that prevent this grander freedom from being attained. It is this negative function, that of removing the causes of misery, which wars are fitted to serve. Most wars are unjustified, but some are, and when they are, they are likely to be the only instrument that can serve the purpose.

PROJECTION OF POWER

In spite of the dismaying frequency of wars, the most common use of the organized forces of mass destruction by nation-states is what analysts term 'projection of power'. National leaders are resourceful at finding ways to make use of military forces for purposes other than all out warfare. Indeed, given the coercive potential of the instruments of mass destruction, it would be surprising if they had not done so. These uses, though, require somewhat greater finesse than does war if their employment is to be successful.

Projection of force is the international deployment of arms for limited acts of violence or simply maneuvering them in a way that signals of threat or messages of support are conveyed to interested parties. The latter, signalling, modes of projection are likely the most widely and frequently used and quite possibly the most benign. The various ways of projecting power, the purposes sought, and their rates of success have all been carefully studied.[13]

When the projection of force involves limited incidents of violence, the acts are not greatly different in nature or in principle from the discrete violence of the weak, the so-called acts of terror. Bombing performed by airplane, for example, seems little different in its nature than from bombing by smuggled suitcase. The release of hostages by commando raid hardly differs from those sprung in a prison break. For a number of reasons, there are likely to be differences both in the manner these acts take place and in their immediate targets. Terrorist groups are less likely to take on military installations, and in consequence more likely to harm civilians by their acts. The violence of nations is most often directed against military targets but is also prone to result in unintended destruction. Both types of violence are probably equally likely to be misused. Nonetheless, in principle it is difficult to see why one class of acts should be thought intrinsically more or less benign or savage than the other. For both, the only ultimate justification can be that the act of violence results in lives being saved or the security of life increased.

Both types of violence are, in intention and conception at least, limited, and therefore ostensibly relatively easy to control. A target is selected, destructive violence is brought to bear, and that is the end of it. Each type can be further subdivided according to whether the desired goal is achieved simultaneously with the act itself or whether the goal is distant or symbolic, intended to be *caused* or prompted by the act but not simultaneous with it. Instances where the goal is achieved simultaneously with the act are the most straightforward and possibly the easiest to justify, if only because the act and its goal are tightly linked so that the act is more likely to secure the goal and the goal is clearly understood – that is, hostages are released, menacing military installations destroyed, or brutal political leaders killed simultaneously with the violent assault. The act brings the goal, the goal is clearly understood, and it can readily be seen whether its cost is justified.

But most often the violent acts themselves are meant to be justified by their linkage to some more distant event. An airfield is bombed, not because it has any great importance in itself, but to send a signal or exert pressure. In such cases it is much more difficult to know whether the physical violence is commensurate with its gain, or exactly what the gain is, or to have any reasonable degree of certainty that the act will achieve its intended effect. In such instances, goals and their relation to discrete acts tend to become obscure – and thus much more difficult to justify either prudentially or morally.

Even when carrying out the act simultaneously achieves the goal, justification can be difficult. Consider the instance where an airfield is bombed in the attempt to destroy warplanes capable of inflicting substantial damage on the attacking nation. During war, it is relatively easy to see how such an act could be justified. In war a nation possessing armaments is extremely likely to use them against an opponent. In times of ostensible peace, the situation is different and more complex. In these cases the attacking nation may sometimes view the mere presence of powerful warplanes as a significant threat to its security, and one which it cannot afford to ignore.[14]

Being 'a threat to security' is a difficult and elusive idea, which involves the interplay of a number of different factors. Coming to terms with the efficiency and the morality of various acts of projection of power requires that these factors and their interaction be understood. To begin with, there must be the capacity to cause substantial damage to the nation that feels threatened. This 'capacity' may take various forms, including military armaments of course, but may also include control of strategic raw materials or simply the fact of lying astride vital avenues of transportation or communication. Nations may also feel threatened in other ways, by ideology or cultural influence. Much Islamic antipathy to the United States stems from fear of its cultural influence – its movies, music and gadgets.[15] The United States itself is not immune from such anxieties, since a good portion of its obsession with Cuba and Nicaragua results from fears of their ideological threat.

A major source of difficulty and anxiety is that 'capacity' is difficult to assess precisely. The exact dangers posed by a given bombing aircraft, for instance, are often difficult to estimate in peacetime both because its speed, maneuverability, accuracy, payload and electronic warfare equipment may be unknown, and also because its effectiveness under actual conditions of war is unknown. (Part of the difficulty of estimating relative American and Russian missile strength and threat is the result of such problems.) But the difficulty does not end here, for the military capacity of a particular piece of equipment depends in large measure on the ability of a given opponent to cope with it. The most powerful nuclear weapon in the world would pose relatively little danger if an opponent could be confident of being able to neutralize it before it could be used. The destructive potential of Libyan SAM-7 missiles in the spring of 1986 was fairly low when matched against the abilities of attacking American bombers, but would probably have been much greater if, instead, Egypt had been mounting the attack. Once again, however, it is often the case that the efficiency of these measures must remain unknown until they are arrayed in hostile activity. Uncertainty thus compounds uncertainty – which is compounded again by the fact that the ultimate effectiveness of inert hardware depends on the skill and dedication of the animate humans who maintain and utilize it. American Phantom jets, for example, appear more formidable when manned by Israelis than by, say, Iranians.

But these uncertainties of capacity mesh with others, those of motive. Great Britain has a far greater capacity to effect physical damage on the United States than does Nicaragua – by anyone's estimate. Yet political leaders in the United States worry endlessly about Nicaragua and not at all about the Anglo menace. The difference lies, of course, in the assessment of the motives of the two nations – their interests, anxieties, goals and attitudes. The US is sanguine about Britain because the two have common interests and a long history of cultural and personal ties. The US and Nicaragua, on the other hand, are sharply divided by ideology and have an entrenched history of mutual suspicion and animosity, which is soured further by Sandinista ties to America's arch-nemesis. Thus Britain, it is supposed, has nothing to gain from attacking the US and no hostile intent, while nothing but the worst can be expected from the Sandinistas, in the view of many in the United States.

Motives by their nature do not lend themselves to precise analysis. Something can be known about them, and they can be analyzed with greater or lesser insight. But they are difficult to pin down because they depend in large part on the psychological processes of national leaders and the dynamics of a governmental system. Who knows, for example, whether the Sandinista leaders genuinely intend to foment revolution throughout Central America? Who knows exactly how Saudi leaders feel about the state of Israel or Palestinian nationalism? Attempts at objective and rational assessment of national interest are one thing, but inspecting the workings of the minds of individual leaders is quite another, and yet motives result from both.

Yet a third level of uncertainty remains. Syria certainly has the military capacity to inflict a great deal of damage on Israel and has the motive to do so, yet does not, at the time of writing, appear to have the intent to go to war. Yet intentions are notoriously volatile and are hidden from external view. Indeed, national leaders often make it their business to keep their intentions hidden from others.[16] Worse, intentions can change in an instant. They depend only on the mental processes of those who hold them and are not directly contingent on more fixed and stable factors, as are military capacity and motive.

These three factors, shadowy and amorphous as they are, react upon one another, so that changes in one bring about alterations in the others. An increase in military capacity, whether real *or* perceived (unless war is actually underway, a perceived increase in power is often as useful as the real thing) can change intentions by opening new possibilities for action. It can also change motives, say, by altering the balance of power so that an erstwhile competitor can now be seen as a subservient ally.[17]

Being 'a threat to security' depends on the complex and imprecise interaction of all of these factors.[18] Judgements of this sort must be imprecise. Yet, because the consequences of failing to appreciate a genuine threat are so great, there will often be pressure to be extraordinarily sensitive to possible threats.[19] But the opposite reaction is also common. That is, a nation may be anxious to avoid becoming enmeshed in hostility and may therefore avoid obvious signs of threats to security, *or* it may be powerless to do anything about them and, because of this, have a strong incentive to view them in other ways. On the other hand, a nation may feel it is in its interest to provoke a confrontation with another and, therefore, may look for threats to security. So these judgements, complex and difficult enough in themselves, are readily subject to distorting external influences.

To believe, then, that a given piece of equipment is a threat to security involves more than only the judgement that it is capable of inflicting great damage without the certainty of adequate response. It must also include the judgement that there is a motive for so using it, and that the intention to do so is close to hand. Israel, for example, bombed an Iraqi nuclear reactor a few years ago because Israelis thought it probable that it had the capacity to produce weapons-grade fissionable material and, if this were so, Iraq would also quite likely develop the intention to employ it, since Iraq had strong motives for wishing Israel's destruction. It is difficult for outsiders to assess the accuracy of Israel's information or the correctness of the inferences they drew from it. This is one of the great difficulties of applying an ethics of international relations under present conditions. Observers must make do with careful estimates and good judgement rather than full information. However, the best judgement of the external world is that Israel's calculations were correct. If so, its strike was justified. Given Israel's size, even a single nuclear weapon could cause great damage. Possession of a nuclear weapon by Iraq would therefore have been a grave threat to Israel's security, given its motives and the history of its government. Iraq's record of using poison gas against Iran clearly re-enforces the correctness of Israel's perception of the threat.[20]

But if it is granted that a particular type of aircraft is a significant threat to the security of a given nation – a judgement, recall, depending on substantially more than the military capacity of the equipment in question – it is still not obvious what sort of response is appropriate. The most direct, and in some ways most satisfying, response would be to use military force to destroy it, to eliminate directly the capacity to cause harm. If the threat posed is quite large and likely to be put to use, coercive action may well justify its substantial cost, as demonstrated in the case of Iraq's nuclear reactor. But there are prominent difficulties even in cases of this sort. For one, destroying capacity does not destroy motive. Israel was able to destroy a substantial portion of Syrian airpower in 1982, yet a few years later Syrian air and missile forces were larger and stronger than before.[21] Because Syrian motives were not destroyed along with their aircraft, Israel's efforts had only a temporary effect. Destruction of capacity may be only temporary so long as motives remain untouched, since motives are frequently capable of generating capacity.

What is worse, the temporary destruction of capacity can serve to re-enforce hostile attitudes and strengthen resolve. The act of destruction itself will serve as a vivid demonstration of the vulnerabilities of the nation attacked, of threats to its own security. The effort to found security on military capacity is a two-edged sword, since greater military capacity for self-defense is easily turned round to become a greater threat to adversaries.[22] Furthermore, hostile action *generates* hostility. It creates fear and anger and so intensifies conflict.

The strength, then, of violent physical action is that it can quickly and decisively eliminate the capacity for hostile activity. Its great weakness is that its effect on national policy will normally be temporary so long as hostile motives remain, and in fact may increase deep-seated antagonism. What overt destruction gains in decisiveness and effectiveness over the short term, it frequently gives up in long term security. Enduring security depends on altering the motives of opponents, and military action short of all-out war with invasion and occupation is unlikely to achieve that.

Sometimes, of course, quick and decisive action is necessary. Sometimes, waiting too long will preclude the chance of an effective response. Sometimes, a striking display of force and resolve will be necessary to upset the momentum of a militaristic and greedy leader and may in consequence prevent future acts of aggression. This latter point is important. The employment of force is dramatic and compelling in a way that few other gestures can be. It is more risky, to be sure, and more volatile, but for just this reason commands attention. The fact that the risk is taken signals commitment and seriousness of intent.

Instances of this sort move beyond cases where the goal is tightly linked with the act. There are several subtypes of these remote consequences. One is where the act itself is seen as part of a coordinated program intended to achieve a larger and more distant goal. The act itself may be futile and costly but is designed to gain its worth through relation to other acts which in turn capture an end of sufficient importance to justify them all. The single act of destroying a missile site, for example, may be insignificant in its immediate consequences, and, in fact, its destructiveness may well outweigh its immediate benefit. But if the single act is part of a coordinated set of acts whose overall result is the abandonment of hostile activity on the part of the target nation, then the set *as a whole* may be amply justified, even though any given member of the set bears only meagre fruit. Thus, when Reagan bombed Tripoli in the spring of 1986, he may well have understood that a single act would have little impact on world terrorism, but he may have seen it as part of a broader program of coordinated activity, of many sorts, which would result in the significant erosion of support for acts of terror. The single act, foolhardy and empty though it may have been in itself, may have made sense as part of a larger effort.

The difficulty with these schemes, of course, is that they only have hope of justification if they work – and if the goal achieved by them is well-defined and clearly justifies its cost. Both of these factors involve difficulty. Reagan's bombing raid on Libya, for example, resulted in a substantial number of deaths and considerable destruction of property. It is highly unlikely that it dampened terrorist activity sufficiently that equivalent lives were saved. The number of assaults did decrease after Reagan's action, but there is little reason to believe that this was the result of the bombing raid.[23] But the claim may also be made that this act was part of a larger effort, whose overall success may have justified the single act. There is no evidence, however, that Reagan had any such larger strategy. Even if he did, there is little reason to believe that the bombing raid played an essential part in it, or a part that could not have been played by another, less destructive act. Furthermore, the success of such complicated operations depends on a large number of assumptions, and probably an even larger number of uncontrollable and unforeseeable factors. Reagan's bombing attack was, therefore, unjustified.

Political and military leaders are often attracted by the elegance and sweep of grand plans and tend to overlook the complex structure of assumptions on which they rest. But schemes which involve certain damage to human life and well-being cannot be justified unless there is substantial reason to anticipate their success. Dazzled by the elegance of their plans, and by the prospect of glory and power if they succeed, national leaders often overlook these complications.

The other problem is with the goals themselves. 'Making the world safe for democracy', 'nurturing international harmony', 'teaching the rascals a lesson' or 'standing tall' are beguiling and heroic. They embody a grandeur which carries its own weight and quiets doubt, but are so vague and abstract as to vanish into ether. There is no specifiable, concrete good associated with their achievement and no clear understanding of the steps required to achieve them.[24] Thus nearly any course of action can be touted as dedicated to their achievement. Such justifications are no justifications at all and cannot begin to compensate for the violence initiated on their behalf.

Until now threats of violence have been classed with violent acts themselves. But there are important differences. Obviously, the threat of murder is less consequential than the deed itself. To some extent, the seriousness of the threat gains its importance from its linked act. This is not universally so. The threat of grievous harm with little likelihood of being carried out is less consequential than the threat of lesser harm which is likely to occur.

This picture is complicated by the fact that threats themselves are rarely straightforward statements of intention. Most often they form part of elaborate systems of signalling and maneuvering, not infrequently in situations where all participants are fully aware that there is no resolve to put the threat into action. This happens quite frequently in relations between the US and the USSR. when statements are issued, troops moved, aircraft launched and ships maneuvered – but with all parties well aware they have no desire for actual hostility.[25] In these instances threats are *only* signals, signs that the situation is viewed as quite serious, indications that the threatening party views the situation as involving its vital interests, *or* signals sent to allies or domestic constituency that resolve is firm and action is being taken.[26]

The threat in these cases is much less serious than the ostensible act. In fact, it becomes part of the normal posturing and bluff of international relations. Nonetheless, because the signal is sent through the vehicle of arms, it is more serious than other modes of communication, and certainly not innocuous. Part of the problem, of course, is that this form of signalling can gain its own momentum, building pressure to force the act. If military gestures are repeated often enough and hostility signalled strongly enough, this interchange may generate pressure for the overt act, as may well have happened in the exchange of threats and bombs involving the United States and Libya in the spring of 1986.[27] Furthermore, the signal sent by this means is hostile, so it injects ill-will, in emphatic terms, into the situation.

The core of the opposed military policies of Russia and the United States is the permanent threat of nuclear war. The very existence of nuclear weapons, their permutation and manipulation, are part of an elaborate play of threat and counter-threat. The ominous and eerily titled Mutual Assured Destruction (MAD) policy of the United States, or its successor, the Counter-Force Strategy, and all the logic of deterrence, are grounded on threat. This strange logic holds that a strong and credible threat of the act can avert the act itself, and so be justified. But the threat is not credible unless the act is seriously intended. So the threat, issued in the attempt to avoid the act, must intend it.

The analysis of threats is made yet more complicated by the importance of including the state of mind and situation of the threatened party in the equation. In part this is because a threat is as serious as its response. A threat, meant in innocuous fashion, which meets an unexpectedly hostile response, or gets put to use by clever politicians for other political purposes, becomes a much more serious matter. Or a mild threat made against a party with few resources for response is more serious than hostile gestures against a well-entrenched and secure adversary.

All of these factors combine to make the business of threatening complex and often quite serious. As with overt violence, it may often happen that a well-timed or well-executed gesture may be quite effective in averting substantial harm. It is possible, for example, that a militant Chamberlain browbeating Hitler at Munich may have made a considerable difference in subsequent history. Threats should not be used routinely and should never be used thoughtlessly. Nevertheless, they are sometimes capable of engendering substantial amounts of good. Furthermore, because threats may *sometimes* be known to be innocuous, it is quite possible that they may be of use in certain cases where human life and security are not immediately at risk. Looser moral restrictions on their use are feasible, but always with the understanding that they have their own dangers, pitfalls, and disruptive pressures.

The projection of force is likely to be effective only in a limited number of situations, and then only for a brief period of time. Where the goal is to encourage some act to take place or to stall action until the capacity to perform it is no longer present, this may be sufficient. When the goal is to prevent action, the effect is likely, at best, to be limited. Sometimes the discrete acts may have a role to play in a larger scheme and may derive their justification from this, but the connections here are multifarious and likely to be missed.

From a moral perspective the salient features of these acts are that they involve the actual destruction of life and property, or the demonstration of the means to do so, or the demonstration of intent. Their justification can come only as a means of preventing the destruction of life or property, either over the short or the long term. Furthermore, their effect is limited and temporary, so they are best suited to meeting immediate threats to life and are unsuited to be used in a positive way to create conditions where it is less likely for human life to be endangered or more likely to be respected. The lesson is that projections of force do have a use, even a valuable and necessary one, but are of limited effectiveness and often unsuited to the grandiose goals which politicians and soldiers are likely to seek by means of them. The Israeli raid at Entebbe, for example, not only resulted in the immediate release of hostages but quite likely served to forestall future terrorist attacks. It is a good example of a justified use of limited violence. It involved great risk, to be sure, but risk which was minimized by elaborate planning and precise execution.[28] However, cases like this are rare. Most instances of discrete violence are poorly planned, shoddily executed, and only tenuously connected to justifying goals – which themselves are often vague and amorphous.

DISCRETE VIOLENCE

In the fall of 1983 a lone attacker driving a truck loaded with explosives killed a large number of US Marines on duty in Lebanon. Several months later, the Marines withdrew. The suicide attack certainly formed a substantial portion of the impetus for the withdrawal, though the Marines' positioning had never been particularly popular in the American Department of Defense and did not have a well-defined role. While it is entirely possible that the intent of the attack was to effect this withdrawal, the exact motives have never been made clear and may have included revenge for Marine killing of militia members or a simple hatred of Americans. Furthermore, it has never been established just which group – or which government – was responsible for the attack. It was widely labelled an act of terror, but probably would not have been if the Marines had been killed through aerial bombardment or even through the commando attack of an established government. So, in current usage 'terrorism' appears to be a matter of how discrete violence is carried out and also of who carries it out.

The use of the term 'terrorist' to describe such acts seems to connote that they are designed to produce fear.[29] But, in the above case, it is unclear just who was made afraid or what the practical effect of this fear may have been. The surviving Marines were likely afraid but also angered, and it is doubtful that such fear as they had was of any practical import. The American public was outraged and humiliated, but there is no clear sense in which they felt afraid. The same applies to American governmental leaders. They may have been 'afraid', in some extended sense of the term, that more personnel may have been killed in Lebanon, but certainly felt no personal fear. Further, it seems unlikely that fear is primarily what sparked the final decision to withdraw. The diverse array of bombings of airplanes in 1985 and 1986 certainly produced fear – and probably had the concrete effect of reducing the number of American travelers to Europe and the Mid-East for a time. It is not clear, however, that causing this fear was the motive for the bombings, which usually are claimed to be retaliatory, or that there are any concrete goals to which such fear may be linked.

The array of acts normally thought of as terrorist usually includes such things as bombings, kidnappings, assassinations, etc. They seem to differ from ordinary criminal activity in that they are ostensibly not performed either for their own sake or for the personal gain of the perpetrators but are in service of political goals or at least undertaken by groups with political aspirations.[30] Discrete violence may thus be characterized as small-scale acts of violence intended to further the goals of a political group. Sometimes the purposes of these acts will include the generation of fear, and sometimes it is expected that this will aid in the achievement of further substantive goals. In so far as violent attacks are intended to produce fear or may reasonably be expected to produce fear as a consequence, they may properly be thought of as terrorism, but this will apply only to a small portion of the acts usually considered as terrorist.

Because such discrete assaults may be carried out with limited resources and small numbers of personnel, they are available for use by miniscule, weak and impoverished groups in a way that conventional military activity is not.[31] Furthermore, and most importantly, the means required for these acts – the equipment and personnel, can be kept hidden until put into use. Conventional military forces are difficult to hide and are removed from the eyes of the public only with some difficulty. This concealability is an important factor for weak groups at work in adverse circumstances. But, in some ways, this limits the usefulness of discrete violence. Massive arrays of conventional weaponry serve as constantly visible reminders of the power of governments, and can thus have a continuing effect on the thought and action of others even when not put to use. Discrete violence, however, becomes visible only when used and is readily forgotten when not employed. Groups wishing to rely on it as a continuing source of power and influence must repeatedly employ it if it is to have continued effect. Nuclear missiles, for example, need not be fired in order to loom large in the thinking of numberless people. The terrorism of the Red Brigades in Europe of the 1970s, however, had to be continually re-employed, or they were quickly forgotten.

As with the mass violence of nations, discrete violence can only hope to have moral justification if it is capable of achieving worthwhile goals. It shares with the former the inability to alter motives, the long-term interests and goals of a target group. Thus, its efficacy will be against capacity and intention.

Obviously, discrete violence has little effect against conventional military armament and so can be of little use in preserving national military security. It is, of course, capable of freeing prisoners or destroying particularly powerful or odious individuals and in that way it can affect capacity. Sometimes discrete violence is capable of affecting intentions, as when it is announced that captives will be harmed unless a certain act is carried out. Or it is possible that a series of killings or bombings will be arranged to put pressure on a target group to perform some act, or refrain from another.

Another important element of discrete violence, in contrast to mass violence, is that it can be narrowly targeted against specific persons. By threatening lives or well-being in this way, it is capable of altering personal intentions – and thus indirectly altering governmental intentions by pressuring the persons who operate it.

Discrete violence can also create fear either by being directed at individual persons or by being random, as through bombing trains or aircraft. There is little doubt that random violence is effective in creating fear, but there is some doubt about whether it can also achieve any positive goal. It may be intended to demonstrate that a government is incapable of protecting its citizens or to cause social chaos, and by this means allow revolution to occur. However, random, mass violence is unlikely to achieve either of these, and is quite as likely to unite citizens against the groups responsible for it. Other than for nihilists seeking chaos for its own sake, mass fear is unable to generate clear-cut results. Like the physical violence that sparks fear, it is better suited for destruction than construction, but it is not particularly effective even for this, unless it becomes so intense and widespread that total social paralysis results.

More broadly, discrete violence is effective in gaining attention. Violent assaults often generate notoriety quite out of proportion to the magnitude of the acts themselves. A common homicide, for example, causes relatively little stir, but a single killing, when revealed to be the act of a political group, rivets the entire world. It is not entirely clear why this should be so. It may simply be that the persons who are most likely to be killed by political groups – government officials or the wealthy and powerful – loom larger in the public eye. Where large numbers are harmed, it may be that the attention is no greater than an equivalent natural disaster. It may be that the threats that often go along with such acts, the possibility that they will recur, increases their fascination. Or it may be simply that such acts, being much rarer than common criminality, fascinate by their novelty.[32]

Whatever the cause, this attention increases the impact of acts of discrete violence either by magnifying their threat or by fixing the operative organization in the public eye, and thus giving it substance, if not respect or admiration. Such acts can have another, not inconsiderable, effect. They can keep a weak and faltering organization alive simply by providing a sense of things being done and of ends being sought. Spectacular violence may move an organization from stagnation and rekindle the sense of purpose and mission of its members. The appeal of these effects is not unknown to leaders of nation-states, who are not always averse to resorting to spectacular military adventure as a means of increasing popular support or boosting national morale.

But the question is whether there will ever be cases where effects of this sort will produce results sufficient to justify morally their cost in human life and human peace of mind. In some respects this sort of violence is easier to manage and contain than the mass violence of nations. Knives, guns and bombs in suitcases allow more limited and surgical destruction than the sort visited by bomber aircraft or masses of infantrymen. Its invisibility after the fact does not invite response with broad military power, and, since it is by nature limited, it is not likely to foment the escalation of force engendered by conventional military confrontation.

On the other hand, it is difficult even to imagine a case where resort to such violence has been clearly justified. Possibly, for example, a program of selective killing and assassination would have mitigated Nazi brutality in some of the countries it occupied, but given the usual Nazi response to such acts, it is unlikely that their cost in human life would have been sufficient to justify them. In principle there may exist repressive regimes where torture, killing and large-scale political imprisonment could be slowed or halted by a careful program of killing and kidnapping, and *only* by such methods. It may be possible that assassination of a particularly cruel and repressive dictator will suffice to change the ways of a tyrannical government. The attempted assassination of General Pinochet of Chile in the winter of 1987 can readily be seen to be justified on these grounds. Such activities are not justified to pursue political objectives, ethnic political aspirations or economic justice, unless these wrongs are so great as to endanger or destroy human lives *and* no other tactics are likely to remedy these abuses. Life-threatening violence, recall, is only justified as a means to save or protect life. For this reason the violent activities of the various groups in Northern Ireland and the Basque separatists in Spain are clearly unjustified. Indeed these instances serve as paradigms of where violence has become entrenched and feeds upon itself without any prospect of securing a justified end. In these cases the struggle has become its own end and has lost any further purpose.

The problems with resort to discrete violence are several-fold. While it is possible to imagine cases where there is clear justification for resorting to such means, they are comparatively rare. But there will *often* be instances where leaders feel they have something to gain by resorting to them. The problem is that they are too easy and too cheap to use, certainly much cheaper than conventional military forces and much quicker and more direct than other means. Furthermore, leaders, and national leaders in particular, sometimes like to try to prevent problems from arising. Thus they may be tempted to assassinate political leaders whom they feel could cause instability. The problem, of course, is that almost anyone could be seen a posing such a danger, and such means are likely to be relied upon not simply where human life and well-being are at stake but to pursue other, more selfish goals.

The greatest incentive for abuse, however, results from the ease of covering one's tracks in such matters. Leaders, whether of nations or of disaffected political groups, are most likely to act irresponsibly when they can act secretly, for this removes them from public accountability. Given the present international situation, world opinion and peer pressure are the strongest single forces for moral accountability. Secrecy and covert activity allow them to be evaded.[33]

The other difficulty is that once such means come to be used by one nation or one political group, others will be tempted to follow suit, with an increase in violence and anarchy the result. If this sort of violence becomes a common tool of international affairs, whatever shreds of civility and decency remain in international dealings will likely be ripped away.

Nonetheless, the counter-examples remain. Surely ridding the world of a Hitler or an Idi Amin would have been worth a great deal. The problem, as the above discussion indicates, is that discrete acts of violence cannot become standard tools of international dealing. For this reason, as will be argued shortly, every effort should be made to rid the world of it, to make it outlaw. Even with these efforts, given the present state of international affairs, leaders, whether of nations or of small political groups, will still be able to resort to it if they so desire. Given the nature of the means and the problems resulting from making it a standard tool of policy, there should be the strongest possible disincentives to its use, even where the use of discrete violence is correct.

ARMS CONTROL

The mass violence of nations is all too easily misused. Even those who are otherwise responsible in their use of military forces sometimes find themselves locked in the sort of conflict with others where resort to arms is a temptation. Given these difficulties, resourceful leaders will seek out alternative ways of dealing with adversity. In addition, of course, all agree that humanity would be better off if the world were free of military weaponry. Failing that, human beings would be better off if they could decrease either the likelihood or the destructiveness of the resort to military force.

In theory there are a number of ways to go about seeking these ends. Control of violence and the instruments of violence by an international agency may ultimately be the most thorough way of effecting this. However, an agency of this sort is unlikely to be established at any time in the near future, primarily because governments are presently unwilling to give up enough of their sovereignty to allow it to operate effectively and are unlikely to agree on specific goals and procedures of control. Given this, such attempts must involve individual governments, acting on their own initiative or in loose confederation with others. They may seek to avoid violence by pledges of non-aggression; by attempts to establish cultural, economic or political ties; or they can attempt to reduce or eliminate armaments. These various strategies thus focus either on intentions (by pledging to forgo developing the intention to resort to force), or on motives (by creating incentives to avoid the use of force), or on the capacity for violence (by controlling armaments).

The instability of intentions, opportunities for deception, and their invisible and elusive nature, serve to make the first approach a slender reed at best. In the long term, and ideally, eliminating the motives for resort to arms would be most desirable, but, given current conditions, hostility, conflicts of ideology or interest, and mutual suspicion limit the potential effectiveness of this approach. The mechanisms available to seek such effects, namely trade and cultural interchange, have generally proven too weak to make any significant difference.

The remaining option is the attempt to control arms themselves. This approach is attractive, since eliminating the capacity to resort to force is obviously effective in preventing violent clashes. Armaments are more stable than intentions in that, once destroyed, they cannot be recreated instantly. They are also relatively visible and hidden only with difficulty, so they can be seen and counted in a way that intentions cannot. Also, and most importantly, they are malleable and vulnerable in a way that, sadly, hostility, suspicion and conflict of interest are not. Weapons can be destroyed. History demonstrates that hostility and suspicion are much more durable. Thus it is easy to see why attempts at arms control have recently received much more attention than other options as a means of attempting to mitigate or eliminate the resort to violence. But it remains important to attempt to understand exactly what arms control is, what it is able to achieve – and what it cannot achieve.

The most prominent method of seeking control of arms is treaty, which can be limited to a few parties or can involve the largest possible number of nations. Nuclear weapons treaties involving only the United States and Russia illustrate the first sort, while conventions dealing with the use of poison gas and nuclear non-proliferation are examples of the latter. As non-proliferation treaties illustrate, such agreements can focus on preventing others from gaining certain weapons in addition to seeking to control the stocks of the signatory powers. Such agreements can also be tacit rather than formal, but, for a number of reasons which will become apparent later on, these are less important than the explicit treaties.[34]

What can such agreements achieve? Once more, it is important to distinguish between immediate and remote results. The immediate results can include limits on or a reduction in weapons, the elimination of certain categories of arms, or pledges to refrain from using them. The remote consequences of these agreements are more varied, more elusive, and yet more important than the immediate. The most concrete and predictable result is economic benefit. Fewer weapons cost less. Sometimes felicitous treaties can prevent spiralling arms races that are capable of absorbing endless amounts of wealth. The importance of economic benefit should not be underestimated. Armaments have the capacity to eat up enormous portions of national economies, as well as tie up scientific talent, natural resources, and hinder efforts at improving the lives of ordinary persons.[35] Nations are often tempted to take draconian measures to finance their arms, and the economic strains caused by these efforts can result in social unrest. Thus, such benefits are distinctly important and the most certain of achievement, though for some reason are often omitted from discussions of arms control.

The very fact of having an agreement may serve to decrease hostility and tension simply through the display of willingness to bargain in earnest fashion. It can, in other words, work on motives. The process of talking, of coming to terms, of straining for mutual understanding, then signalling good-will by coming to agreement, can all help dissipate the psychological climate that fosters war. What is more, the disposition to reach agreement seems to indicate the absence of determination to initiate conflict, though the history of the twentieth century shows that this need not be so. It is likely that these atmospherics account for a large portion of the popularity that arms control agreements have for the general public. Leaders who achieve or seek them are perceived as being committed to peace, while those who avoid them are suspected of belligerent intent. It is difficult to gauge the importance or substance of this psychological climate. Leaders who seek these agreements certainly seem to be working for peace and against war, and it is possible that this perception can create its own reality. Working towards such agreements does normally preclude the usual sorts of hostile gestures, the name-calling, propaganda, military feints and maneuvers that increase tension and can spark open conflict.[36] So these things seem important and may well be so, but it is difficult to judge how much substance they have, and, of course, they can easily be used to mask other more sinister preparations. Still, by working on motives, these can possibly have the most significant and permanent effects of all.

Finally, the agreements may make it more difficult for nations to go to war or less likely that they will do so. A nation with only a small number of bomber aircraft, tanks or naval ships will have more difficulty in projecting force beyond its borders than otherwise. If arms agreements serve to limit significantly the numbers of these weapons, the chances of war may decrease. The cautious 'may' is important here, for history has a way of circumventing such designs. Nonetheless, treaties may also serve to eliminate certain types of weapons that can cause instability – either by making aggressive attack much easier or by becoming useless and hazardous if not used until an opposing party attacks. Before the development of radar, for example, bombing aircraft could readily carry destruction to an opponent but could also be easily surprised on the ground and destroyed. Therefore, there was substantial reward to use such craft first and substantial danger in restraint. Such armaments thus caused instability. If such weapons were eliminated, or reliance on them decreased, one incentive to initiate war would be eliminated.

It is worth noting that much of the attention given to arms treaty negotiations recently has focused on numbers. In some cases concern for numbers is appropriate and fruitful. A nation which agrees to make a sharp reduction in the number of its bomber planes, tanks or naval ships significantly limits its ability to carry destructive force to others and may, as a result, become less of a threat. However, this need not be so. Sometimes reductions in numbers will have essentially no effect on destructive capacity. For example, a nation may have many times the number of bombing planes necessary to inflict substantial damage on another. If it agrees to reduce this force, even in half, essentially the same power remains, and it is not thereby less of a threat. The same sort of logic applies to nuclear weaponry. The United States and Russia, for example, possess such massive numbers of nuclear weapons that reduction to a half or even to a tenth of their number will still leave each with overwhelming destructive power.

Furthermore, reductions in numbers of arms need not increase stability. That is, such reductions need not reduce the incentive of nations to initiate war. Pressures to initiate war are more due to the vulnerability of weapons or their suitability for aggressive purposes than simply numbers. For certain kinds of weapons, such as bombers, a reduction in number below a certain threshold may eliminate their utility for particular purposes, but, given their destructive power, this hardly applies to nuclear weapons. The current fascination with numbers need not result in greater stability or warrant feelings of greater security.[37] If negotiators are genuinely concerned to stabilize relations between Russia and the United States ('stability' meaning creating conditions where neither has the incentive to initiate war), they should focus on issues of precision, vulnerability and verifiability – and remove their attention from numbers alone.

It is also extremely important to understand what such agreements cannot do. They cannot, by themselves, either prevent war or achieve durable peace. Nations that are determined to go to war will do so, with or without such agreements. Treaties cannot erase the conflicts of interest or the hostility that serve to nurture war. Arms agreements can create conditions which make these events less likely. They can serve as part of the process leading to the achievement of genuine peace. But they cannot do the job alone.

In fact, thoughtless or hastily contrived agreements can increase hostility and increase the chances of going to war rather than the reverse. If treaties lack provision for monitoring compliance with their provisions, hostility, accusations and suspicion may increase. Similarly, arms reductions thoughtlessly carried out, can increase instability. For example, if all nuclear weapons are eliminated, with the exception of those which are both highly accurate and vulnerable to destruction in a pre-emptory strike, instability will be increased. This is because there will be an incentive for each side to use its weapons first and grave danger in pausing until the opponent has struck. It often happens that some classes of weapons are militarily more important to one side than another, so that reductions in numbers of that weapon make one party proportionately weaker, even if the same numbers are given up on both sides. For example, if one nation depends heavily on submarines for its military power, it will be weakened in greater measure than an opponent that does not, even though both forfeit equal numbers of such craft. A realization of this may tempt the weakened nation to strike first to gain the advantage of surprise. Or, of course, it may tempt the side with its newly gained military edge to press its advantage.

The complexity of contemporary military establishments and the mutual interplay of elements make it difficult to be sure that some advantage has not been inadvertently bargained away. The issues are sufficiently ephemeral that there may be leeway for protracted debate within a nation over whether a given treaty does or does not give away too much. This legitimate uncertainty indicates the hazard of such agreements and shows that reluctance to take part in them need not be without rational foundation, and need not be motivated only by hostile intent.

Determining exactly which types and numbers of weapons lead to stability and which do not is complex and difficult. As the above discussion shows, the wrong choices can actually lead to greater instability. In the euphoria of the period between the two world wars, it was thought this difficulty could be remedied easily. Weapons would be classified as essentially offensive (that is, most suited for attack) or defensive (best fitted to repel a would-be invader). Bombing aircraft were regarded as instances of the former, while fighter-interceptors were the latter. World peace, it was thought, could be secured if offensive weapons were banned, thus effectively eliminating the capability of nations to initiate offensive war.

The basic difficulty with this scheme is that the distinctions are not easily or simply made.[38] All too often weapons are made most suitable for defensive use by being highly effective for offense as well. Mobile artillery may be thought offensive, while fixed guns are most certainly not. But purposes of defense are best served if weaponry can be maneuvered into places where it is needed, so that offensive mobile artillery becomes the best defensive weaponry too. Furthermore, the military cliché is that the best defense is a good offense. The most effectively fought wars will include offensive strategies, even if their ultimate goals are essentially defensive. The distinction cannot be made in wholesale fashion. Even if it could, technological advancement would continually upset the apple cart by introducing new weapons and new ways of using them. The implication is that effective treaties must take careful account of place and circumstance and will require periodic re-evaluation and renegotiation if they are to remain useful. In itself, this need not be a bad thing, since it will require that the process of discussion, mutual understanding and mutual negotiation will have to continue and that continued vigilance is required to preserve peace and stability. But it further underscores the limitations of arms treaties and the conclusion that no ultimate or final solutions are to be had.

Wisely crafted arms control agreements, founded on good will, are thus capable of increasing stability and reducing incentive to go to war, as long as they focus on the features of weapons systems which increase the temptation to initiate hostility. Haggling about numbers in many cases will not address this issue. Nonetheless, the basic force of these agreements is on the *capacity* to initiate war. To a lesser degree the process itself can operate on motives, by creating an atmosphere of greater trust and understanding. Such treaties cannot by themselves avert war. There will always be strong pressures working to undermine them. Arms control treaties can play a role, perhaps even a crucial one, in creating a more stable world order, but they are not capable of doing the job themselves. They are worth pursuing because they are capable of achieving substantial benefit at little cost, but it would be unwise to expect too much from them.

CONTROL OF DISCRETE POLITICAL VIOLENCE

In the nature of things discrete political violence must be controlled by the governments of nation-states if it is to be controlled at all. For one thing, governments themselves are often implicated in acts of discrete violence, whether by helping to instigate, finance, or plan them, or by carrying them out themselves. Recent efforts by the international community to come to terms with such acts bear witness to this, for they have acknowledged the governmental tie in such matters. Nonetheless, it remains true that many of the incidents of discrete violence *are* the work of small factions without governmental ties, and these, obviously, will not be controlled unless by governments. Small groups of this sort pop in and out of existence in rapid fashion. They are apt to exhibit wide ranges of seriousness or desperation and are often anarchic by nature. However, they are capable of acts of violence of sufficient magnitude to inflict significant damage to life and property and, sometimes, to create a climate of fear. In the summer of 1986, for example, American tourists all but deserted Europe for fear of terrorist acts, even though only a very small number of American travelers had been harmed in Europe in such incidents. The events themselves, however, created great publicity and generated substantial anxiety.

The numbers of people killed in attacks of this sort is quite small.[39] If numbers alone are considered, these attacks would count for little in the scheme of things. Yet the reaction to them makes them serious, since people, particularly in the United States, *believed* that their lives and personal security would be at risk if they ventured to Europe. By any rational assessment, however, this threat was small, much smaller than the risk of harm from injury in traffic accidents, pollution or disease. Yet people are accustomed to these latter risks, as in the case of motor vehicles and disease, or are simply unconcerned about them, in the instance of pollution.

In a number of ways the strange, and perhaps irrational, dynamics of fear at work here mirror those of concern for national security analyzed earlier. In each case, the anxiety generated may be only tenuously related to plausible threat. Yet in each case as well, this unreasoned anxiety can generate important consequences. Numbers of deaths, in themselves, would not justify the elaborate expenditures on security that have been made at airport terminals, for example. More lives could be saved by spending the money elsewhere, on improved roads or more elaborate emergency medical facilities. However, it is true that, lacking such precautions, the number of incidents could well dramatically increase. Human peace of mind is important, and all human death is important. Given this, and given the potential for large increases in destructiveness, acts of discrete violence justify more concerted action. But the magnitudes are not sufficient to justify draconian measures. They certainly do not morally justify activity that will endanger human life or compromise civil rights to the extent that the personal security of citizens is imperiled.

The events themselves are not likely to achieve political, economic or social goals of any great consequence and, in fact, seem to have gained nothing positive at all beyond publicity for the groups that have carried them out. The acts of discrete violence, in other words, have not been morally justified in any but the rarest of cases. But this moral wrongness does not justify significant compromise of human security in return. Spectacular though they may be, the acts themselves are much less important for general human life and well-being than other problems, such as environmental pollution or disease.

In addition, it is important to consider the potential diversity of this sort of violence when contemplating possible responses. Recently the violence that has captured the public consciousness of Western Europe and the United States has primarily involved political and religious groups of the Middle East attacking Israeli and Western European airlines and airports. In a decade or two the context and mode of this violence could be entirely different. It could involve Far Eastern political groups, European ethnic minorities, American political radicals, or some completely novel manifestation. Presently the preferred mode of attack is bombing and kidnapping. But this could easily change. There is great concern about nuclear weaponry falling into the hands of such groups. Or attacks could focus on water supplies and power stations. Biological experimentation may also open possibilities for mayhem. Terrorist groups may emulate the ploy of poisoning medicines or foodstuffs. The possibilities are nearly endless.[40] The lesson is that responses made to present groups and current forms of discrete violence may become completely irrelevant a few years hence.

It is highly unlikely that any particular mode of response is capable of being adequate to deal with all forms of discrete violence at all times and places. It is also possible that these acts and these groups will wither away and simply cease to cause difficulty in a decade, as American radical groups have become nearly extinct.[41] They may flare up once more in the future, or they may not. The present discussion can only focus on current problems and current groups. Some features of its analysis may hold good for all future outbursts, but it is unlikely that any and all of its aspects will remain permanently viable. The temporary and fluctuating nature of these threats again underscores the point that draconian measures of response are unwarranted morally as well as practically, both because the threat may evaporate spontaneously and because particular counter-measures can be effective only against particular modes of discrete violence.

The moral and practical problems of controlling discrete political violence break in two. They can be called problems of response and problems of association. The problems of response are focused on means of reacting to acts of violence themselves. They include passive preventative measures, such as monitoring devices, security checks and armed guards at airports or other public centers, as well as security measures for embassies, until recently another popular target. Though cumbersome and expensive, these measures of passive prevention are unproblematical. It is fairly easy to know what is required, and little more *is* required than setting up a protective system and maintaining it. The material cost may be considerable, but the risk to human life and well-being entailed by such measures is small.

Another set of problems of response include those of managing crises in progress – events such as kidnappings and hijackings, or the Iranian hostage crisis – which extend over periods of time and require continuing attention. Many of these difficulties are purely practical ones of discovering the most effective strategies for dealing with kidnappers. This body of knowledge is growing, and techniques are becoming more effective.[42] Difficulties of a more pointed sort arise when hostages are being held in another nation either under that nation's auspices, as in Iran in 1980, or with the collusion of that nation, as at Entebbe. It is implausible to believe that force should never be used in such situations. Sometimes that is the only way to bring the crisis to an end. Sometimes it will be the only hope of saving captives. Sometimes, as evidence shows, a strong and decisive response will be necessary to deter future acts.[43]

This analysis is not greatly changed when the government of a nation is itself a party to the event, as it was in Iran. As will be argued in the following chapter, national sovereignty is not sacrosanct and can be overridden on occasion. Certainly such occasions include those where a government is taking a part in actively mistreating foreign citizens. Governments gain whatever moral claim to sovereignty they possess by looking after the welfare of their citizens or of aliens legitimately within their borders. Where they fail in this, their sovereign privilege may be overridden to the extent necessary to give aid where human life and well-being are at hazard. Jimmy Carter's helicopter raid on Iran may be criticized on a variety of grounds but not because the attempt violated national sovereignty. Iran had simply forfeited its sovereign inviolability by its conduct in that instance. The problem is different where a nation is doing all it can to remedy a difficult situation or where there is disagreement because its methods are at variance with the nation whose citizens are in custody. Where a government is not in active collusion but is simply indifferent, it is abrogating its responsibility to safeguard the lives of those within its borders and has also forfeited its sovereign inviolability in such cases. The moral problem is not with violations of national sovereignty but with the much more fundamental problem of whether the risk to human life was counterbalanced by an equivalent gain. In the instance of Carter's helicopter raid, it quite clearly was not. Though the lives of the hostages were in constant threat, there is no reason to believe they were in immediate danger. More importantly, the risks of the raid were considerable, and it is likely that many more people would have been killed than saved if the raid had been carried to completion.

Carter was certainly correct in believing he had a duty to look after the welfare of American citizens and in thinking his responsibility here outweighed his responsibility to safeguard human life generally, including Iranian. As pointed out in Chapter 1, there are good utilitarian grounds for imposing special responsibility on national leaders and in giving these responsibilities greater weight than some of their general obligations as human beings. However, in this instance, he was significantly endangering both Iranian and American life, with the hostages in no immediate danger. In fact, the raid would have been wrong even if they had been in immediate danger because of the much greater risk to other American lives (those involved in carrying out the assault), the substantial odds against success, and the peril to Iranians.

As in the case of Margaret Thatcher and the Falkland Islands, Carter's personal guilt is small. He should have done otherwise, and he should have considered the matter in terms of the human lives at stake. However, there is little precedent for doing so; rather there is a propensity to consider these matters in terms of the rights of sovereign states or the obligation of national leaders to look after the lives of their citizens. In addition, there is often strong political pressure to use armed might in these circumstances. Had the raid been successful, Carter's popularity would have soared, and the United States as a whole would have been hugely elated. Still, this pressure could have been resisted by Carter without undue heroism. Cyrus Vance, for instance, was strongly opposed and resigned his post as Secretary of State in response.

The most difficult set of problems of response concern after-the-fact measures. Should terrorists, for example, be classed as common criminals, and punished in the way any ordinary violator of the law would be? Terrorist groups tend to argue not. After all, the defining feature of their violence is that it is in pursuit of political goals. They often wish to be considered prisoners of war. Of course, they do not fit neatly into that category either: they are not representatives of legally recognized governments; they will often be incapable of engaging in activity which approaches the level of organization and intensity of guerrilla war; and there will be practical problems of distinguishing political groups from common bandits. From the perspective of the activists themselves, however, a more basic problem is that prisoner-of-war status is a double-edged sword. Prisoners of war, in accordance with the standards of the Geneva Convention, lack a number of the rights and legal safeguards enjoyed by common criminals, and have special obligations in addition. Prisoners of war, for example, are not assigned lawyers, are not given trials, and do not receive fixed-term sentences. Further, under the Geneva Convention prisoners of war have special obligations toward their captors and toward one another which do not burden ordinary criminals.

The situation of the agent of discrete political violence is a difficult one, falling between the clearly defined lines of ordinary criminal and agent of an alien power. There is no precise way to resolve the issue. Political activists will understandably wish to distinguish themselves and their activity from that of common criminals. It is understandable that they do not wish to be considered *guilty* in the manner of ordinary criminals and perhaps wish for some recognition of the risk and sacrifice they may have undergone on behalf of their ideals. Yet without the protections of the criminal justice system, with its established modes of proceeding and presumed independence from other branches of government, it is highly likely that innocent persons will be harmed, that the web of repression and violent response will widen, and that the police apparatus of the state will become increasingly powerful and oppressive. Activists may welcome this, as hastening the downfall of their declared foe, but it is by no means certain that this will happen, and it is by no means certain that whatever political goals are possessed by activist groups will justify this cost – particularly in light of the uncertainty that their goals will be achieved even if their revolution is successful. The desire of political activists that the purity of their motives be acknowledged is understandable and important. Such concerns, as pointed out earlier, are foundations of the theory of moral agency necessary for any moral perspective. However, these concerns, and whatever other political goals such activists possess, should not be allowed to obscure the fundamental concern for human life and security. These must always remain the ultimate basis of analysis. Thus, for the protection of all concerned, including that of innocent citizens who may be caught up in violent activity, resort to the criminal justice system is preferable to the very different conditions of prisoner-of-war status.[44] Like others in this work, this is a solution which is imperfect and unsatisfying. It lacks the purity which moralists understandably seek, but it is all circumstances allow.

Further difficulties arise over the issue of active response to the violence of the weak. Disaffected political groups functioning within nations can expect to be fought by police and military forces. Few question this. There are special problems, however, when groups operate by the sanction of other states or with the active support and nurture of alien governments. In these instances armed response to activists is much more controversial. Reagan's bombing of Libya in the spring of 1986, for example, caused a great outcry. Apart from the details of justification and execution in this particular case, it is worth asking whether such acts can be justified in principle. When nations either tolerate or actively support the activities of violent groups, they are contributing to undermining the sovereignty of the target state. Since they are already party to interference in sovereignty, there can be little complaint if the target nation, in defense of its own perquisites, responds by incursions. It is difficult to see how the Sandinistas' incursions into Honduras in 1985 and 1986 or the United States' incursion into Cambodia in 1970 are in principle unjust. Of course, such actions substantially increase the hazard and level of conflict and can never be automatically or easily justified in any given instance. It may well be that, when all the facts are known, most such incursions have been unjustified, but this does not imply that they are wrong on the basis of the principle that they violate national sovereignty.

A number of nations, France in particular, have traditions of giving asylum to political exiles.[45] There are difficulties with such traditions, however admirable they may be. Activists will certainly be able to carry on organizational and resource-gathering activities while in exile, even if they refrain from violent acts. To grant asylum is thus to support activists, even if only indirectly. Granting even-handed asylum to all may even exacerbate the problem by allowing the entry of groups whose methods and goals one deplores. Or opposing groups may carry on their conflict while in exile, thus making their host nation a stage for their own violent activity.[46]

There is little reason, however, why asylum must be given to any and all groups. Nations could, for example, use the standards of respect for human rights embodied in the United Nations Universal Declaration of Human Rights as a test of the moral propriety of various groups. Groups not pledged to accept such standards, or for which there is good reason to believe are in violation of them, need not be given asylum or any other form of assistance. Groups which do respect them should be aided to the extent of granting asylum, even if their political aspirations are at variance with those of the host.[47]

A related and particularly difficult problem concerns the extradition of those charged with committing political crimes. Many nations, for example, allow extradition only for criminal acts and not for political ones. This has caused some difficulty and some violation of international law. Israel, for example, has kidnapped former Nazis to spirit them back for trial. The United States has recently become involved in controversy by agreeing to extradite IRA members accused of political crimes.[48] Again, nations may wish to support some groups but not others, and may want to preserve the distinction between criminal and political acts. Also, in the murky international arena, some acts are crimes in one nation but not in another, and there are the difficulties of trumped-up charges, widely variant types of groups, and diverse systems of law. To allow such extradition in wholesale fashion will gut the practice of asylum. If armed struggle is a legitimate part of such programs, then it will be unlikely that any exile is not linked somehow to acts of violence.

There is a twofold solution, albeit an imperfect one. For one thing, there are some types of acts which may not be committed in service of any goal. The bombing of public transport or poisoning of water supplies, for example, should be considered outlaw for anyone who practises them. While utilitarianism cannot claim, in principle, that such acts are inevitably morally wrong, it is clearly difficult to imagine any cases in practice where they are likely to have utilitarian justification. In the same way that, on the domestic level, it is reasonable to outlaw acts which inevitably have ill consequences which will be outweighed only rarely by some greater good, so the above sorts of discrete political violence are gravely harmful and unlikely to be justified by any redeeming benefit. Persons who commit acts of the above sort should be extradited, whether their ultimate goals are admirable or not. Even where the ultimate goals of such groups are laudable, it is highly unlikely either that such atrocities will be necessary to secure them or that other, less destructive means will not serve them equally well. It is a grave error to believe that in utilitarian theory the ends justify the means. It is a basic requirement of utilitarian thinking that means must always be carefully and precisely balanced against ends – *and* that careful thought must be given to questions of whether a particular means will in fact serve a given end, or at what cost. Much of the political evil and human suffering of the world results from the failure to practise these very basic principles of utilitarian thought.

A second part of the solution is to work to achieve international standards of recognition for resistance groups. Criteria could include some sort of statement of grievances, goals and charter, pledges of standards of conduct, and standards of membership. Resistance groups are a fact of life at the present time and are likely to be so for the foreseeable future. Furthermore, nations often find themselves actively supporting some groups and combating others. This is inevitable. Nations have ideals as well as political interests, and will encounter others that support or are in opposition to them. Work to regularize acceptance of them could serve to resolve a number of international problems. It is highly unlikely that all nations would accept such a standard, but, even if only a few did, or some were adapted by single nations on an *ad hoc* basis, there would be some benefit.

It would be ideal to have a broadly accepted international agreement on terrorism, with acts understood as terrorist, procedures for dealing with them, and rationales for both clearly outlined. Even merely advisory standards would help, so that *all*, whether governments or terrorist groups, knew where they stood and *what was expected of them*. To be effective, an agreement need not involve *all* the nations of the world, but some critically important nations would have to be part of any agreement made for it to be more than only rhetoric.

The practical problem at present is that discrete political violence is seen to be a difficulty only for Western European nations.[49] Others, either from indifference or antipathy, are not likely to be helpful. This is not an insurmountable problem. If the nations directly concerned develop common approaches and standards, an effective response can be made. The problem has been that they have been fragmented, lack consensus, and some have attempted to make their own peace with terrorist groups. If they pull together, they may be able to make an effective response, and may also be able to involve the USSR or other Soviet Bloc or Middle Eastern nations.

Part of the problem, but perhaps also part of the solution, is that the *current* net of terrorist groups is supported in various ways by an array of governments.[50] Governments can be approached and dealt with in a way that shadowy terrorist groups cannot. An important factor is that none of these governments are willing to reveal publicly their support of this activity; indeed, all of them publicly condemn it. This hypocrisy can be a useful tool for exerting influence on them.

Given the obvious ills which international violence entails, and given the propensity of national leaders for its use, it may seem that the only solution is to renounce it entirely, in all its forms. Unfortunately the present international situation does not allow this response, a response as simple and satisfying in its way as the resort to violence itself. The world is, and is likely to remain for some time, a cockpit where many nations and many groups of people have access to means of violence and the incentive to use them. It is also a world of numerous independent and sovereign nations displaying a broad range of moral sensitivity and responsibility. This spectrum includes the relatively enlightened and the absolutely tyrannical, those actively working for the benefit of their subjects and those who are a great menace to the lives and well-being of their citizens. It is a world where many governments, and many peoples, have deep-seated and bitterly-felt antipathies to one another.

With the violent nature of the world, resort to violence is often necessary, morally, to save lives, nurture human security, or create order – and the refusal to countenance the means of violence will often result in increased loss of life and the erosion of security. So some violence is justified and may sometimes be morally obligatory. Nonetheless, because of its deficiencies as a means, the narrow range of goals which it is suited to achieve, and the permanent danger that it will be misused, it is important to seek means to control it. The thesis of the present work is that reasoned criteria for the proper use of violence can be established, it is reasonable to expect leaders to adhere to these criteria, and that there are feasible means of controlling violence available. These measures fall far short of what might be sought in a more highly structured world, but they can be achieved in present circumstances – and the world would benefit considerably if they were.

3 Sovereignty

There are some 165 independent nations in the world. Many are quite small, both in physical size and in population. Some would not fill a respectable American suburb.[1] Nonetheless, all are held to be sovereign over the territory and people of their domain, and this sovereignty shapes many of the characteristic problems of the ethics of international relations.

The principle of respect for the integrity of national sovereignty is deeply entrenched in the international law and diplomacy of this century – in theory if not always in practice. The charter of the United Nations, as well as those of regional associations such as the Organization of African Unity or the Organization of American States, mandate that the sovereignty of nation-states shall not be violated.[2]

The precise boundaries of this principle are unclear. Roughly, it requires that nations do not intervene in the domestic activity of established governments and that they do not attempt to undermine them or otherwise work for their abolition. Furthermore, its prohibitions are absolute and without exception. In terms of the position of this work, it is one of the fundamental prescriptions of *intuitive* morality operating on the level of international relations. In so far as statesmen avow any principles of morality at all, respect for national sovereignty is likely to be included among them.

This intuitive prescription is not the result of a process of explicit moral reflection. As with many common beliefs, it has been shaped by the pressure of events. The difficulty is that the pressure of more recent events has strained its intuitive clarity. As shall be seen, these developments have generated sufficient doubt that it is now appropriate to perform critical thinking both to see how respect for sovereign autonomy can be more firmly grounded and perhaps how it should be revised or limited.

It is not difficult to understand why the world should have come to view sovereign inviolability as possessed of fundamental importance. A substantial portion of the history of the past century is shaped by multifarious struggles against colonial domination. In this context the rhetoric of sovereign autonomy has had an important role to play. People striving to free themselves from foreign domination have naturally turned to this rhetoric, and coupled it with the principle of the right of self-determination, to fashion a theoretical basis for their aspirations. What is more, the nation-states resulting from these anti-colonial struggles have often been weak and fragile entities, artificial creations resulting from the contingencies of imperial domination. They often lack stable political institutions or administrative expertise and find themselves adrift in an environment of national upheaval and fluctuating borders. In these circumstances, the sense of stability and security afforded by mutually acknowledging respect for sovereignty can be a rare and highly prized commodity. Even nations that are older, more firmly established and more powerful can appreciate the value of enjoying freedom from external manipulation in return for the pledge of similar restraint.

It is also easy to understand why this principle should be considered absolute and without exception. Were exceptions allowed, it is highly probable that they would be distorted and misused by powerful, aggressive nations seeking their own ends. Given the chaotic nature of world affairs, it is difficult to imagine that there could be general agreement on allowed exceptions. This is not only because nation-states may feel their sovereignty jeopardized as the result but also because significant differences in ideology, governmental structure and social conditions make it difficult to establish a single set of standards of governmental conduct.

In the usual course, furthermore, nations appear less interested in manipulating others' internal affairs than bullying them externally. They are more likely, that is, to be interested in international trade, access to resources, military operations or international population flow than the details of a nation's governmental structure or the way it treats its citizens. This is not to say that nations are never interested in such things or never attempt to manipulate others. Rather, the claim is that their interests are more likely to range elsewhere *and* that they are less likely to expect any great benefit from internal manipulation. But, most fundamentally, as recent experience with South Africa and earlier attempts at forcing change in Rhodesia show, the attempted manipulation of domestic affairs by outside governments is unlikely to be successful.

Given this perspective, it is easy to see how the ordinary pressures of events have prompted the international community to endorse the principle of sovereign immunity in wholesale fashion. This intuitive clarity has, however, been shaken by recent history. The world has been faced with instances of tumult within nations which it is unable to ignore, either because their scale demands international attention or because the larger community has, willy-nilly, become caught up in essentially domestic conflicts.

When the Khmer Rouge initiated a program of wholesale liquidation of Cambodian citizens in the mid-1970s, many outsiders felt they did not have the option of standing aside. By some estimates the toll of Cambodian dead runs to a million or more in a nation with a total population of perhaps 5 million people.[3] Crime of that magnitude could not be ignored by the world community. But Vietnam's invasion of Cambodia made discussion of an international response moot, and political manipulations have subsequently ensnared moral deliberations.[4] The salient case of the present day – one on which the world seems to be acquitting itself with only slightly greater honor than in South-east Asia – is South Africa. Though the international effort is flawed by self-interest, inertia and petty politics, the world seems finally to have its attention clearly focused on a situation which it managed to ignore for a long time.[5] It remains to be seen what sort of action the world community will take, whether it can be effective, or whether it is not simply too late to forestall violent upheaval. But the fact that the community of nations now appears to recognize that the situation in South Africa is clearly a moral problem, *and* one which it is no longer at liberty to ignore, is clearly a positive sign and a step in the right direction.

Nations of the world must also contend with other issues of a more subtle and perhaps more difficult sort. There are instances where they have become enmeshed in disputes which ought, it would seem, to be of primarily domestic or strictly local concern. But because they are thus involved, they face moral problems related to national sovereignty which they might otherwise feel they could legitimately ignore. France, for example, is entangled in the struggle of the ETA movement of the Spanish Basques. It has become involved by physical proximity, the fact that it has Basque communities of its own, and because it has a long tradition of providing haven for political exiles. The unfortunate result is that partisan violence has spilled across French borders, and France has become a staging ground for ETA activity in Spain.[6] Though France has been innocent, even commendable, in its response to this struggle, it is enmeshed, both in the sense that its policies, whatever they may be, will in fact assist one side or the other, and its citizens and territory are inextricably affected. While the wish to remain neutral in the Basque conflict is understandable, France can neither divorce itself from it nor pretend that its policies are of no consequence. So it is forced to come to terms with issues of Spanish sovereignty it might prefer to ignore – and must recognize that attempting to avoid the conflict will also have its effect.

On a larger scale, nearly the entire world is involved in the national aspirations of the Palestinians and the concomitant Israeli struggle to survive as a state and a people. International motives are considerably less innocent and more self-interested than the French quandary over the Basques. The United States, for example, has a mixture of interests, including the laudable desire to preserve the state of Israel, the less laudable but understandable desire to safeguard the oil resources of the region, and the more self-interested desire to forestall Russian activity in the Middle East. The states of Europe are less interested in Russia and less interested in Israel, but more desperately interested in Middle East oil. They are also more immediately caught up in the conflict, both because of their physical proximity to the region and because their past colonial adventures have resulted in intricate ties with Arab states, along with substantial populations of expatriate Middle Easterners. The importance of the oil resources of the region, the interest of the great powers, the identification of Third World nations with Islamic aspirations, international concern for the fate of Jews, and politics in the United Nations, have resulted in a tangle of moral concern, national self-interest, political rivalry, and jealousy in which the difficulties of a comparatively small number of people in a small corner of the globe have moved to the center of world attention.

In different fashion, the United States has become deeply entangled in the domestic politics of such nations as South Korea and the Philippines. Its monetary assistance, myriad cultural and governmental ties, and military presence have fixed the belief that it is responsible for the actions of the governments of these nations – both in the view of the citizens of those countries and of the larger world. It is presumed by many to have the power to make those governments more democratic and more responsive to citizens' concerns – and has the moral obligation to do so.

Cambodia, Uganda, South Africa, the Basques, the Palestinians, the Israelis and others vividly demonstrate that, however much the nations of the world may wish to ignore problems of sovereign autonomy or uphold the principle of sovereign inviolability, the pressure of events now prevents them from doing so. They must face these issues and must face them as *moral* issues. As yet, though, they are poorly equipped with the theoretical or conceptual apparatus for this.

Ethics for a Shrinking World

Before the moral issues can be met, the conceptual and theoretical ones demand attention.

THE NATURE OF SOVEREIGNTY

Governments come in various types and often – as illustrated by federal systems – have complex relationships with one another. Nonetheless, in a given territory only one government will enjoy ultimate legal authority. This ultimate legal authority over persons and institutions in a particular domain is sovereignty, understood internally, from the perspective of those within the state. Externally, the picture is more complex. When nations formally acknowledge the sovereignty of a government, it is not entirely clear what commitment they have made.

They must recognize the ultimate legal authority of a particular government over a given territory, to be sure, but it is not obvious what all this entails. A natural answer is that they acknowledge that they have no legal authority to intrude in domestic affairs. The current practice of nation-states, however, appears to include two additional elements. One is that sovereignty entails being recognized as the international representative of the people of a given area, authorized to articulate and press their interests, to speak for them.

Several reasons exist for this. For one, individual persons are poorly equipped to press their own concerns in the international arena. They simply do not have the resources, strength or institutional means for doing so. In part this is because nation-states have guarded their prerogatives closely and have worked to undercut attempts to dilute them – as demonstrated by the experience of the United Nations in the matter of enforcing human rights.[7] Allowing people to press their individual causes beyond the confines of the nation-state would circumvent governmental sovereignty by giving them avenues to challenge or escape its authority. And, of course, international bodies with recognized authority to judge cases and mandate remedies or punishments would clearly erode some of the sovereign authority now possessed by governments. This reluctance is not only a matter of narrow self-interest. The past forty years of attempts at international regulation show that these measures are easily politicized and readily become means of asserting self-interest. National governments have legitimate grounds for being suspicious of the fairness and impartiality of many international regulatory agencies.

Furthermore, a nation will have interests which do not distribute in any straightforward fashion to its individual citizens. A few years ago, for example, the United States engaged in much soul-searching over the question of whether to agree to return control of the Panama Canal to the nation of Panama. Very few private American citizens had any particular interests served by the Panama Canal, yet the nation as a whole clearly had. Part of the difficulty of this issue lay in the problem of determining just what these interests were and how they could best be served. National defense possesses this quality as well. The protection of each individual citizen is only indirectly related to the protection of the nation – in whichever of its senses 'nation' is understood. The nation of Germany was defeated at the conclusion of the Second World War and many of its governmental and cultural institutions destroyed. This did not result in doom for its individual citizens. But clearly these collective national interests do exist and are often highly important, and national governments are best situated to look after them.

In practice recognition of sovereignty also encompasses acknowledging that a particular government is entitled to the rights and privileges enjoyed by other nation-states (the entitlement, that is, to take part in international organizations or make treaties with other sovereign states) and is to be counted, officially at least, as their peer. This last element often prevents nation- states from formally recognizing the sovereign status of antagonistic governments elsewhere. The status of sovereignty need not be in question. Rather, their reluctance may derive from a hesitation to acknowledge that they possess the entitlement to enjoy the prerogatives of recognized nation-states. Sometimes, there is the hope that the reign of a particular government will be brief. Formal recognition is then withheld as a way of demonstrating lack of support. Conversely, prompt recognition of a new and precarious government may be a signal of good wishes and approval. These contrasting attitudes are vividly illustrated first by the response of the United States to the successful Communist revolution in China in 1949, where formal recognition was delayed for nearly twenty-five years, and secondly its quick recognition of the new government of Cory Aquino in the Philippines in 1986. Bitter antipathy and hopes that the Marxist triumph would be temporary caused the delay in the first case, while fond wishes sparked prompt recognition in the latter.

Finally and most importantly, recognition of sovereignty amounts to *acceptance* of the sovereign status of a particular government, with the implied obligation to refrain from efforts to overthrow it.[8] Current practice, as claimed earlier, has no theoretical or principled basis for this response. It is simply the result of pressures of circumstance.

With few exceptions, the usual habit of nation-states has been to grant recognition of sovereignty to those governments that *in fact* enjoy legal dominion over a territory. The discussion of previous pages shows that there are very good practical reasons for this. Most basically, like it or not, nations must deal with one another, and recognition is part of the price they must pay for doing so. Western European nations and the United States demonstrated this fact of international life by finally recognizing the triumph of the Communist Revolution in Russia, though this recognition took decades in some cases. The fact that governments must deal with one another and have few effective measures for coercion short of all-out warfare, entails that they are generally obligated to treat one another as equals and display at least formal courtesy. Where coercion fails, the appearance of good will and mutual respect is all that remains where there is hope of influencing the behavior of another, a truth reflected in the canons of diplomacy.[9]

LEGITIMACY

Nonetheless, scholars are prone to insist that there is a fundamental conceptual distinction to be made between mere *de facto* sovereignty and the moral entitlement to rule, or 'legitimacy'.[10] Governments recognized as legitimate are acknowledged to have a moral entitlement to retain sovereignty, which has force against domestic groups as well as foreign governments.

Positions on issues of legitimacy range across a spectrum of options. The tacit presumption of international law and diplomacy is that all governments that achieve sovereignty have the moral claim to retain it, at least in so far as the international community is concerned. A claim which is theoretically different but practically similar is that sovereign governments must be presumed to be entitled to retain power unless specific criteria demonstrate otherwise.[11] A third position, popular with theoreticians of the present, is that governments are entitled to sovereignty only if they meet certain minimal standards of justice or moral probity.[12] This position is close theoretically to the second but differs in the practical matter of determining which governments can be presumed to enjoy legitimacy. The former presumes all are legitimate unless it can be proven otherwise, *and* it presumes that outsiders are unlikely to be situated, or have the information, to make this decision. The latter view presumes that none is legitimate until it can be established otherwise, and presumes that outsiders can be sufficiently informed to make these decisions. The final position, the position of this work but perhaps shared with some others, is that *no* governments are legitimate, not in the sense that all governments deserve to be removed, but in the sense that the notion of 'legitimacy' is not a fruitful one for working out these issues.[13]

Legitimacy has not been discussed much outside academic circles in recent years, perhaps because this century's tumult of war, revolution and post-colonial adjustment has drained the idea of any significant application to events, and because there are many parties with an interest in submerging it. The pressures that established the consensus that sovereign autonomy should be respected by the community of nations also militate against the introduction of a concept that would require the distinction between a moral entitlement to autonomy and its simple *de facto* possession. Consensus on such a criterion would be difficult to achieve, possibly have little practical effect, and could easily be manipulated to serve as a cover for aggression or international bullying. Present international conditions may not allow such refinement.

Whatever the rhetoric of diplomacy, nations have commonly chosen sides in the civil wars or revolutions of others, and have often done so on the basis of self-interest or perceived affinity with the favored party. Concern for legitimacy has apparently made relatively little difference in the actual practice of states. Perhaps this has always been so. In the past though, these matters have received theoretical scrutiny. Centuries ago, the Western European focus of attention was the manner in which governments came to hold power. A government which came to power in the correct way, using the correct means, was legitimate. One which failed these criteria was a usurper and had no claim to sovereignty.[14] These theories were developed during the time when the rule of monarchs was taken for granted and were commonly focused on acceptable rules of succession from one monarch to the next. Legitimacy understood in this sense, as referring to rules governing the correct succession of governments, remains today in the rules of transition in democratic governments or the procedures regulating the replacement of one group of leaders by another in Marxist nations.

When legitimacy was understood in this archaic sense of rules of the succession of individuals to governmental office, it was often presumed that the person holding ultimate power, the prince or monarch, *was* the government in all its aspects. A single individual was the supreme office-holder and also the final source of law – as well as a symbol of the governmental order of the nation. When all these aspects of government are combined in the figure of one person, it is plausible to believe that legitimacy is simply a matter of rules of succession – and that rules of succession involve more than simply the ascension of one person or another to political office. But if these elements of government are broken apart, it is not quite so apparent that rules of succession can encompass the entire picture. Legitimacy then becomes more complex and requires more subtle analysis.

As the above intimates, 'government' is an ambiguous term which can have a variety of referents. In broadest terms, it may encompass the political culture of a people, their habits and expectations of political activity, their hereditary rights and obligations, and their traditional parties and institutions. In this sense it will be nearly equivalent to 'nation'. More narrowly, the term may refer to the formal structure of government, what Aristotle termed the 'polity' or 'constitution'. This may include reference to the broad principles of government, the abstract conception of the relation of various governmental institutions to one another and to the citizens at large, as well as the fundamental laws of the land. Or 'government' may refer, in its narrowest European parliamentary sense, to the particular persons or political groups that hold office and the preponderance of political power at a given time. Sometimes people use the term to refer to none of these in particular but to indicate government agencies, the departments of agriculture, finance or education, manned by civil servants and leading an existence insulated from the usual push and shove of political activity.

If the people ascending to office, unlike medieval monarchs, are not the bearers of the full range of governmental authority, the rules of legitimate succession become far less consequential. To say that sovereigns are in office legitimately means only that they have followed the rules of succession of their nation. Possessing legitimacy in this sense is the basis of a substantial moral claim to power by those holding office, that of fairness. By following the publicly accepted avenues to power, they can claim to have fulfilled their part of the public agreement and for this reason are entitled to their reward.

But office-holders are not the only claimants established by acceptance of rules of succession. Citizens at large will have legitimate expectations founded on *their* acceptance of these rules. It is certainly of significance if these rules are violated by individuals who usurp the offices of government. No governmental culture can survive for long where there are continued and uncontrolled struggles for possession of sovereign power. So rules of succession are important – and they are important for the long-term well-being of the people of a nation as a whole. Though, as claimed above, they are not of the very highest importance, it is apparent that the rules themselves and the people holding office by means of them should be insulated from abrupt or capricious buffeting. The long-term welfare of the citizens themselves depends upon this.

The upshot is that governmental leaders who have come to power following legitimate rules of succession have some claim to remain in office, the claim of fairness. But it is apparent that this claim does not have overwhelming moral weight. It is reasonable to believe that this entitlement would be invalidated if leaders overstepped the bounds of their authority or caused grievous and unjustified harm to their citizenry. Ferdinand Marcos of the Philippines was originally elected to office by democratic means. He later declared martial law, a move which was quite popular at the time, but he then used its prerogatives to establish himself as dictator.[15] Marcos offers a clear example of an individual who came to office legitimately but by his later conduct forfeited any moral claim which this accorded him.

Rules of transition cannot, therefore, be the whole story of legitimacy. A government such as that of Ferdinand Marcos may satisfy these rules, yet fail in other ways which could negate its moral claim to power. In Locke's view, for example, legitimacy is produced from the mingling of two factors whose relationship is not precisely defined. Ultimately Locke believed that government's legitimacy must rest on the consent of the people, whether explicit or tacit. In this his views continue in the tradition of earlier thinking about rules of succession, since they delineate the proper means of coming to hold power, viz. by receiving the consent of the citizenry. But he also clearly believed that in practice consent would be granted only to governmental leaders who provide peace and security for their citizens by enforcing the laws of nature. When office-holders perform these functions badly or attempt to usurp more than their legitimate power, people would withdraw consent and rise in revolt. Locke presumed that people would *in fact* respond so because they are rational *and* would reason in the manner he envisioned. Because he viewed the matter in this way, he did not see that the two elements are distinct . . . and that each might pull the theory of legitimacy in different directions.[16]

If people did not reason in the fashion Locke foresaw, they might endow consent to a government which had commandeered more than its just share of power. They might, as in the case of Ayatollah Khomeini's Iran, *demand* such a government as their due. Or people might, for their own reasons or because they are caught up in the dynamics of popular movements, withdraw consent from a government of modest and limited pretensions. There has never been a government quite like that, of course, but something of that sort occurred when the modestly liberal but ill-fated Weimar Republic was displaced by Hitler's National Socialists. There have also been cases where a roughly Lockean government has been imposed on a people without consent. The American occupation forces in Japan could certainly claim to be Locke's heirs in a number of ways. The principles of government of the Founding Fathers were distinctly Lockean, and the second paragraph of the Declaration of Independence is as eloquent and succinct a summary of Locke's political philosophy as is likely to be found.[17] General MacArthur was certainly no Thomas Jefferson but apparently did find that Locke's views came quite as naturally as both Locke and Jefferson might have hoped. The Japanese people accepted the new form of government, but did so because of Confucian views that the Mandate of Heaven had passed to the Americans – and because their Emperor commanded it.[18] This is choice of a sort, but clearly not what Locke had in mind.

Locke thus had two different criteria of legitimacy, criteria that could operate independently. He failed to see this because he presumed people would only choose governments narrowly devoted to the enforcement of the laws of nature, and they would only withdraw consent where this authority was exercised improperly. In the event of conflict, however, it is not clear which of the two criteria he would have weighed more heavily. Where it becomes necessary to choose between them, it is necessary to go beyond Locke.

Possibly the decision is made easier as the result of substantial criticism of the criterion of popular choice. One basic problem is that there is no clear sense in which the great majority of the people of the world have consented to the governments which rule them. Save for adult immigrants, the citizens of nations do not select the governments they have. Even adult immigrants often do not have distinct choices of where they wish to live. They head for nations they can physically reach or ones that can be expected to accept them. For most refugees, and even for most other immigrants, there are no significant options. Many have not made the free choice to leave their home nations. Many are forced out by repression, political upheaval or simple poverty. Most, perhaps, would not have migrated had domestic conditions been tolerable.

If personal choice is the criterion of the legitimacy of governments, it is unlikely that any clearly attain legitimacy. But, Locke might rejoin, it is *tacit* rather than explicit choice that matters. Most, he might claim, have tacitly chosen to accept their government by, like Socrates, remaining when they could leave, by refraining from revolt, and by, without undue coercion, following the laws of the state or taking part in its political institutions.[19] The difficulty with these responses, as noted above, is that most people really do not have any significant option for going elsewhere. There is no assurance that anyone else will accept them. Furthermore, most will for all practical purposes have their lives destroyed by leaving their homeland and be faced with the prospect of beginning entirely anew. Or they may detest their government but remain because they love their families, friends, career – or nation. Where residence continues for these reasons, it can hardly be construed as tacit support for government.

Of course, disgruntled citizens could rise up in revolt rather than simply leave. As the previous chapter demonstrates, however, violent response has its own costs, costs that are substantial and difficult to control. Many governments are distinctly unsavory, but few achieve the level of tyranny that would clearly justify the resort to violent, life-threatening insurrection or the cost in human suffering it would entail. But the fact that their failings are petty rather than enormous need not imply that they have a strong moral claim to remain in power.

People do more than obey laws. They often go beyond obedience to participate actively in their government. Again, this is not necessarily endorsement of the government in question. Laws are obeyed for a variety of reasons. It has been claimed, for instance, that most people obey laws simply from habit or inertia.[20] For other, more reflective sorts, laws may be obeyed because individuals agree with the laws themselves rather than the virtue of the government that instituted them. Furthermore, the experience of Lebanon, and possibly the South Bronx, is sufficient to demonstrate that almost any government is better than none at all. Acknowledging the need for *some* government is quite distinct from endorsing the one at hand. People, in addition, have private goals and needs. In many cases, to serve these they must work through the government that is available. Doing so need not be an endorsement of that government but rather the acknowledgement that government is often a means necessary to attain one's ends. It is always possible that a different government would be better suited for these purposes than the one at hand, but, no other being practically available, the one that is must be relied upon.

What is more, minimal conditions of genuine choice require a variety of distinct options. In the matter of government this is almost never the case. Even the resort to revolution contains no assurance that one specific type of government rather than another will result. Revolutions are often negative reactions directed against particular governments rather than positive struggles founded on a clear conception of the features of a new one. The most direct result of revolutions is that they transfer a new group of *people* to power, and even this is often uncertain, as the Russian Revolution illustrates. Further, since they are often violent, revolutions are better suited for destruction than reconstructing new government. As the Sandinista experience in Nicaragua shows, mass uprising can be initiated with only the vaguest idea of what government will be established should the insurrection prevail.[21] Indeed, it is normally impossible to judge just what sort of government will result from a given revolution. They generate their own dynamic and are subject to abrupt and unforeseen twists. The sort of government foreseen at the beginning of a revolt may be quite different than the one in place at its end.

Of course, most people probably accept the government they have, in the sense of passively accepting it. Many even endorse their government wholeheartedly.[22] But neither of these responses is equivalent to free choice. People, for one thing, are conditioned from birth to appreciate the virtues (whether genuine or imagined) of their inherited government and overlook its deficiencies. Few have the sort of acquaintance with other systems of government, with their particular virtues and deficiencies, that would enable them to make a clear choice.

Ordinary people, and even politically sophisticated people, often fail to distinguish the various aspects of 'government' mentioned earlier, so that their endorsement of government may not be precisely directed at any one of them. Furthermore, when 'government' is understood in the broadest sense of 'political culture', it will, for those nations with ancient and settled political and social institutions, be closely bound up with the common life of the people. Where this is so, it may well be impossible to change one aspect or another of government without destroying or substantially altering the nation as a whole.

Simple endorsement or approval of government is therefore normally imprecise and must be distinguished from genuine choice. These matters are sufficiently complex when attempting to unravel individual choices, but become much more diffuse and unwieldy when stretched to cover an entire people, considered as a collectivity. The collective preference of a people is commonly referred to as 'the will of the people', a phrase which has perhaps come to have too large a role in the political rhetoric of this century. 'The will of the people', in other words, is another of the major icons of the intuitive international morality of the present era, and deference to it is nearly axiomatic.

In practice the criterion of 'the will of the people' has proven sufficiently difficult to measure and apply that it has provided the basis for all manner of self-serving rhetoric and maneuver. Even political upheavals with demonstrable popular and broad-based support, such as those in Nicaragua and Iran of 1979 or the Philippines and Haiti in 1986, did not necessarily reflect the determined resolution of all or even a substantial majority of the people of these nations. In any case, it is probably impossible to tell whether this is so and would not matter much if such a determination could be made. Even the hallowed American Revolution did not have overwhelming popular support.[23] What seems to have mattered in these instances is that a sufficiently large number of people was motivated to act in circumstances where their numbers made a political difference, and *this* qualifies them as popular revolutions. However, disorganized and ill-directed numbers of people may not suffice for political change. The people must be organized or must be deployed under conditions where their massing can have political effect. Such movements should be distinguished from 'the will of the people' as a whole, though they may certainly qualify as popular movements. A 'popular' movement does not signify an entire population but only a massed group that is able to deploy its numbers in such fashion as to have political impact.

Nonetheless, there are instances where elaborate efforts have been made to discern the will of the people, though they are comparatively rare. These include cases where plebiscites have been held on issues of government, where people have voted and expressed their preferences. It is natural to wish to count these as genuine expressions of the will of the people. But this view can only be accepted after pointed questions are asked about the context in which such polls are taken. Governments are adept at pressuring citizens and structuring plebiscites to elicit the outcomes they wish. Even where bias or coercion does not mar schemes of voting, ballots count for little if citizens are illiterate, uninformed or unable to scan a roster of genuine and distinct options. Nor will voting be significant if there is not free and open public debate with sufficient time for contending options to be developed and aired.[24] Even then, people are likely to opt for the institutions to which they are accustomed and have been conditioned to accept.

The above are essentially practical considerations. They may well be sufficiently intractable that the consent of the people is not suited, given the conditions of the world, to serve as the criterion of legitimacy. Nonetheless, it remains possible in theory to discern the will of the people clearly and unambiguously. It is possible as well that this will is not so fragmented and diffuse that it is unsuitable for the purpose of selecting a government for an entire people. It is also possible that this will is not sufficiently fickle that no government resting on its foundation can expect any degree of stability. If all of these difficulties are surmounted, would the consent of the people *then* qualify as the ultimate criterion of legitimacy which should override all others? The theoretical issue remains and demands attention, if only for the sake of conceptual tidiness. But it is also important because of the substantial worry that the alternative to basing government on the will of the people is *not* basing government on the will of the people – and no sensitive commentator would feel comfortable with that.

It may be, therefore, that in an imperfect world imperfect consent is the least unworkable of possible foundations of legitimacy. The converse case has arisen frequently enough. That is, there are instances where a particular government is widely unpopular and where it is plausible to claim that the consent of the people has been withdrawn – acknowledging the aforementioned difficulties of maintaining this judgement. In so far as these matters can be discerned, consent was withdrawn from the governments of the Shah of Iran, of Somoza in Nicaragua in 1979, and most recently from the governments of Duvalier in Haiti and of Marcos in the Philippines in early 1986. Should it be the case that wherever popular will is clearly and unambiguously expressed, it must be respected and given greater moral weight than other considerations?

Addressing this issue requires that attention be given to the question of just what sort of choice the choice of government is. The common impulse to believe that people have the right to select the government which will direct and manage their lives appears to be founded on the principle of respect for individual autonomy.[25] Conventional wisdom has it that respect for personal autonomy requires that people be allowed to make their own decisions and act upon them. It seems a short step from this to the belief that, since the choice of government is of great importance and consequence, people should have their choices in this matter respected above all others.

However, on second glance, the choice of government is quite different from the choices people make in the direction of their personal lives. Choice of government is a choice for all and not just the individual. When a fundamentalist Muslim pushes for the establishment of an Islamic republic, which is both a theocracy and follows the Law of the Sha'ria, he is not choosing just for himself but for all. If he is in the majority, or simply a member of a dominant faction, his choice will prevail, but not just for him. His choice will carry also for those who are greatly opposed to such a government and for those whose lives will be greatly changed by it. It will, for example, be of great concern for women, who will be frozen out of public life and political activity by such an arrangement.

Furthermore, this choice differs from plebiscites organized *within* a governmental structure on more particular matters of national concern. Choice of government determines the context and shape of the future choices citizens will be able to make and is, therefore, much more fundamental. The picture is further complicated by the fact that under the conditions of the actual world the choice of government is in general not simply the choice of fundamental laws and institutional arrangements but is *de facto* a choice which elevates a particular group or individual to sovereign power. So the decision is normally a choice about political domination within society.

Because choice of government fixes political responsibilities, civil rights and social domination, it is a choice in which people will have a great deal to lose. In fact, they may have more to lose as individuals than can be morally justified. Given these complications, it is not obvious that popular choice of government should be free and unfettered.[26] Neither can it be presumed that whatever government results from the operation of the will of the people is legitimate in the sense of possessing an overwhelming entitlement to exist, an entitlement which outweighs all other moral claims. This does not imply that the will of the people should have no moral weight whatsoever. Personal preferences are, after all, the basis of the utilitarian perspective of this work. But, given this perspective, it is reasonable to presume that governmental structures should be instituted which will satisfy more of the preferences of more people of a nation rather than fewer. Popular choices of government which deviate strongly from this standard may in some cases be overridden by other concerns.

Thus, where there are established rules of succession to office, the immediate 'will of the people', in and of itself, may not necessarily outweigh them. Removing persons from office is not justified if performed capriciously, both because of the value of having stable rules of governmental transition and because of the difference between the personal choices people make for their own lives and the choices they make for the society as a whole. It is unjustified also because of the difficulty of determining what the general will requires – *and* because the general will may be significantly divided or fragmented.

If popular will is unsuitable as a single abstract standard of legitimacy, 'justice' serves little better.[27] It is difficult to formulate a conception of justice which has real substance but which will not suffer from Western European biases – which, that is, will be sensitive to important cultural and political differences of non-Western societies. It will be difficult to formulate a conception broad enough to accommodate this diversity, yet specific enough to have real bite in assessing concrete cases. Reliance on an abstract standard of justice must obscure the fact that there will sometimes be good reasons for establishing, or recognizing, governments which are from certain perspectives unjust or working to remove those that in many respects *are* just.

Reference to an abstract ideal of justice glosses the fact that governments can be just and unjust in many ways and that governments are just and unjust in varying degrees. No government is purely just or unjust. The government, in *all* its aspects, of the United States was seriously unjust in fostering segregation several years ago. Yet it was just in its general rule of law and usual protection of individual rights. The government of the Soviet Union has been unjust in its treatment of political and religious dissidents and its cavalier attitude toward civil liberties. It has also been unjust in working to maintain an oligarchy and restricting the benefits of power to that class alone. Yet it has been just in working to provide the basic requirements of well-being for all its citizens and in attempting to provide them with rewarding lives that include more than only the means of subsistence.

Both these governments are unjust in a number of ways and very probably will continue to be so, but it is not apparent that their failings are sufficient to justify a violent effort to depose them. It is easy to imagine a government that would attain a higher standard of justice than either, but it is not obvious that such a government is in fact achievable in these nations or that it would justify whatever cost in coercion or violence may be required to install it.

In the past few years several scholars in the United States have developed positions which begin to meet these problems. They have elaborated the idea that all governments have the obligation to provide minimal justice for their citizens or insure that they possess what are called 'basic rights'. The work of Henry Shue is representative.[28] In Shue's view basic rights include the right to life and security. The difficulty with these positions, however, is the same as those that plague theories of legitimacy generally. Since Shue acknowledges that he wishes to establish only a minimalist ethic, it is not obvious that he would wish to claim that any government which satisfied his minimal standards should be morally immune from attempts at overthrow, whether from within or without.[29] But neither is it apparent that he would wish to say that governments falling below the standard should be considered fair game for overthrow on those grounds alone.

More fundamentally, there are problems in determining just what constitutes meeting this standard. Governments seldom directly threaten the lives and security of an entire population, though the Pol Pot government of Cambodia came close. Rather, they threaten some portion of the population, such as particular ethnic groups or troublesome political activists, and leave the great majority alone. Even in notorious cases of repression, such as Chile or Argentina, only a very small portion of the population was in direct peril. It is not clear whether Shue wishes to say that these governments met his standard simply because the great bulk of the population was generally secure or whether he would wish to say that they failed the standard and were therefore legitimately subject to overthrow by any and all comers. Yet if his standards are genuinely rights and are therefore the solemn entitlement of all persons, it would seem that Shue should be committed to the position that a government falls short of legitimacy if the basic rights of even one individual are violated in even one instance. Anything less would constitute the very balancing of life against life that rights theorists decry in utilitarianism. The rigorous insistence on full satisfaction of these rights for all results in an extreme position that lacks plausibility. Attempts at melioration, however, would move his position disconcertingly close to utilitarianism.

Casting issues of entitlement to sovereign power in terms of legitimacy encourages the tendency to believe that governments either have it or they do not. If they do, the implication is that they have an overwhelming moral claim to retain power. If they do not, they have none. But thinking about legitimacy is misguided and unhelpful if cast in terms of the search for a single criterion which, if met, will confer an absolute entitlement to sovereignty. As the discussion of this section illustrates, the usual candidates for such a criterion, those of individual choice, popular will, rules of succession, or meeting standards of justice, are not capable of providing such an absolute entitlement.

Where legitimacy is understood as equivalent to absolute entitlement to sovereign power, it is at best misleading, and at worst confuses thinking about the status of governments. It is more reasonable to claim only that governments have stronger or weaker moral claims to retain sovereignty. Even where these claims are weak, the costs of working to remove particular governments will often be great enough to make such an effort unjustified. Furthermore, even governments with strong claims to sovereignty may, on occasion, find them outweighed by more pressing concerns. The issue is further complicated by the fact that where 'government' refers simply to the particular group of people holding power, the claim to sovereignty may be comparatively weak. Where 'government' is understood in its broadest extension, as equivalent to the established political culture of a people, the basis of its authority becomes much stronger.

In the final analysis, then, it is Locke's second criterion, revolt for the right reasons, which must be the ultimate basis for moral claims that governments should either be removed from power or should be allowed to remain. Sometimes right reasons will include reference to 'the will of the people', however this may be understood. But the discussion of this section shows that this endorsement cannot be an automatic warrant either of legitimacy or its absence. Neither can reference to abstract standards of moral propriety, such as justice or basic rights, serve this purpose. The position of this work is that utilitarian analysis of cost weighed against probable gain must be relied upon to determine whether the effort to remove a particular government from power, whatever aspects of it are of concern, is justified.

In principle it makes no difference whether the above analysis is carried out by citizens or by outsiders. Neither does it matter whether efforts to initiate change are undertaken from within or from without. The reason for this is the fundamental distinction between the fate and interests of governments and those of individual persons. In a few cases governments will directly serve the interests and concerns of citizens in such fashion that overriding their efforts would genuinely count as violating the wishes of their citizens. In other cases governments may be so tightly linked to the common life of their people that they can be considered extensions of their agency. However, these examples will be few and far between. In most instances government and citizenry will be distinct and largely independent of one another. These distinctions, however, are blurred by an established sense of national identity. Citizens of a nation presently tend to identify with one another and with their government, so that they view an external affront to their government as directed at themselves. But this sense of identification, as will be claimed in the next chapter, has only practical and not moral importance. It does not, in other words, establish any genuine link between the personal autonomy of individuals and that of their governments.

Governments, as argued earlier, can function as moral agents but have no status, by themselves, as moral patients. That is, their fates and prospects are only of moral concern in so far as these affect the welfare of individual persons. The difference between internal and external is extremely important in practical terms, however. Because of this, the following sections are devoted to the various facets of these problems.

DEPOSING GOVERNMENTS

Foreign groups often have considerable interest in removing one group of people from office in a nation and/or installing another. Some of the more infamous maneuvering of the American CIA, for example, has been directed to these ends.[30] The Ayatollah Khomeini once stated that his terms for ending Iran's war with Iraq included the removal from office of his arch-enemy President Hussein.[31] Multinational corporations have sometimes been involved with these matters as well, as in the notorious instance of the role International Telephone and Telegraph played in the removal of the Chilean President Allende from office in 1973.[32] It is common for nations to become embroiled in the revolutions and civil wars of others and even to foment them. Talk of sovereignty and legitimacy aside, efforts to remove governments and install others are a distressingly common feature of the international scene. Most often, it is true, the grounds for this interference are selfish and callous. But this does not touch the conceptual issue of whether such activity can ever be justified.

From a strictly theoretical perspective, as the discussion of legitimacy demonstrates, there is no reason to believe that it is always wrong in principle for outsiders to work for the removal of a particular government. The focus on legitimacy has been valuable in concentrating attention on the point that governments are not automatically morally entitled to sovereignty simply by virtue of possessing it. Asking these questions, in other words, has made the intuitive view of the present day less tenable. There are often morally sound reasons for seeking to remove governments from power.

In the above examples of Iraq and Chile, outside efforts were directed at removing governmental leaders. However, as the discussion of the previous section illustrates, efforts to change government need not be directed at simply removing particular leaders from power. At the present time, for example, the ostensible policy of the United States is to alter the institutions of government in Nicaragua, by forcing it to become open and democratic rather than remain a narrow oligarchy, but *not* to remove the Sandinista leaders themselves. There is reason to doubt the veracity of these announced aims, but conceptually the distinction is perfectly sound. The occupation forces in Germany and Japan following the Second World War successfully changed all three aspects of government – that is, leaders, institutions and political culture.

Because the practical and theoretical issues of working to depose different aspects of governments vary, they will be discussed separately. In addition, it will be necessary to discuss the proportionality of means to ends. The importance of these considerations is masked when the discussion of sovereignty is framed in terms of legitimacy, since governments lacking legitimacy are deemed to have no claim at all to sovereign power while legitimate ones have the absolute entitlement to office. Where the issue is cast in stark terms of black and white, concern for proportion of means to ends seems out of place. But if there is no absolute entitlement to rule, if there are only stronger and weaker claims, the focus on proportion is natural and important.

It would seem that the clearest case in which external pressure for the removal of national leaders from office may be justified, and where even the extreme means of mass violence would be justified to bring about change, is where heads of state are responsible for causing a great deal of human suffering abroad, and the only way to halt their activity is to expel them from office. If such a case arose, working to remove even those leaders who enjoyed broad domestic popularity would seem warranted. What is not clear is whether any such cases are likely to arise. If Iran's war with Iraq was prolonged simply as the result of the Ayatollah's antipathy to President Hussein, then his policies were clearly wrong. It was unlikely that Hussein's removal was necessary either to end the Persian Gulf War or to prevent new ones.

But war is both a clumsy and costly instrument. While there was little reason to believe that Hussein's removal was necessary to end the war with Iran, working to remove him would be justified if it were true that he was the major obstacle to peace. If this were so, however, other methods, such as assassination or stirring political pressures against him, would be preferable to full-scale war – assuming there were reason to believe they would be effective and that these measures would not be likely to cause more disruption than they would cure. It is reasonable to believe that the assassination of Hitler in 1943 would have greatly helped bring about an early end to the Second World War. In cases such as this, note, even the extreme measure of assassination would be warranted, because of the toll of human life at stake.

National leaders may be coerced in various ways, and there are several means for resolving problems they cause. Pressing for their removal from office may well move them to desperation, to cling to their prerogatives at any cost, and thereby increase the difficulty of resolving their mischief. Where this is so, it is necessary to keep in mind that the major goal must always be that of halting life-threatening mischief or preventing future outbursts. Seeking removal from office is only justified as a means to seek this end, and not as an end in itself. Under the usual conditions of personal ethics where there is some organized social authority to establish order, it might be reasonable to seek the punishment of every miscreant and to demand strict adherence to principles of conduct. In the international arena, where conditions are presently quite different, such expectations are not similarly reasonable. Assigning blame, seeking punishment or pressing for strict adherence to standards are only possible where institutions and authority exist to support these efforts. It is surely worthwhile to work to establish such conditions, but they do not exist at present. Because of this it is often feasible to seek only the more modest goal of halting present abuses or working, over the longer range, to establish a global consensus on standards of governmental behavior.

Cases where a particular set of national leaders is a menace to its own population are more difficult to manage – not in theory but in practice. Recent history gives plenty of examples of brutal governments causing domestic turmoil which the outside world was unable to ignore. The instances of the Khmer Rouge in Cambodia and Idi Amin in Uganda come readily to mind. But there are other, in some ways more difficult, instances. The regime of Baby Doc Duvalier in Haiti was characterized by enormous cruelty. Yet the greatest suffering of his people was not caused by his armed militia, the Tontons Macoutes, but by the corruption and nearly incomprehensible incompetence and stupidity of his reign. The greatest misery resulted from Haiti's economic shambles and Duvalier's thorough milking of its resources.[33] Incompetence and greed work their ill effects in less spectacular and direct fashion and, because they are indirect, lack the riveting quality of consciously intended abuse. Their toll in human life and well-being can easily be greater than even the most determined campaign of repression. Yet absence of spectacular violence or intentional harm has the consequence that the outside world will be less clearly agreed that destructive harm exists, harm that requires a determined response. Where there are no international structures with authority to deal with miscreant governments, only outrageous wrong is likely to produce the consensus and motivation sufficient for the world community to act. It is not immediately apparent that a government which causes suffering as the result of incompetence or stupidity has any greater claim to remain in power than one oppressing its citizens by means of overt physical violence.

There *are* differences, of course. Suffering resulting from incompetence or greed is not normally directly intended. Assuming that most governments have reason to wish their citizens to be healthy and prosperous, rather than the reverse, it may seem plausible to assume that they will welcome assistance and expertise from outside and will not be intentional obstacles to improvement. Where this is so, they *need not* be removed and need not be confronted with force. Furthermore, conditions within nations are frequently such that the removal of one incompetent indigenous government is likely only to make way for another of the same kind. The particular individuals who are members of government may not, in other words, be the fundamental problem. Rather, the nation's political and economic infrastructure may be so decayed that competent institutions as well as qualified people to fill them are lacking. The problem may lie with 'government' in its broadest sense rather than with the particular individuals in power. In the Haiti of Duvalier, for example, the legal system was in such disarray that it was rare for members of the legal profession, whether judges or lawyers, even to possess copies of Haitian lawbooks, which at $25 per copy were too expensive for most to afford and which, dating from 1939, were hopelessly obsolete in any case.[34]

Even with the exile of the Duvalier family, Haiti remains an economic and political shambles, often skirting dangerously close to brutal anarchy. Where problems are of this depth and magnitude, it is difficult to imagine that outsiders would be able to do much to improve the situation. It is much more difficult to change people's ways of life and political culture than simply chase a few miscreants from office. Doing so would require a long-term and thoroughgoing intrusion into their lives. In the case of Haiti, with the cruelty and incompetence of the Duvalier government, even extreme measures, including life-threatening violence, would have been justified to depose Baby Doc and his kin. Given the disarray of the nation, it is unlikely that violent means would have made the situation *worse*. The exit of the Duvaliers clearly could not solve Haiti's problems, but it was both a necessary and a beneficial first step.

In a similar case, that of Idi Amin's government of Uganda, violent means were used to depose a vicious dictator, and it is unclear that anything less extreme would have sufficed. It is entirely possible that pressures of different sorts would have sufficed to remove Duvalier, but violent means would have clearly been justified had none other offered a reasonable chance of success.

It is relatively easy to remedy harm when directly caused by the willful viciousness or greed of specific individuals holding the reins of power. When they are removed, it is reasonable to believe that the harm will cease. Even with the uncertainties involved in attempting to install new members of government, steps can be taken to ensure that the failings of that sort are avoided. That is, it will be difficult to ascertain in advance whether a proposed government will be competent, inspired, able to maintain the confidence and patience of its people, or whether it will be able to restore order and weather the crises of inflated expectations which often attend the removal of a particularly detested group of leaders. None of these factors can be gauged with any degree of accuracy. However, steps can be taken to help ensure that the new group of governmental leaders will not replicate the physical abuses of the old. Leaders can be chosen who are known for their restraint. Strict rules can be established governing the use of force. Actions can be taken to ensure that there is a rule of law rather than of individual whim. In other words, both the personnel and institutions of government must be changed. None of these measures can *absolutely* ensure that abuses will not recur. Neither can they ensure that the new government will be competent or inspired in its leadership. These are matters which as yet lie beyond the reach of precise human control and that is part of the reason why it is important to exercise restraint. With all this uncertainty, however, it remains plausible to assume that some measures and some persons will be more likely to succeed than others.

It is more difficult to justify the removal of a government for incompetence, since it will be uncertain whether the problem can be remedied by mere change of governmental leaders. It is much more difficult to judge competence in advance and more difficult to orchestrate the institutional structures which will allow such competence to become effective than it is to prevent physical abuses. Furthermore, competence in one area, such as managing the economy, does not necessarily indicate the competence required to deal with popular unrest. Yet both types may be required for the success of a new regime. To make matters worse, the competence of individual persons may be effectively undermined by the political culture and social practices of a nation. If, for example, bribery is an established feature of the political culture of a nation, it is highly unlikely that simple change in government personnel will suffice to eradicate it.[35] Or if a nation has a long history of rule by a small elite group, it is unlikely that a vigorous party system, responsive to citizens' needs and demands, will spring up overnight. There is, in other words, a complex interplay between the personnel of government, its institutions, and the political culture of a nation. These can react upon one another in intricate and often unpredictable ways. Individuals can sometimes be molded to competence and moral sensitivity by the institutions which envelop them, or their personal abilities and energy can be dissipated by those that are corrupt.

What is often required, therefore, is change in the political culture of the nation, as well as in governmental structure and the personnel holding power. Such changes may require long years of altering practices and re-aligning expectations, goals not easily accomplished by anyone, and therefore especially outsiders. Even in the cases of revolutions as abrupt and thoroughgoing as the Russian and Chinese, astute commentators have maintained that the operation of their new governments is better understood in terms of the entrenched history of these two nations than of global features of the Marxism espoused by victorious revolutionaries.[36]

Change of this latter sort is much more difficult to manage, therefore, and it is easy to understand why the removal of cruel, oppressive governments is easier to justify, in practical terms, than that of incompetent ones. It can also be seen that deposing good, or even moderately good and responsible, governments is unlikely to be justified. The reason is *not* that their removal is necessarily more difficult or costly than that of tyrannical governments. A humane and conscientious government may in some cases be easier to overthrow, since it may be unwilling to resort to the mass violence and oppression commonly used by despotic governments to retain power. This holds true even where government is relatively popular, since the mass of people may be uninterested in, or unwilling to take, forceful action to save it. Furthermore, even comparatively humane governments can become distinctly unpopular, sometimes through no fault of their own, as in the case of the Weimar Republic. Unfortunately, given the nature of world affairs, decency is neither a necessary nor a sufficient condition for a government's remaining in power.

The reason why justification of the overthrow of moderate governments is difficult is not that it is impossible to imagine that they could be made better. Every government has warts which are readily visible to all.[37] Only a decided lack of insight and intelligence could prevent people from discovering any number of ills in a particular government. The difficulty is rather that, where a given government is reasonably good and humane, the odds are against installing a new one sufficiently better than the old to justify the inevitable costs of bringing it into existence. This, allied with the great difficulty of knowing how good a future government is apt to be and the threat to stability which always accompanies transitions in government, makes any real-world attempt to justify the destruction of decent governments very difficult indeed.

Modestly good governments ought generally speaking to remain in office, but not because they have some fundamental moral entitlement to do so. Rather, the reason is that the array of conditions in which their removal would be justified are exceedingly rare. If such could be conceived, they would have no claim to remain in office and could legitimately be removed – and this applies to all actual governments.

Nonetheless, there have been cases where all the elements of government have been removed on the grounds that, as a group, they were morally deficient. Following the Second World War, for example, not merely the leaders, but also the political institutions and political cultures of both Germany and Japan were self-consciously, successfully and permanently dismantled by the Allied Forces to be replaced by Western-style liberal democracies. These instances demonstrate that drastic transformation of government can occur – and can do so successfully and permanently. Marxist revolutions of the orthodox stripe have the same goal of wholesale transformation, since they aim at overthrow of an entire ruling class, along with its apparatus of government and attendant political ideology.

In the case of the Axis powers at least, conventional wisdom has it that these wholesale transformations were both morally legitimate and morally required. It is worth having a closer look at them to see how they may have been justified. Effecting these transformations required an enormous cost, the struggles of the Second World War resulting in unconditional surrender followed by occupation. It is highly unlikely that these changes in government could have occurred without extreme measures, and it is reasonable to ask whether it would have been worth prolonging the war in order to be able to achieve them.

The leaders of the Axis nations were responsible not only for the crime of wrongful war, that is, wrongfully initiating aggressive war, but also for war crimes, atrocities committed during the course of the conflict. Clearly, taking measures to halt such activities and attempting to ensure that they did not recur were important and well-justified goals. But they are not goals which would justify *any* and all costs which might be required to achieve them. If it had been possible to secure these ends in some other way and at less cost in human life and well-being, the Allied insistence on unconditional surrender and its drive for invasion and occupation would have been unjustified. If the attempted assassination of Hitler, for example, had been successful and the participating military officers had been able to secure power, sue for peace, and install a new government, then continuing the war in Europe would have been clearly wrong. Nonetheless, it transpired that the Allied leaders deemed it necessary to follow the war in both theaters to the end. It is *not* obvious that their insistence on total and complete victory was morally warranted. But where removal of officials of government could be achieved with little additional cost, since invasion and occupation were already set as goals of the war, these efforts were justified. This would have been the case even if these leaders of government had continued to enjoy considerable domestic popularity. This is because the enormous harm they were capable of achieving would have outweighed the preferences of their citizens on this matter.

But more than only governmental leaders were removed. The institutional apparatus of the Nazi Party and the militaristic government of Japan were thoroughly ousted as well and replaced by democratic governments of the Western liberal style, at least in Japan and *West* Germany. In *East* Germany the Marxist government installed was a radically different but equally abrupt change from what had existed before. Certainly the pre-war institutions of government these nations possessed were deficient in a variety of ways, and it is quite likely that they contributed impetus to brutal and aggressive war. Japan and West Germany ended up with more decent and humane governing institutions than before, and the transformation has been a success – in retrospect.

The Axis powers are easy cases in some ways. Their leaders, political institutions and political culture all interlinked to spark the great suffering and abuses these nations caused. Their removal would have been worth even extreme costs, but not the costs of the Second World War. The war was justified only to end their abuses and would not have been warranted had it been possible to stop the atrocities by some other means. Even the drive for complete victory and unconditional surrender would clearly not have been warranted simply for the purpose of deposing these two governments. However, since there is probably no way the war could have been avoided, with the intransigence on both sides, the imposition of liberal government was clearly worthwhile.

The institutions of government can be defective in a variety of ways. They can fail to ensure proper representation of the masses of their citizens. They can fail to establish and nurture basic civil rights and liberties. They can fail to secure the basic requirements of due process or competent legal representation. But these are seen as deficiencies mainly from the perspective of Western liberal democracies. The Ayatollah Khomeini established an Islamic republic in Iran. As such, its standards of government and justice are different from those in Western European nations. Nonetheless, the Shi'ites possess a coherent and defensible conception of government which, though quite alien to Western perspectives, has a moral foundation that deserves respect by others. If the Ayatollah's plans enjoy the broad support of the people of Iran, his Islamic republic has a considerable moral claim to its sovereignty, though, as pointed out earlier, not an absolute and overwhelming entitlement. It would be wrong either for outsiders or for Iranians to seek to impose one of a different sort simply on the grounds that the Ayatollah's government differs in its fundamental perspective from the Western model of liberal democracy.

However, the situation in Iran is complex. Its people are entitled to an Islamic republic, if that is what they desire, and they are entitled to the Shi'ite glorification of martyrdom, even to the point of sending their children off to death in battles with Iraq.[38] So long as the Iranian people accept these practices and values – indeed, cling to them with fervor – they have a significant moral claim to them, one which outsiders have the obligation to respect. Furthermore, given Shi'ite views of the relationship between religion, law and government, it would be facile to argue that they are entitled to choose this way of life for themselves and perhaps for their families but not for their nation as a whole. The distinctive Shi'ite practice requires a unity of religion, law and government. Its values cannot be fully obtained without this unity. But the matter cannot rest at this point, for conservative Shi'ites are choosing this system not only for themselves but for all the people of Iran, including political and religious minorities. Thus there remain the issues of Iranian persecution of the Bahai religious group and the brutal oppression of dissenting political organizations. The desire for an Islamic republic can neither justify nor require such measures. It is one thing to extol the value of martyrdom for oneself and one's family, but it is a different matter to suppress a distinctive or dissident minority.

There is a substantial difficulty here, one which is noted elsewhere in this work. Sovereignty is not merely ultimate legal authority over discrete individuals but is power over *all* those residing in a given territory. For this reason there are always likely to be groups or individuals within a territory who are at odds with the values or practices established as the norm for the whole. People are entitled to have their preferences in government respected, just as any other human preferences merit respect. These preferences carry added weight when they are closely linked with religious and cultural values, as they are in Iran, since these are likely to be of considerable importance for the people who hold them and because they have broader impact on personal life than more limited and mundane preferences. Within the conceptual scheme of this work, however, these preferences are secondary. They cannot be given greater moral weight than the fundamental needs of life and its means, and it is these which religious and political minorities are denied in Iran. Human decency requires that the latter be accommodated even where, as in the case of the Shi'ites of Iran, some compromise of fundamental belief may be required. But there is little reason why the creation of an Islamic republic or preservation of its values requires the sort of persecution the Iranians have undertaken. Neither does it justify vilification or oppression of other sorts. An Islamic republic can be established, in other words, which can accommodate the decent treatment of others who are also citizens. This accommodation, though, would still allow the Bahais to be second-class citizens in the sense that there would be certain positions and certain decisions of the state as a whole from which they would be excluded. So long as they are essentially able to live their own lives, such arrangements need not be *prima facie* morally wrong. They should be suspect in the way that all inequitable arrangements are suspect, but they may be the best that conditions will allow.

Neither can Iranian treatment of dissenting political groups be condoned. These organizations appear to be composed of urban, educated people whose values are out of sorts with those of the Iranian people as a whole.[39] Their desire to impose their own system of government and their own perspectives on the entire nation is without strong moral claim. In part this is because there is little reason to believe that the various Marxist and socialist groups that constitute the opposition would be more likely to safeguard human rights than the mullahs they detest. But, more important, the values and ways of life they wish to establish through their proposed institutions of government are clearly out of sorts with the preferences and common life of the great mass of the Iranian people. Their programs do not necessarily deserve support by outsiders, but their treatment at the hands of the government is another matter and *does* warrant rebuke.

The case of Iran illuminates the problems of legitimacy and sovereignty in particularly vivid fashion. By most criteria its government, in all its aspects, has a substantial moral claim to retain sovereignty. It enjoys the support of the great majority of its people and offers political institutions which mesh tightly with their values and ways of life. While its concerns are far removed from those of Western liberal democracy and it certainly does not safeguard civil or human rights in any Western European sense, it is closely in tune with the needs and aspirations of the bulk of its people. Yet it is treating distinctive minorities with brutality and vituperation which clearly extend far beyond what is necessary to maintain Shi'ite culture.

It is clear that this widespread and systematic brutality is wrong. It is also clear that its harmfulness is of sufficient magnitude to justify even extreme, life-threatening measures in response. Beyond this, not much is clear. None of the presently viable alternatives to the government of the mullahs is likely to show greater sensitivity to human rights and none is likely to be as closely in tune with the aspirations of the bulk of the Iranian people. Even if something resembling Western liberal democracy could be installed there, it is unlikely to last long. (In part, this is because the oppression of the late Shah and the fundamentalist zeal of the mullahs have decimated the classes of people and the political organizations which would allow democratic institutions any chance to function.) Invasion, followed by long-term occupation, might suffice to make the change, but the cost would be unjustifiably enormous and would have only the slimmest chance of success.

In situations of this sort talk of legitimacy seems wildly irrelevant. The present government of Iran is a major part of the problem, but it is unlikely that its removal would go far towards a solution. The most that present circumstances allow is that the present government should remain but cease its abuses. But it is also apparent that there is little the outside world can do in this matter. Resort to military force is unlikely to be effective and would be enormously costly. Supporting Iraq's battles with Iran is unlikely to have the desired effect of freeing beleagured minorities. The Ayatollas, furthermore, are sufficiently narrow and rigid that they are likely to be immune to any but the most draconian attempts at coercion.

Several measures can be taken, however. World-wide recognition of the treatment of minorities within Iran can easily become more focused and consistent. While the nations of Western Europe have little influence with the Ayatollas, there are several nations, Pakistan and Japan for example, that have cordial relations with Iran and are well placed to exert quiet pressure to mitigate persecution or allow minorities to leave the country in orderly fashion. Such responses are neither fully adequate nor neat and thorough, but they are probably the best that can be achieved in a disorderly world.

In similar fashion the Marxist and quasi-Marxist governments of the world have standards of justice and citizens' rights that are at variance with those of Western Europeans.[40] While many are scarcely models of probity, they are often distinct improvements on the governments they replaced. For the most part, these governments appear reasonably dedicated to meeting the basic needs of their people and improving their lives. Once more, though the moral perspective of Marxism is different from that of liberal democracy, it is a coherent and defensible position. It would be mistaken to claim that governments of this sort are essentially defective or that concerted efforts to replace them are always justified. Even Soviet dissidents and refuseniks claim for the most part to be loyal citizens and fervid supporters of their system of government. They press only for reform, not for abolition of the Marxist system or the removal of its leaders.[41] While some share a number of political values with liberal democrats, their perspective also diverges in significant fashion. While Andrei Sakharov's views, for example, appear close to near those of the West, Solzhenitsyn's are quite distinct.

Other examples can be drawn from the experience of Third World nations suffering through the turmoil of post-colonial adjustment. While there is little to admire in many of these governments, it is important to recognize the distinct pressures of the circumstances they face and to acknowledge the element of truth in claims that the Western-style governments many inherited from their colonial overseers were simply unsuited for local conditions. Furthermore, in spite of periods of colonial domination, they often retain distinct political cultures, such as those of tribalism, which do not mesh easily with liberal democratic systems. Of course, these factors do not neutralize their more extreme failings. Rather, they serve to warn that what may appear as a deficiency from a liberal democratic perspective may be revealed as both important and defensible when viewed in context. Once more, this acknowledgment does not amount to relativism but a recognition of the validity of different sets of values and of the pressures of local conditions.

As the fate of the Axis powers following the Second World War illustrates, there are some governments and some circumstances which combine to justify efforts by outsiders to overthrow them. But this example also shows that such instances must be rare, because of the substantial costs of working to achieve upheavals of government and the uncertain prospect of installing a new government that is significantly better than the old. Of course, there are various ways of working to remove governments. The use of military force, guerrilla warfare or terrorism are only the most costly and least easy to justify of these means, but they are also capable of being the most effective. Political manipulation and economic pressure may sometimes suffice to bring down a government, in the sense of forcing those in power from office. Or assistance can be provided to opposing political groups in the hope that they will be able to force their way into power. But these methods are difficult to manage precisely and can lead to unpredictable results. Further, they must depend on the presence of just the right conditions within a nation, so that a shove here or a hint there can make a difference. The United States was able to exert such pressure in the Philippines in early 1986 by advising Marcos that it was time to go and giving ostentatious support to Cory Aquino. However, this case clearly illustrates the limitations of these efforts. In the case of the Philippines, only the United States was situated to provide such impetus. No other nation could have done it. But even the efforts of the United States were parasitic on developments within the Philippines. It could only move to assist a process already under way – and it is not at all obvious that its actions made any crucial difference in the final outcome.

The revolutionary efforts of those within nations are easier to justify and more likely to succeed simply because they are less likely to require violent means and to have closer access to the levers of political power. Political activity or mass pressure may suffice. Further, where pressures are exerted from the outside, people are more likely to band together and identify with their government, however inept, to resist external pressure. The influence of national identification is powerful and too often overlooked in analyses of international relations. Where opposition arises from within, people are not so likely to perceive the threat to government as also directed against the nation as a whole.

One implication of this analysis, however, is that many of the violent revolutions of the world have been unjustified. This certainly applies to the American Revolution. British rule was imperfect in many ways, but it did not threaten the lives or security of the Colonists. As pointed out earlier, the revolution did not even have a clear majority of popular support. To point out that violent revolution was unjustified, however, need not imply that working for the liberation of the colonies was unworthy or unjustifiable. It only means that violent means of seeking it were unjustified.

Where the outside world is essentially a bystander to political currents within nations – and this is the most common state of affairs – they may sometimes be justified in attempting to exert influence in the hope that better rather than worse governments will result. Or where governments are unstable and insecure but essentially decent, there may be good grounds for outsiders to do what they can to preserve them. The turbulent post-Marcos Philippines of 1986 again provides a case in point.

Early in 1986 Ferdinand Marcos was forced to abdicate as the result of popular unrest, and a new regime, headed by Cory Aquino, took its place. The new arrangement was imperfectly democratic, yet appeared humane and genuinely concerned to establish democratic institutions. This effort met considerable difficulty, not only because democratic institutions and practices had been thoroughly rooted out during the years of Marcos's rule, but also because considerable numbers of his supporters remained at large and in positions of power. They were not reconciled to the new regime and had a vested interest in returning to the old arrangement. In the fall of 1986 Ponce Enrile, Marcos's former defense minister, who had played a large part in making the revolution possible by switching allegiance from Marcos to Aquino, began to cause a stir. His actions led many to believe he was preparing for a coup to put himself in power and perhaps return to the old ways of doing business.[42]

A transformation of this sort clearly would have been retrograde and was therefore quite properly opposed by outsiders, including the United States.[43] Of course, this situation would not have justified use of military violence. But clear declarations of support for the Aquino government and disapproval of those pressuring for retrograde change were in order. Even displays of military force, if there were reason to believe they would have been helpful, could have had a proper role. This external resistance would have been morally justified even if there were evidence of overwhelming popular support for Enrile's maneuvering. It would be justified on grounds that a return to a Marcos-style government would have had a long-term adverse effect on the satisfaction of the preferences of individual persons and on the Philippine people as a whole. This factor carries sufficient weight to outweigh the transient, and possibly ill-considered, momentary preferences of the masses of citizens. The Philippine situation differs quite clearly from that of Iran in that the unrest of the fall of 1986 was not a quest to establish a distinctive set of plausible values but was a fleeting response to political opportunity. In contrast to Iran, all in the Philippines profess adherence to the values of liberal democracy. In addition, as the response to the constitutional plebiscite of February 1987 demonstrated, the great mass of the people of the Philippines did in fact support the government and the values of Cory Aquino.[44]

INTERVENTION

The focus on abstract standards of legitimacy may cause an important distinction to be overlooked. There is a considerable difference between believing that a particular government ought to enjoy sovereignty and believing that its legal authority may, on occasion, be overridden. Sovereignty overridden is not sovereignty dissolved. Even where governments have strong claims to retain sovereignty, there may be occasions when there will be good reasons for overriding it, without making the attempt to remove the government itself from power. There ought to be pressure on the Soviet government, for example, to allow greater freedom of emigration and to adhere more closely to the requirements of the Helsinki Accords. But to acknowledge this is not to imply that the Soviet government should be removed from power. Prior to 1987 there should have been more pressure on the Chun government of South Korea to allow greater democracy and a more active opposition, but this would have been different from attempting to push Chun from office. The emphasis on legitimacy seems to have engendered the presumption that a government with a strong claim to sovereignty may never have its sovereignty overridden. More importantly, perhaps, it has engendered the converse belief that any attempt to override sovereignty must amount to a denial of the claim to sovereignty, and is a blow against sovereignty itself.

In the above cases of the USSR and South Korea, governments, understood narrowly in the sense of persons holding power, were acting amiss and should have been the objects of attempts at external intervention. Where intervention is directed only against those in power, it need not be a threat to the interests and lives of ordinary citizens. Cases of this sort do arise, and when they do intervention is comparatively unproblematic. However, there are also cases where government in its fullest sense is involved in wrongdoing. The racism and segregation in the United States thirty years ago provide a case in point. Enforcing segregation was not merely an affair of the persons holding governmental power but encompassed the very structure of American laws and governmental institutions, as well as being firmly embedded in its social and political culture. Segregation ran deep into the fabric of American society. Action effectively directed against it, therefore, had to strike deeply into the lives of ordinary people, affecting their preferences and desires. External intervention in such cases would be highly problematic and extremely difficult to bring to fruitful conclusion.

Among the central facets of this issue is the question of just what activities are to count as intervention. Some wish to define intervention narrowly, to refer only to military (that is, physical) coercion. Others wish, more broadly, to include any form of clearly coercive activity, such as threats or economic embargoes, on grounds that all such ventures cause harm and may result in human suffering. Yet others would define intervention quite broadly, including any attempt to alter the ongoing policies or courses of action of other nations.[45] This definition would encompass-behind-the-scenes diplomatic maneuvering and public posturing as well as private exhortations and messages. The justification for this broad categorization would be that *any* attempt to alter the ongoing course of action of those in other nations represents an intrusion in their affairs, and may have implications for the way they conduct their lives.

There is much to be said for this latter definition. Common sense would seem to support the view that any action agents take which is intended to influence the internal affairs of another should properly be classed as intervention. It is clear, furthermore, that this sort of activity is the very life-blood of international relations. It occurs routinely and in myriad ways. For this reason, a distinction must be made between routine efforts at influence and persuasion and those that require explicit moral justification. Moral justification of intervention, in any of its guises, is required when measures of intervening are likely to cause harm for the people of target nations and where some significant cost will be required to resist them. There are, of course, important differences among the various types of intervention, both in the amount of harm they may cause and in the comparative ease with which they may be resisted by the target party. Justification of *some* sort, therefore, is not the justification of recourse to any or all of the above measures.

As always, there must be proportionality of means to ends, so that life-threatening measures or those likely to cause human suffering are warranted only where human life and security are at stake. Where other, less than vital concerns, such as freedom of speech or religion, are imperilled, only less severe responses are in order. What all these measures will have in common is that they will be coercive in some way since their purpose is to pressure target nations to change their course of action. Only rarely will nations be in a position to provide leverage for change without resorting to coercive activity. Though the role of the United States in the transition in the Philippines from Marcos's rule to that of Cory Aquino does provide an instance of this.

Given the lack of established international authorities and procedures for dealing with the misconduct of governments, there are clear constraints on what can be done by the nations of the world when these issues arise. For one thing, among the gravest problems impeding effective action is likely to be a simple lack of adequate information concerning abuses. Domestic courts could not hope to operate fairly without full information and the apparatus for its collection. Justice requires firm and complete evidence, rather than uncorroborated hearsay or partial facts. Yet access to such data is likely to be controlled by the very governments whose activities are suspect.

Furthermore, the methods of coercive intervention, whether physical or otherwise, are crude and often require a long time to have significant effect. Because they involve the prospect of some harm for the target nation, there is always a considerable cost, both to the target and the agent nation – in case of backlash or a hostile reaction. If there were international agencies with a clear monopoly of physical power and a clear authority to take action, costs of this sort could be greatly mitigated or eliminated altogether.

Finally, without precisely defined and commonly accepted standards of governmental conduct, there will be wide divergences of opinion about what is right and proper. Without an established body of cases, which serve to specify exactly which concrete acts violate standards and which do not, there will be frequent disagreement about compliance and non-compliance, even where general consensus about standards exists.

These considerations also delimit a perspective which can be used to understand the difference between failings which are of sufficient importance to require international attention and those which are legitimately of domestic concern only. Domestic failings of the usual sort cause relatively little harm, are not likely to be cured by outside intervention, and are of insufficient importance to justify the cost of attempting to eradicate them. There is no fundamental difference in principle or in kind between these issues and others which are legitimately subject to international scrutiny. The difference is only of degree. The instance of corruption in local police forces illustrates this point. Normally infelicities of this sort would be considered domestic matters. However, if corruption becomes sufficiently malignant, if killing and torture become commonplace and widespread, if financial corruption seriously undermines the lives and well-being of ordinary people, then the problem would be legitimately subject to international scrutiny and possible response. The difference lies in the magnitude of harm and its relation to the costs of intervention.

Rights theorists, along with other reflective individuals, might respond that the above analysis is the wrong way of looking at the problem. They may argue that, in the example of errant police forces, the difference between cases where intervention is not justified and those where it is lies in the fact that significant human rights are being violated in the latter case but not in the former, where corruption is most likely to manifest itself in such peccadilloes as bribery or fixing parking tickets. This is not a useful way of looking at the matter, since corruption of insufficient weight to justify external intervention often involves wrongful killing and the physical abuse of prisoners. This type of activity is common among police forces in all parts of the world, including those of what are commonly termed 'advanced' nations. But the world community has neither the institutions nor the resources to attempt to ensure that all police forces avoid all abuses. The attempt to do so would require broad and systematic intrusion into nations on a scale which would cause great disruption and which the world community could not presently support. If the world were more tightly organized and possessed institutions empowered to enforce standards of police conduct, such scrupulousness could reasonably be expected. But that is not the world we presently have.

In the cases that do exist, important rights of human individuals are being violated, and because they are, the serious rights theorist must be committed to intervention, whatever the cost – even where one such instance of abuse is recorded. For the serious rights theorist human rights are solemn entitlements whose violation cannot be weighed against the costs of preventing or rectifying them. Magnitude and extent of harm cannot enter into their deliberations, since deontological theories must provide at best only a secondary role for consequences.

In short domestic issues are those that do not readily yield themselves to international effort or scrutiny. Matters of intervention are further complicated by the fact that individual citizens commonly have a sense of identity with their nation. Though they may scrap interminably among themselves, they tend to band together in solidarity when faced with external criticism.[46] This feature of human psychology complicates matters considerably, because citizens may react defensively and thoughtlessly to criticism which they may have considered seriously were it to come from their fellows. The effect is that positions can harden and problems become less tractable when they are the focus of international scrutiny. The exception is where the members of a government are so thoroughly alienated that citizens no longer identify with them. Other difficulties resulting from this identification will be examined in the following chapter. The pertinent result for this discussion is that national identification, by raising the cost of intervention, makes international intervention more difficult to justify.

International activity requiring the cooperation of a number of independent nations is difficult to sustain for long periods of time, and there is no international mechanism for continuing to coordinate and plan such undertakings. Broad international cooperation is most likely to congeal to meet obvious crises where decisive action is clearly required and where explosive violence makes the need for action clearly apparent. Of course, international cooperation is not particularly effective even in these cases, but it *is* better suited to meet crises of this type than the long-term and careful action required to cope with more deep-seated issues resulting from established cultural practice.

With these constraints in mind, it is apparent that intervention can only be a rough and crude instrument. Because the costs are great, it will be suitable only for use against the most serious abuses. Because methods of intervention require long periods of time to be effective, it will be of use only against established practices of abuse rather than against isolated incidents. Because of disagreements over standards of conduct, intervention should be relied upon only in the most obvious and widely deplored abuses, where there will be a substantial measure of international consensus that such conduct is wrong. Only in such instances is there the prospect of support for those wishing to take action and some hope that action will be effective. Where consensus is lacking there is broad range for political entanglements or simple disagreement to scuttle effective response. Finally, given difficulties caused by lack of information, action can be justified only in those particular cases where clear-cut data are present.

The above analysis applies only to instances where intervention is undertaken with the clear goal of bringing abuses to a halt. However, there are grounds for responses of various sorts even when there can be no serious intent to end abuses. This might occur where it is apparent that the costs of effective action will clearly outweigh any foreseen benefits, where there is no prospect of any significant change in abusive practices, or where the agent is not sufficiently powerful and secure to make an effective challenge to the target nation.

In such cases, simply speaking out, making one's position known, and making use of non-coercive methods of pressure can be valuable. It can be important simply to let errant nations know that their actions are apparent to the rest of the world and that they are condemned.[47] It is a rare nation, even the most brutal, that has no concern at all for its reputation in the world. Even where nations continue their wrong-doing, to avoid seeming to back down in the face of pressure, public outcry may serve to prevent new abuses or the spread of present ones. It may also serve as a deterrent to those who may otherwise be attracted to such methods. There are clear cases where public awareness together with long-term pressure have had significant effects, as in the case of the USSR's release of well-known dissidents.[48]

However, there is a more fundamental reason for registering these objections. The outcries serve to further the establishment of genuine international standards of moral propriety. Complaints may register in international consciousness even if they do not have immediate effect. Discussion of such matters serves to nurture international awareness of them and can perhaps increase sensitivity as well. The more of this sort of discussion there is, the more probable it will eventually come to be viewed as a legitimate and serious topic of concern. If conditions finally evolve to the point where enough nations complain in sufficiently consistent fashion, the foundation for a genuine international ethics will begin to develop. Thus even futile and ineffectual complaint which falls short of coercive intervention can have a significant role to play.

CLAIMS TO SOVEREIGNTY

Preceding discussions have not touched on the problem of just what groups or what claims are sufficient to justify the entitlement to sovereign autonomy. Possibly as the result of the struggles against colonialism of the twentieth century, it has become almost axiomatic that 'a people' is entitled to sovereign autonomy, since this is the rhetoric in terms of which such struggles have been waged. Yet, on examination, this idea yields significant difficulties.

A fundamental problem is simply determining what constitutes 'a people'. In a number of current struggles, common language, as in Quebec or Wales, is claimed to be the decisive factor. Yet there are obviously many groups sharing common languages that are not constituted as a people. The English, French and Spanish speakers scattered across the globe certainly have a variety of ties with one another, but they clearly do not constitute 'a people' and do not share any significant measure of political cohesiveness. Furthermore, the barrios and Chinatowns in New York and Los Angeles have clear linguistic affinity along with geographical proximity, but only the most reckless would claim that they are entitled to sovereign autonomy.

The response might be that it is not language as such that determines a people. Rather, language makes possible a common life and culture, and it is these bonds which make sovereignty possible.

Aristotle, for example, argues that part of what is required as the basis of the state is a common life and a shared conception of the good, for it is these things which meld individuals together into a unity.[49] Perhaps this is the claim which grounds the nationalistic struggles of the Basques in Spain and the Kurds of the Middle East. This claim yields difficulty as well. The United States, for example, while in some ways more nearly homogenized at present than in past years, is clearly a cultural hodgepodge. Yet few would argue that it should be broken up into a myriad of small cultural and political fiefdoms. Furthermore, the United States and Canada share a great number of cultural elements, but not since the nineteenth century has anyone claimed they should be united; indeed such a proposal would be met with outrage if pressed at the present time. In a few cases, such as Japan and Iceland, there is a distinct and close fit between national culture, language and political structure. These, however, are notable exceptions. Most nations of the world do not possess anything resembling this sort of unity, and it is not particularly obvious that they should seek it. What is worse, many of the new nations of the world, those established since the Second World War, are linguistic and cultural polyglots. An insistence on cultural homogeneity would erode their own claims to exist as distinct national entities. Thus if legitimate claims to sovereignty depend on cultural unity, the world would have to be completely broken up and re-constituted as entirely different and much smaller political entities, and no one would be exactly sure where to draw the boundaries.

There are additional difficulties with this idea. For one, there is no obvious sense in which cultural unity provides a basis for claims to political sovereignty. The view is not held universally, and there are alternatives. Those in a number of Islamic nations, for example, would claim that religion should be the deciding factor – that there should be one overarching nation of Islam.[50] Prior to the religious battles of the sixteenth and seventeenth centuries, Christians of varying stripes could be found who would urge the same thing. Some Marxists and socialists would argue that none of these factors are relevant. What should matter, in their view, is possession of a common political ideology. They would claim that there should be one sovereign confederation of Marxist or socialist states. (Recall that the connection between Marxism and nationalism is of comparatively recent, largely accidental vintage and runs counter to major elements of Marx's own belief.)[51]

The basic problem is that there is no clear relation between respect for the choices and preferences of individuals and the goals, needs and entitlements of cultural units. Individuals should have their preferences acknowledged, but this does not give *them* claim to sovereign autonomy since most agree that there are good grounds for establishing governments with authority over persons. There is also good reason to believe that cultural groups have less claim to have preferences respected than do individuals. Cultural groups are not individuals writ large. They are, rather, numbers of individuals related in certain ways, and it is not clear what it is about them that should entitle them to sovereign autonomy. Cultural groups have varieties of interests and personal ties in common, of course, but so do milk producers, university professors and newspaper deliverers. It may be said that they have an encompassing sense of identity, but so do these other groups. It may be said that cultural relations touch all aspects of the individual's life, but the same can be said of these other groups.

It is plausible to assume that both individuals and individuals banded together into cohesive groups deserve to have their interests respected and to have some influence on the political decisions that affect them and their lives. But this does not amount to a justification for an absolute entitlement to political autonomy, any more than similar claims of milk producers and college professors would.[52] It should be noted along this line that Basques do not live only in Spain; they are also found across the border in France, yet the French Basques have neither joined the struggle of their linguistic kin in Spain, nor have they pressed similar complaints and demands against France.[53] Of course, it may be too late for the Spanish to reach an accord with the Basques, and it may prove impossible for the needs of the Kurds to be met within present national structures. It may be that, given present circumstances, no accommodation with them can be reached which will both satisfy their aspirations and preserve existing political arrangements. At most, these arguments about autonomy are capable of demonstrating that, where human preferences and well-being are not well served by existing political arrangements, there are good reasons for establishing others. In some cases, given the conditions of the world, it may be that a given people can have its needs met only through possession of sovereign autonomy. But these scattered cases do not demonstrate the abstract conceptual point. They do not prove that cultural unity embodies a universally valid moral claim to political sovereignty.

They prove only that people and groups of people have strong claims to political structures which are suited to provide them with decent lives.

The current political divisions of the world are largely matters of historical accident and military conquest. It is only a historical accident that the world has evolved into a group of distinct nation-states each possessing its measure of sovereignty. The world's face has not always been like this and will quite likely evolve into different political shapes in the future. It is quite possible that future political, cultural and economic developments will make nation-states and national sovereignty largely irrelevant to the lives of ordinary people. In such circumstances, sovereignty will be a historical relic of little significance. Given this possibility, it would be nugatory to claim that human cultures are possessed of an abstract and universal right to political sovereignty.

It follows that no one and no group has an abstract right to sovereign autonomy. People and cultural groups of people do have a strong claim to have their interests met and respected, and it may sometimes be the case, as a matter of historical accident, that the only way this can be achieved is through possession of sovereign autonomy. But this does not establish any fundamental conceptual connection. Neither, of course, does this conclusion grant a blank check to those plotters wishing to deprive nations of their sovereign autonomy. Military coercion and economic buccaneering remain wrong for the harm they inflict on ordinary persons and the way of life they enjoy. Governments that are competently meeting the needs of their citizens do have a moral claim to remain in existence, but this does not amount to a universal and inalienable right to sovereignty.

If it were possible to establish world government, for example, with the likely prospect of meeting more of the needs of more of the people of the world than the present arrangement, there would no nothing amiss if national leaders were to transfer sovereignty to such an entity, even where these national governments were decent, humane and competent. Furthermore, there would be nothing amiss if the world community were to exert pressure on recalcitrant governments to join the larger entity. World government is not likely to develop in the foreseeable future. Circumstances simply do not yet allow it. But if it were to develop, there would be no basis for a principled objection founded on a fundamental entitlement to sovereign autonomy.

The discussions of this chapter serve to re-enforce one of the recurrent themes of this work. Nation-states are tremendously important both theoretically and practically, but they have few overwhelming moral claims. They are important theoretically because they are the basic structures of human political order, and their existence serves to define the issues of the ethics of international relations. They are practically important because their control of physical power and legal structure has the consequence that they are they most significant actors on the international stage. Whatever is accomplished in this arena must normally be directed either at or through them. But there are few significant moral claims to be made on their behalf.

These points are amply illustrated by the topic of sovereignty itself. The power and authority which allow nation-states to claim sovereignty for themselves are basic in shaping international relations. But these features do not give rise to overwhelming moral claims. They do not, for example, have any absolute moral entitlement to retain the sovereignty they enjoy. There may be morally compelling reasons why a given government should continue to enjoy sovereign authority or why it should not be deposed. But these reasons are always a matter of degree, and though the degree may be greater or lesser, it never reaches the absolute. It is always reasonable to wonder whether a given government should be deposed. The greatest obstacles to this are likely to be practical, the huge costs of working to dislodge governments and the uncertainty of replacing them with anything better. Even where there is no justification for removing governments, there may be strong grounds for intervening in their affairs, though there are grave practical difficulties confronting these efforts as well.

One result of the present analysis is that there is no profound theoretical or moral difference between those within and those outside a given governmental structure. The important differences are practical ones of the relative costs of introducing change or being well situated to bring it about. A consequence is that, as sovereignty is never the absolute entitlement of governments, neither is it the absolute entitlement of a people – however 'a people' is understood. It has been argued that people – human individuals – have strong claims to life and its means and therefore have a strong claim to political institutions which meet them. People also have strong claims to be able to join together in unity with others with whom they share language and culture. These groupings have the claim to enjoy protection, but this is not the same as the claim to sovereignty.

Nonetheless, the difference between those inside and those outside the borders of a nation has commonly been thought to be of central moral importance – another of the deep-seated moral intuitions of international affairs. It has been thought, that is, that those within national boundaries have greater obligations to one another than to aliens. It is also commonly believed that they have an entitlement to whatever wealth they enjoy and an entitlement to prevent outsiders from gaining access to it. The following chapter will address these predilections in more direct and detailed fashion.

4 National Boundaries

It happens that the sovereignty claimed by nation-states is at present always over a piece of territory.[1] However, there is no conceptual reason why sovereign authority should necessarily encompass a particular area of land. It would not be conceptually absurd if governments claimed sovereignty over nomadic tribes who laid no claim to specific stretches of terrain. Nor would it be conceptually absurd if sovereignty were claimed only over specific individuals who were scattered among others with differing sovereign allegiance. There seems little reason in principle why Jewish people, for example, could not hold allegiance to a Jewish state wherever they are found or why the scattered Kurds or Armenians could not have the same arrangement. Of course, as the previous chapter illustrates, there is no reason why ethnic or linguistic affinity should be the only factors deciding matters of sovereignty. Religious conviction or political ideology could serve as well. All socialists, for example, could consider themselves bound together under the sovereign domain of the International Socialist Brotherhood.

But these arrangements would be practically absurd, in part because the inhabited territory of the globe is presently taken up by governments that stake their sovereign claims not only to people but also to territory.[2] This is very probably a historical accident. It came about only when human culture evolved to the point where land became a sufficiently valuable resource that differing cultural or ethnic groups became motivated to stake claims to it and fight over it. Nonetheless, this development has made it practically difficult to exercise claims of sovereignty within the physical space held as the sovereign domain of another government. The present conflicts of nomadic Kurdish tribesmen with the governments of Iraq, Iran and Turkey are the vestigial result of just this sort of situation. Over the years the various settled governments of the world have made their accommodations with nomadic groups, mainly by assimilating them. The issue was finally and firmly decided with the appearance of conditions which spawned the contemporary nation-state and its present monopoly of material resources and physical power. The current aspirations and difficulties of the Kurds vividly illustrate, however, that the connection between sovereignty and physical space is a contingent development of human culture rather than a conceptual or a historical necessity.[3]

Even if all governments did wish to claim only people and not land, it would be very difficult to establish distinct sovereign relations with people who live in close physical proximity to one another. It is true that human organizational ability has developed to the point where it is now possible to undertake transactions and create institutions structuring the lives of people who are far removed from one another in space. The disconcerting vitality of multinational corporations amply illustrates this point. But it remains the case that the most fundamental and vital dealings of human beings are with those other individuals who are in close physical proximity, and it is *these* relationships which governments are most especially fitted to control.

At some point in the future it is entirely possible that all of this may change yet again. It is possible that culture, technology or economics may evolve to the point where it is not necessary to control masses of land in order to enjoy power. Nuclear power, for example, or advances in the techniques of producing food may make dominion over vast physical spaces unnecessary. Or these products may be created in such abundance that control over them is no longer a significant source of power. From another perspective, it is conceivable that communications technology and human culture will spawn modes of association that will make possible relations of sovereignty in which spatial relationships become essentially irrelevant, where it will not matter how near or far away people are. Under circumstances of this sort, it is likely that the connection between sovereignty and territory would become trivial and irrelevant, a mere vestige of an earlier order – and as useless and unimportant as medieval suits of armor.[4]

It is simply a matter of present fact that governments are motivated to claim sovereignty over specifically bounded ranges of territory as well as over particularly delineated groups of people. While it is true that governments cannot claim sovereignty over all of the persons within their area of control at any one time, since not all will be citizens, particular people will nonetheless continue to be identified with a particular place. As things stand, government which is government of *them* must be government of their place as well. Because governments structure individual lives within their sovereign domain, legally recognized inhabitants become interlinked with one another in ways channeled by sovereign authority, and these relations extend far beyond the bare political relation of citizen to non-citizen.

'National boundaries', then, are of two sorts. They can be the spatial boundaries of territory, delimiting the physical space that is under the jurisdiction of a particular government, but there are also the legal and political boundaries distinguishing citizen from non-citizen. In each case the boundaries determine what is inside and what is outside. At present the two sorts of boundaries roughly coincide, so that those residing in a given area are for the most part also subject to the same government.

It is plain that this connection between sovereignty, citizenship and territory has created special relations among the people who reside within a given political domain, along with distinct relations to those who do not, which raise substantive moral issues. The fundamental questions are whether these citizens and neighbors owe special responsibilities and rights to one another which can be denied to others and whether they have some special entitlement to the benefits of their citizenship which may also legitimately be denied to others.

THE TIES OF CITIZENSHIP

Clearly citizens, simply by being members of a distinct nation-state, come to have ties to one another, depend on one another, and become accountable to one another in ways that do not encompass outsiders. Because nation-states regulate economic traffic and because of legal entanglements inhibiting the movement of people, goods and business institutions across national borders, these political entities tend to become distinct economic units as well.[5] Politics has a central role in establishing the overall structure and ground rules which shape economic activity. Governments can determine whether a nation shall be essentially capitalist, essentially socialist, or some intermediate combination of these two. They have the power to determine how property shall be used and who shall use it. They have the ability to nationalize companies, or return them to private control. The way in which business is conducted and the role which persons play within it are to a large extent determined by political authorities, and these influences are largely coterminous with national boundaries.

More fundamentally, perhaps, the ways of doing business, the skills, expectations and habits of economic activity, which develop independently of direct governmental control, will nonetheless be shaped by it. And they will be distinct from those of other economic cultures, at least in part, because of the legal bounds established by sovereign authority. One result of the interaction of these factors is that people who have attained wealth or satisfying positions within an economy – or those who have not – will have done so because of the manner of operation of that economic system and the manner in which they followed its practices.

This coherence of economic ties with political boundaries has several implications, for while nation-states are clearly interdependent in many significant ways, they continue on the whole to remain distinct economic structures. It is true that there is essentially one world market for many products, and the scope of world trade is likely to increase in the future. It is also true that there is an increasing number of corporations that routinely conduct business in a variety of nations, and this includes not only the huge multinational corporations but also small and middle-size concerns. Nonetheless, the world is, and for the foreseeable future is likely to remain, an aggregate of distinct economic units which are shaped and defined by the political space in which they are found. At present there is a relatively free flow of capital across national borders and less fluid transfers of technology and material resources. Labor is much less mobile, not only because governmental regulation controls it tightly, but because personal ties and training, skills and cultural habituation often impede its movement across national boundaries.

Furthermore, economic infrastructure – the communications, transportation, manufacturing and social environments of nations – are not readily transferred and cannot easily be created where they are lacking. In addition, business is acutely sensitive to what is called the 'business climate' – the willingness of local governments to accommodate business activity, their political and social stability, and the presence of fixed rules of the game which allow corporations to understand the conditions under which they must operate. All these must in general be taken as they are found and cannot be easily created or readily transferred. Much of what influences these factors is under the direct control of governments, who jealously guard their sovereign prerogatives in matters of law and policy. It is likely that these factors will continue to work together to preserve the array of essentially distinct economic units the world now possesses. They are highly interdependent, to be sure, but interdependence is not homogeneity.

This economic heterogeneity has significant consequences for individual human lives. It is widely appreciated that the prospects of human individuals for a materially comfortable and satisfying existence are determined to a large extent by the conditions of the nation-state into which they are born. Any child born in the United States or West Germany, for example, has far rosier prospects than almost any born in Bangladesh or China. It is not merely more likely that they will be able to enjoy the basic necessities of life, but also that they will have a far wider array of opportunities for a satisfying existence. Even within nations, accidents of birth contribute in significant ways to prospects for material well-being. Those born into wealth and comfort are far more likely to continue to enjoy these advantages when they reach adulthood than those whose lives begin in poverty. This holds true whether the nation in question is the United States, the USSR, China or Egypt. Nonetheless, inside each of these economic microcosms there is latitude for individuals to move up or down or, in some cases, to jump from one microcosm to another.

Because of this latitude and the broader set of conditions determining economic relations and welfare, individuals are likely to think they are *entitled* to the benefits they receive from their activity. They may have followed the rules and have done what was expected of them. They may, for example, have conducted themselves fairly, honestly, skillfully or industriously, and therefore believe they deserve to keep what they have. People may be entirely *correct* in all of this, including their belief that they have a claim of entitlement to the material and social goods they have accumulated. But the question is whether outsiders have grounds for making claims to these goods as well and whether these claims may sometimes have sufficient strength to outweigh their own.

Furthermore, members of a single nation-state have substantial grounds for believing they are all in the same economic boat. When the gross national product or the value of the local currency or the level of employment rise, all are likely to *feel* elated, whether or not their individual fates are directly affected, simply because of their common sense of identification with the national whole. This perceived identity is an important factor in preserving a sense of the economic distinctness of nation-states. But it is also the case that developments in one sector of a national economy genuinely are more likely to affect other sectors than events outside the realm. Often this keen sense of identity can serve to create its own reality, as the crash on Wall Street in October of 1987 was significant mainly for its psychological impact on investment and spending for people across the United States. It had this effect on people apart from whether their individual wealth or that of their local economy had been significantly affected by the turmoil in New York.[6]

Apart from the above, the presence of distinct political entities and the social institutions that accompany them means that people within them have clearly established procedures for making decisions and for making agreements or commitments. They can plausibly believe that they have special ties to one another because, perhaps, all have paid taxes, served in the armed forces, or cooperated in other ways to seek goals of mutual benefit. Because of this, and because the established conditions of distribution and decision are ones they are likely to understand and acknowledge, if not accept, they are prone to believe they have special obligations to one another which they do not have to other persons in the world.

Human cultures have means for generating obligations that are specific and explicit, such as mechanisms for accepting or throwing off obligations – as when people marry or divorce or accept or disavow office. The conditions of human culture are such that these mechanisms usually operate within the boundaries of nation-states. Governments themselves have specific responsibilities to clearly defined groups of people and means for receiving complaints or responding to pressure from them. When there is hunger, for example, in depressed farming communities in the American Mid-West or extensive earthquake damage in California, there are designated governmental agencies charged with making an effective response. If they fail to do so, governmental leaders are acutely aware that they will be held to account by citizens for their lapses. There are, in other words, both clearly defined lines of responsibility and of accountability which are understood on all sides.

There are no similar mechanisms and only the vestiges of such institutions operating on the international level. Consequently, there are no authoritative groups with acknowledged responsibility for dealing with specific problems of international need. The absence of clearly authorized institutions for dealing with suffering, combined with the problems of coping with armed states loath to yield any portion of their sovereignty, has the consequence that human needs often are not met even when there are material resources for doing so. Consider examples of urgent and clearly defined need, such as the starvation and torment caused by civil war in the Eritrea district of Ethiopia, where efforts at response are being undertaken by a variety of agencies. None of them have either the clear authority or physical power to meet needs effectively in the face of disruption and harassment from both the government of Ethiopia and the Eritrean guerrillas.[7] This is a clear instance of where the material resources to prevent suffering are available but cannot be distributed to the people who require them because of problems of sovereign authority and lack of physical might on the part of those wishing to help.

Ordinary people, furthermore, do not have a developed sense of fixed and defined responsibility for responding to human want which lies beyond the reach of their immediate experience. People in the United States or Western Europe, for example, may be well aware of suffering in places like Ethiopia but often lack a sense of responsibility to do anything about it. They may argue, for example, that they have done nothing to cause the problems, that they do not have any dealings with the people in those nations of the sort that would cause them to have responsibility for them, that they do not have access to governmental bodies authorized to cope with such matters, and, finally, that there is little they could hope to do to resolve such large problems anyway. Any response they make, therefore, is likely to be seen by them as charity, as morally optional, and not the fulfillment of pressing moral obligation. From this perspective it is easy to understand why they should believe they have no responsibilities at all in such matters, why they should believe that any acts of care and concern they perform for those in distant lands are strictly supererogatory.

The sorts of human needs that arise on the international level cannot for the most part be adequately met simply by a developed sense of personal moral responsibility. The difficulties are large and far away in space and culture. They are the sorts of problems that are best met by political institutions with fixed responsibilities and established authority. The international arena also lacks institutions of another sort, those which generate a sense of moral responsibility and generally accepted moral principles for guiding conduct and policy. Mankind is as yet poorly equipped, institutionally, culturally and morally, to deal with international problems of human need and human suffering. Once again, it is easy to understand why people should feel that they have no moral responsibility at all in such circumstances and why special argument is necessary to demonstrate to them that such obligations can exist.

The above discussions illustrate the ways in which membership in a distinct economy can generate legitimate claims and expectations which have moral weight. Since economic systems tend to be shaped by political power, these claims to material resources are commonly, though not necessarily, generated within political borders. But the fact that governments exist and have acknowledged responsibilities and mechanisms for responding to need creates yet other claims, ties and expectations which, once more, have moral weight. In addition, political unities tend also to shape distinct cultural unities, which have the means of generating obligations required for all segments of ordinary human life. The moral weight of the responsibilities generated in each of these areas is substantial and gives credence to the widely accepted, common-sense view that citizens have special moral obligation to one another which they lack with regard to aliens. These are real, palpable, and cannot be ignored, but it is possible that they may sometimes be overruled by more weighty claims. This issue will be addressed later in this chapter.

First, however, a closely related arena of possible moral responsibility requires attention: the strong sense of identification people come to have with their nation. Distinct from all the specific ways people have of becoming obliged to one another, this encompassing perception of unity, the sense of being akin to fellow citizens in some special way not shared with aliens, has a central role to play in shaping people's sense of moral accountability.

NATIONAL IDENTITY

People identify themselves as American, French or British and therefore identify themselves with the actions and fortunes of their country and of their countrymen. This sense of identity is bolstered not only by such factors as those of citizenship or having a role to play in national affairs, but by other means of identification, such as the Olympics Games, military and diplomatic presences, or cultural exchange programs. Furthermore, this identification sometimes appears to have distinct moral implications, as the common feeling that Germans ought to feel guilt for the Nazi atrocities of the Second World War or the, quite different, feeling that members of nations are morally obligated to give higher priority to the difficulties of fellow citizens than to those of aliens.

It is quite common for governments to work to nurture this sense

of national identification by their citizens. It is not difficult to understand why this should be so. Governments have a vested interest in
bolstering such identity – in part because the ready conflation of
nation and government means that pride in, and concern for, the
nation is often readily transferred to the government. Feelings of
national pride can be harnessed to support a government's own goals
or to instill obedience and a sense of responsibility – which can then
be mobilized in times of national crisis. This, of course, is part of the
problem. Governments have the ability to absorb their entire nation
in crises of their own devising – to make issues mainly resulting from
the initiative and interests of those holding governmental office into
problems for the nation as well. Thus the Reagan Administration's
invasion of Grenada became the American invasion, and whatever
shame or pride resulted from that venture was not confined only
to those members of government who planned and executed it
but was shared by the citizens of the nation as a whole. In part
this identification results because the government is the nation's
agent of action. Also, the scale of governmental authority will
involve many different segments of the nation, and will therefore
genuinely *be* the activity of a significant portion of its population.
This identification of government and citizens, furthermore, is not
confined to the nation but will be shared by other people of the
world. In other words, Germans, Poles, Japanese and Indians all
viewed the activity in Grenada as American, and often directed their
approval or opprobrium of the act towards individual Americans.[8]

This sense of identification has both a bright and a dark side.
Individuals possessing a sense of identity with their nation are more
likely to feel responsible for it, to feel its problems as their own
and seek ways of meeting them, to be willing to contribute when
cooperative action is necessary, or to be motivated to stand up and
fight against abuses when the nation goes astray. The development
of a national and political culture will re-enforce and channel this
identification. As claimed in the previous chapter, it is important for
the health of the national entity that a viable political culture should
develop, and it is difficult to imagine how it can do so without this
sense of identity.

From a utilitarian perspective, therefore, it is easy to explain
why it is important that this identification should occur and why it
is a necessary condition for the long-term well-being of the citizens
of a nation. Hence, it is good, morally, that people feel a special
sense of responsibility for other members of their own nation, that

they feel unwise governmental actions are *their* problem which they must act to rectify, and that the functioning of national institutions is *their* affair.

There is also a dark side to the lure of national identification. Part of the dark side of nationalism is that it may nurture an us-against-them mentality, a feeling that all responsibility is owed to the nation and its interests, that the external world is united against it, and that members of the external world have no moral claim on its citizens.

Another aspect of the dark side is a primal emotional desire for national identification which appears to surge beneath the constraints of national patriotism. It seems there is a widely felt drive to identify closely with a group, to merge one's identity with it, to feel the power of association with a larger whole, and to rally to its support on occasions of threat, stress or simple competition. Furthermore, this sense can best operate, apparently, only through a vivid perception of exclusion. The unity is cemented through negation of what is outside and beyond. It is quite likely, for example, that a compelling sense of world unity, the perennial cosmopolitan dream, can only be achieved by the perception of a distinct threat which confronts all human inhabitants of the world. The UFO invasion endlessly predicted in the tabloids may be what is necessary to knit the members of the human race tightly together – but then, of course, it may be too late.

The origins of this drive are obscure. They may possibly be found in the pack and herd origins of the race. Certainly there is nothing primordial about the patriotic attachments of nation-states which have arrived late on the scene. Nations serve more to provide the present-day focus and occasion for these communal attachments than an explanation of their origin. It may be difficult for independent-minded academics to grasp this attraction, just as it was difficult for Bertrand Russell to grasp the enthusiastic British surge into the First World War.[9] But, of course, *his* attachments lay elsewhere, in the embattled militancy of the pacifist movement. He certainly appreciated the value and the attraction of giving his all for *that* cause. But perhaps scholars will understand this drive better if they reflect on what happens when they step outside their offices on recreational jaunts to sporting events. The close identification of fans with teams and the almost palpable sense of unity felt in cities where teams are caught in a significant series of sporting events – such as close competition for the World Series or the Super Bowl –

demonstrates the reality, and the very great attractions of this close sense of unity.[10] The vivid sense of common purpose and the keenly felt stake in a common outcome, the bracing awareness of belonging where ordinary barriers are broken down and the encompassing spirit of unity and exhilaration this brings, are sources of exultation for all who participate in them, though observers may be dismayed by such primal goings-on.

Yet World Series Fever must be a close kin to the tribal enthusiasm that both fascinated and horrified Russell on the eve of the First World War. On such occasions rationalistic carping or hesitation or identification with the opponent can be submerged – or simply vanish – in the overpowering urge to join the unity generated by mass movement, and in response to the constant and overwhelming pressure generated by the masses to enlist. Personal cavils may not so much be forgotten as dissolve in the push toward mass unification. This is something similar to what Hegel had in mind when he applauded the *unifying* effect of wars, their ability to break down social divisions and reconstitute the seamless unity of the whole.[11]

This visceral patriotism is part of what makes mass wars possible, and yet the swelling of the mass unity erases doubt and criticism, not so much through conscious confrontation as through the dissolving wash of the tides of national identification. In this regard the official rationale for the Olympic Games appears an odd and interesting anomaly. The purported justification of the Olympics is that it will increase world understanding and harmony by bringing the nations of the world together in peaceful competition. Yet sending teams to compete has had the effect of generating something of the fervid patriotism that heretofore could only have been engendered by warfare. In fact, modern communications technology exacerbates this effect by making possible mass participation and visceral identification in a way that could only be achieved by war in recent times. A few years ago, only the athletes themselves and that comparatively small group who were able personally to attend the competitions could be merged in common feeling. For most people in most of the world, the Olympics was an abstraction, insufficient to generate visceral identification. Television and radio have changed that. The 1984 Summer Olympics at Los Angeles in the United States clearly generated much of that same vibrancy for Americans.[12]

The surge toward national identification is both powerful and troubling. It seems to emerge from human emotional drives in ways which preclude the sort of vivid sense of identification with the human race as a whole which is much sought by utopian writers. The conditions that are likely to nurture it must be described in terms that are borrowed from science fiction. The conditions of the world do not appear well-suited to bring it about at any time in the near future. The surge toward national identification certainly does not appear to provide the basis for any distinct moral claims of citizens upon one another, nor does it provide the basis for limiting the sense of moral accountability to the near side of national borders. In this regard emotional patriotism is unlike the ties generated by economic, political and cultural systems. Yet it clearly looms too large to be ignored altogether and must be accommodated in any moral analysis which purports to be grounded in the real situation of the world.

EMIGRATION/IMMIGRATION

A substantial portion of the human misery of the world today – along with knotty issues of international relations – results from from the fact that many people are not able to be where they want to be or are unwanted by the people who find them where they are. These problems take the varying forms of people who wish to leave the nations where they live but are not allowed to do so; people seeking temporary refuge from war, famine or social unrest; families divided by international politics; those who wish to escape economic deprivation; or those simply wishing for a better or a different life.

It is important to keep one feature of this issue firmly in mind. Emigration and immigration must be considered together. Persons who leave one nation do not simply disappear. They become problems or windfalls for another nation, or for the international community. For most people, in most parts of the world, it is much easier to remove themselves from their home nation than find space, acceptance or new lives elsewhere. Too many emigrants find themselves in the disturbingly permanent limbo of refugee camps, unable to build new lives for themselves yet unable to find permanent places.

It is therefore simply not enough, even if it could be achieved, for all nations to agree to allow free emigration, and to make such an agreement genuinely effective. This is only the beginning of an adequate response to the problem. It is often easy to forget that the really huge problem for the world is not that of emigration. Most of the people of the world suffering from being out of place are not those who wish to leave their home nation but are unable to do so. The plight of the Soviet Jews wishing to emigrate and other Eastern Europeans, including East Germans, who wish to leave their home nation but cannot is both genuine and important. Their anguish clearly merits the world's attention and action. However, in terms of sheer mass of human suffering and magnitude of physical deprivation, the greatest problems of displaced persons involve those who have left their home nation but are unable to return or to establish lives elsewhere. These problems are larger both in terms of numbers of persons involved – they run to the tens of millions – and also in terms of degree of physical deprivation. Refugee camps are sometimes able to offer only the most minimal conditions of subsistence for a portion of the refugee population while many others have nowhere to go – and many more perish or suffer greatly en route to comparative haven. It should be kept firmly in mind that several *million* Afghans alone, one-third to one-half the population of that nation, have become refugees seeking to escape the hazards of warfare in their nation.[13] An entirely plausible argument could be made that the greatest sins of the Soviet Union at the present time are not those of preventing the emigration of its own citizens but the scorched-earth policies which have driven millions of Afghans into forced exile. Their strategy in the latter days of their conduct of the war in Afghanistan was to drain the ocean of people in which guerrilla fighters can move and survive. This policy of forced emigration generated enormous human suffering.[14]

The problems of those who are out of place therefore direct attention to two distinct, yet closely united, sets of issues. The first has to do with the obligations of governments to those who wish to leave. The second is the complementary, and perhaps more difficult, set of obligations of governments and of individual persons toward those seeking space to establish a life.

These issues are complicated by the fact that there are important differences among those wishing to emigrate both in intent and character. There is not, in other words, simply one problem of emigration and immigration but several which differ in accordance with the nature, aspirations and circumstances of those who are out of place. First, emigrants have markedly different aspirations. Probably comparatively few of those who are out of place have any strong desire to remain in permanent exile. Most are seeking only temporary haven from war, internal upheaval or famine. They been driven out, and aspire to return to their home nations when conditions permit.

As a matter of historical fact though, the great bulk of them will not have the opportunity to return, since the conditions that drove them abroad will remain or will evolve into other arrangements, which pose equally effective barriers to their return. A war destructive enough to drive a substantial proportion of its population abroad, for example, will probably also be sufficiently destructive to erase provision for them to return once the war runs its course. Furthermore, people, like wandering species of other types, tend to take root where they land. Early plans for eventual return are transmuted or overshadowed by other, more pressing concerns, and never come to fruition. In some cases political conditions prevent the return of those who have been driven off. It is worth recalling that many Palestinians in the camps of Lebanon or the Gaza Strip have been refugees for nearly forty years, with little prospect of either being absorbed elsewhere or returning to their original homes. They have, in fact, become pawns in larger struggles, and this has done nothing to ease the precarious nature of their existence.

A second class of people are those who move elsewhere in the hope of economic improvement. These people need not have been driven out by life-threatening poverty but may simply leave in hopes of better and more rewarding prospects elsewhere. The United States is currently on tenterhooks in its relations with Mexico over the continuing flow of illegal workers across its borders. Not all Mexican immigrants are unemployed or displaced peasants. An increasing proportion is comprised of skilled and prosperous middle-class professional or managerial sorts.[15] These are people who are not fleeing poverty but are looking for better opportunities to pursue their careers or advance their commercial aspirations. Migrants of this sort are not a burden but a windfall for the United States, but they are precisely the people Mexico can least afford to lose. Yet it is quite likely that the great bulk of these people will never return. While for unskilled Mexican laborers there is often regular two-way traffic across the border, with temporary jobs punctuated by temporary visits home, many settle down and become a permanent underclass of illegal aliens residing in the United States. On this note, it is worth recalling that many of the earlier immigrants to the United States had no intention of remaining in permanent residence. They planned to stay only long enough to make their fortunes before returning to their native lands.

There is another class of transients, those whose status is precarious by not being accepted, even in principle, as immigrants by the nations that house them. These include the previously mentioned group of illegal aliens, those who have entered a nation illegally and established lives there but are officially unwanted and unwelcome. The other, newer group are the officially transient 'guest workers' of Europe – those imported from abroad on a strictly temporary basis to labor and then be returned to their homelands when the need for them no longer exists.[16] There are important differences between these two groups, of course. For both, though, questions can be raised concerning whether they are entitled to the full array of rights, privileges and protections of citizens, or which of these can be enjoyed and which not. For both, it is important to understand that human lives and human environments are at stake. In these cases, too, temporary stays tend to evolve into permanent ones, both because there is little place for them in their home nations and because people tend to take root where they land. For them, forcible removal to their homeland would be a substantial burden indeed.

The final class of migrants includes those who leave for reasons of politics, who either do not accept the nature of the regime in power or are made to understand that they are unwelcome by it. For most of these people, as for others, leaving is not desired. Many would certainly prefer to return to their homelands if they could. In the case of many of the Soviet dissidents, for example, exile is unwelcome and is imposed upon them. For most political exiles, the prospects of a change in regime sufficient to allow them to return are dim, though there are notable exceptions, as seemed to be the case in Haiti after the fall of Duvalier in 1986. For most of them, what is initially seen as a temporary escape to safe refuge becomes permanent exile.

It is difficult to know how to classify the case of the Soviet Jews. Apparently all see exile as a permanent and not as a temporary matter, though this may in part be due to their perception of the permanent nature of the Soviet regime and the enduring anti-Semitism of Russian culture. Many, perhaps, desire to leave because of a wish to join the Zionist movement by living in Israel or to participate more fully in Jewish culture and ways of life. Many, however, apparently aspire to leave because of the anti-Semitism of the Soviet regime and the feeling that their prospects for satisfying lives are constricted simply because they are Jews. This view is corroborated by the discussions of the recently freed Soviet dissident and activist Anatoly Shcharansky and by the fact that significant numbers of Soviet Jews finally settle in places other than Israel.[17]

The above typology of those who are out of place indicates that the discussion of emigration and immigration must be complex, involving diverse groups of people with varying motivations and aspirations. Few wish to leave voluntarily and few initially plan for their departure to be permanent. However, new situations can generate new aspirations and new habits. If all the political barriers in the way of emigration were removed and if all could be assured of finding a stable place to live elsewhere, it is possible that large numbers of people would take advantage of this freedom and that massive and abrupt population shifts would become commonplace. The importance of such migrations for human life and human society should not be underestimated. Demographers and historians can all point to massive changes in the course of human life and the course of human history which have accompanied significant shifts in population. The potential explosiveness and unmanageability of this issue should be neither underestimated nor lightly dismissed.

However, there are many barriers to massive population shifts other than the political. Individuals have strong ties to the people and ways of life of their nation. They will have built a life there and understand full well that building a new life in an alien place is a difficult and uncertain undertaking. It seems likely that people who choose to leave a nation with some sense of genuine freedom do so only because they are unable to make a life for themselves or for their families there *and* because they have a clear sense that there are particular destinations where their prospects will be significantly better. There is not much evidence that major population shifts occur because of political repression, of which there has been no lack in this century. So long as they can make a living, the bulk of people either suffer in silence or stay and fight. Only those who feel they are singled out for repression or whose lives are in immediate danger and feel they have no adequate response are tempted to leave. It is not that these problems are unimportant. Rather, the numbers appear rather small in terms of the overall picture of emigration and immigration.

Though emigration and immigration are closely linked, some

clarity can be gained by discussing them separately, and establishing their links as the examination proceeds. Further, as the above illustrates, people who are out of place do not constitute one homogeneous group, but have different characteristics and aspirations. Thus the nature of their claims on others and the sorts of problems they pose will vary.

The right of free human movement across national borders is widely agreed, on the intuitive level, to be a fundamental one. It is one of those listed prominently in the United Nations' Universal Declaration of Human Rights. It is easy to understand why this should be so. The ability to control human movement across borders is one of the major sources of the power over individuals and institutions that governments possess. By ensuring that they can keep their populations where they want them and being able to exclude others, governmental resources of human control are greatly enhanced. On the other hand, if individuals had the unimpeded ability to cross borders whenever they wished, take up residence wherever they wished, and establish patterns of trade and communication as they wished, they could well enjoy far greater freedom then they do now. It would seem that the control governments would have over them would greatly decrease. People could easily escape the harsh rule of tyrannical governments, for example, simply by leaving. If individuals genuinely had the ability to vote with their feet to register approval or disapproval, it is plausible to assume that governments would be under pressure to become far more receptive to their wishes and more expert in providing the special services only governments can provide. If the market for governments were open rather than fixed, people could choose among them, and governments would have to be receptive to their wishes or be faced with the prospect of ruling a nation filled only with the aged and infirm. What governments would lose in coercive power would be directly gained by human individuals.

But free and open borders would offer an important benefit for governments as well. With absolutely free emigration, they would have some justification for presuming that the individuals residing within their borders have freely chosen to do so. The moral basis of governmental authority would be greatly enhanced.

These are obviously compelling arguments. In some ways their attractiveness for governments is enhanced by the previously catalogued facts that people are tied to their nations by far more than just political barriers to exit. Even repressive and inept governments are unlikely to suffer the embarrassment of mass exodus, given the realities of human life. So free emigration would be no great threat to them, even though it might therefore be less effective as a means of keeping governments on their toes.

Furthermore, freedom to emigrate ideally should also include freedom to stay in place. It is not simply the freedom to leave but, fundamentally, the freedom to be where one wishes, since, depending on circumstance, the harm of being forced into exile can easily equal the harm of being forced to remain. From this perspective, then, forced exile is as grievous a harm as being forced to remain. The considerations of human need and desire that support the one also support the other. It is worth noting that the Soviet Union, which is a primary offender in the former at the present time, is also a primary offender in the latter, by occasionally forcing dissidents into exile as well as forcing Afghans from their homes. So the argument for freedom of emigration is not open to the rejoinder that it may make things easier for repressive governments to force dissidents into exile, and allow only the passive or inert to remain. Such freedom should not give governments the entitlement to tell people to leave if they don't like the status quo. Those who wish to stay to combat abuses, or simply push for a different arrangement, have a strong moral claim to do so, on the same grounds as support their claim to leave, if *that* is what they wish.

With all of the above, it is worth asking what arguments can be made against the general right of free emigration. The basic claim of the foregoing paragraphs is that the choice of where to live is fundamental to many of the other choices one is able to make in life. The reality of the present world situation is that the nation where one lives determines a great deal about how one can live. Furthermore, there will be instances when life and well-being will depend on the ability to escape tumult in one's homeland. So this is a fundamental choice which must be given considerable weight. But the question remains of whether there are other considerations which may sometimes have sufficient weight to override these.

The salient instance here is the Soviet Union. It stands out as an example of a nation that has only recently begun to reconcile itself to the idea of free emigration.[18] Because of its opposition to the article endorsing free emigration, the USSR was one of the few nations to refuse to sign the United Nations' Universal Declaration of Human Rights in 1948. At that time its opposition grew from its reluctance to allow citizens who had married foreign nationals to join their spouses abroad. More recently the issue has concerned Russian Jews who desire to leave. When it has deigned to present arguments to defend its position on these matters, it has usually claimed the right to receive service from those whom it has educated and nurtured, and argued that it has legitimate reasons for wishing to prevent the unrestricted movement of those who possess secret information.[19] These arguments can be viewed as specifications of a more general argument that governments have the morally justified entitlement to restrict the movements of people where their absence is likely to cause harm to citizens or where their presence is important for the well-being of the nation as a whole.

Both arguments, considered in the abstract, have genuine substance. Developing nations in particular have suffered greatly from the loss of skilled and highly educated individuals on whom they have lavished great expense. Under present conditions, economic development depends in large part on human capital – that is, people possessing the skills, talents and discipline required to operate institutions and develop technologies needed for economic advance. Without these people, nations are essentially doomed to backwardness until they can recruit or nurture others to replace them. So these people and their abilities are genuinely important for the welfare of others in their homeland. Particularly where nations have gone to some trouble and expense to educate such persons, with the understanding that they would remain and put their personal resources to work, there is a strong *prima facie* argument that they have a moral obligation to remain.

Of course, the validity of these arguments depends on the claim that governments really are making concerted efforts to improve the lot of the nation and that the skills of the persons in question genuinely will be drawn upon for this effort. Where, as is all too often the case, nations have no use for the advanced skills their students develop, where students with engineering degrees, for example, can expect only unemployment or gross underemployment if they return to their native countries, these arguments lose much of their force. Furthermore, where there is controversy in cases of this sort, governments should bear the burden of proof in showing that the presence of particular persons is genuinely needed *and* that there is reasonable prospect that their skills will ve put to use.

Only where there is clear reason to believe that the presence of a person will assist the nation are there definitely grounds for overriding their personal preferences to leave. The reason for establishing the priority in this way is that the individuals are suffering a certain and clearly defined harm, not being able to reside where they wish, in return for a much more amorphous and problematic benefit, service to their nation. Also, nations and persons are obviously unequal in resources and coercive power. In cases where there is great disparity of this sort separating two contestants, fairness is most likely to be achieved when the burden of proof is placed on the stronger and better situated party.

It is understandable as well that a nation should wish to keep those who possess secret information from drifting off. Given the importance of technology and expertise for economic advancement and social welfare, it is easy to understand that information is highly important, and can sometimes be crucial for the prosperity of a nation. This is particularly true, of course, of military information. As the celebrated spy cases of 1986 and 1987 in the United States reveal, it is necessary for millions of people to have access to highly classified information, which might be at risk if they drifted off to other nations after leaving governmental service.[20] Once more, however, the burden of proof in cases of this sort should be on those government agencies that wish to override personal preferences. To justify the obvious harm of preventing persons from residing where they wish, there must be a clear demonstration that their migration creates the plausible risk of harm. For example, there is clear evidence that both the Soviet Union and the United States – and possibly other nations as well – greatly inflate the category of secret information. Where this is so, where there is doubt that the information in question genuinely is sensitive and important, there is much less reason for restricting movement. Furthermore, given the rapid pace of technology, the crucial importance of particular items of information often quickly becomes outmoded, so there is little reason for restricting the movement of those whose expertise is fifteen or twenty years old. Finally, there is little point in trying to restrict the flow of information whose secrecy is already compromised by having become generally known.

Generally speaking, there are usually good reasons for respecting the wishes of those persons who wish to leave their homeland. There may be grounds for specific exceptions where the departure of particular individuals can be demonstrated clearly to cause harm to others in the nation, so the harm of restricting their movements is counterbalanced by the greater harm caused by their migration. Fundamentally, though, these exceptions must be overridden when a nation violates basic human requirements, those of life itself and its security, in wholesale fashion or mistreats those who wish to leave. The touchstone of this work is that the security and means to life of individual humans are basic. Where these are not nurtured, or are abused by governments, officials can have scant morally compelling grounds for wishing to restrict the movements of persons.

However, as emphasized previously, the right to leave a nation means little if persons can find no other nation to accept them. This is the way in which issues of emigration and immigration are tightly linked. The general argument for allowing persons to immigrate into a nation is that their lives will be improved, whether economically, politically or socially. The *prima facie* obligation of the citizens already in the state, and their government as their representative, is to allow such entry. For those allowed entry, the benefit will often be substantial, while for natives and the nation as a whole the burden will normally be minimal. Those wishing to enter, for example, are often fleeing poverty, war or famine. Their needs in a host nation are unlikely to be more than basic material subsistence. Sometimes this *can* be a considerable burden for host nations, but it is unlikely to equal the suffering of those who wish entry. Sometimes, of course, those who desire entry will be competing for jobs and resources with natives and may cause social disruption by their presence. In these cases the cost for the host nation is greater, as will be seen, but is still unlikely to burden individual citizens in ways equivalent to the suffering of those who wish entry.

From a global perspective, it is also plausible to believe that greater economic equality will result from such movement. If people were able to move freely from areas with low standards of living and little employment to regions with more jobs and wealth, it is reasonable to believe that the troughs of poverty would be flattened somewhat. For those citizens of wealthy nations who have something to lose by such flattening, and are therefore opposed to unrestricted movement, there is some consolation even here. For it is unlikely that the peaks and valleys would be totally flattened, with total equality resulting. Within the United States, to consider one example, where there is relative ease of movement from area to area and certainly no *political* barriers to such migration, there are still pockets of regional poverty and areas of regional wealth. As pointed out earlier, there are many barriers to human movement other than political ones. Nonetheless, free immigration would be likely to erode some of the disparity between wealthy and poor nations.

It remains true that massive or even substantial shifts in population could have serious effects on recipient nations in a variety of ways. Social services, normally stretched thin in most nations, could be overwhelmed. Further, a great influx of aliens could disrupt long-established and carefully balanced political culture, particularly where groups of aliens bring their own organizations or hostilities with them. Finally, there are arguments that large influxes of aliens will destroy the social and cultural homogeneity of a nation, and the valued ways of life that accompany them. All these considerations are serious and merit further attention.

It is true that waves of immigrants have sometimes nearly drained the resources of those nations who have received them. This is particularly evident in poorer parts of the world that are both more susceptible to turmoil and less equipped to deal gracefully with it. Presently Pakistan, Thailand and Somalia are host to large numbers of refugees and have nearly exhausted their resources for assisting them. Here the answer is simple but difficult to implement. The problem is not merely confined to those host nations but is a moral burden for the entire world. All nations have the obligation to assist with material resources and devise programs of resettlement when it appears that refugees will not be able to return to their homes. This is because, as claimed earlier, all human individuals everywhere have the strong obligation to provide the basic necessities of life to human beings. It is an obligation which obviously transcends national boundaries, though it may be an obligation which is best met through the agency of national governments, which serve in this instance as the representatives of individual persons. As has been argued before, there is no great practical barrier to this, as the material burden will be quite small for most nations and the burden will be less onerous still if managed in cooperative fashion by the nations of the world as a whole.

It is true also that substantial influxes of immigrants will place strains on established political cultures. The problem is serious but not insurmountable. It requires concerted attempts at political re-education as well as reasonable efforts to integrate migrants into political life.[21] The latter is an important point. Disruption is most likely to be avoided if persons feel they are part of the system and have some sense of how to operate effectively within it. It is when they continue to feel alienated that they are most likely to turn to unrest.

A more serious argument is that allowing free immigration

may destroy the established culture of a nation. Australia, for example, once defended its policy of excluding Asians on grounds that a massive Oriental influx would significantly undermine its British culture.[22] Close-knit, homogeneous nations with distinctive national cultures, such as Japan and Iceland, have strict immigration laws for just this reason.[23] If it is presumed that the way of life of a people is an important source of value to them – and to the rest of the world – and that a strong political culture is a major factor in producing national stability and political harmony, then arguments of this sort must have great weight. Massive and unpredictable shifts in population are likely to have just this disruptive effect. National cultures require long periods of time and of social stability to grow. It is quite plausible that large influxes of aliens, who have different cultures, could seriously threaten those of host nations. It is reasonable to believe they may be legitimately subject to restraint for just this reason. However, restraint and control are not equivalent to total closure of immigration.

The difficulty is in determining just what counts as a genuine threat to the viability of a culture and how much weight should be given to culture when balanced against basic human wants. Human life and securing the means to life must always be fundamental. Of course, long-term political stability and social harmony are necessary prerequisites to these over the long run. In this regard Iceland, small in territory and small in population and resources, *does* seem vulnerable to a foreign influx. This does not absolve it from all responsibility in these matters, for there remain other ways in which it can be of assistance. Japan is a somewhat different case. It is larger both in territory and population, and is active on the international scene, as Iceland is not. There seems little reason to believe that an influx of even several million people should pose a serious threat to its distinctive and highly intriguing way of life. There seems little reason, furthermore, why its culture must remain completely pure and homogeneous for this to occur. The culture is under pressures of stress and adaptation in any case, as Japan becomes an increasingly prominent citizen of the world and undergoes the social transformation endemic to all modern industrialized societies. What is more, Japan is already host to a substantial minority, that of Koreans, a legacy of its colonial era, to which it has adjusted with more or less grace.[24] For a given nation, in other words, there will be a point beyond which increased immigration will genuinely constitute a threat to national culture and social stability. However, this threshold will differ from case to case.

Certainly Iceland will be more vulnerable than Japan and both more vulnerable than the United States. But none of these nations would suffer greatly from allowing at least some immigration. So, once more, while there are strong arguments in favor of the restriction of population movement, there are no arguments which adequately support banning immigration altogether.

The problem of emigration/immigration is another of those that could be handled much more neatly if there were some sort of world government with authority to coordinate human movement. This could prevent tides of humanity from swamping national economies and prevent some nations from bearing too much of the burden of human dislocation. But the temptation to reach for neat and pat solutions must be resisted when, as at present, humanity simply does not have such institutions or the authority to support them. This means that even the response of morally responsible nations will be messy and uneven. It means also that it cannot be said, flatly, that all human individuals should have the unrestricted right of emigration, or that any and all nations must allow unencumbered immigration. Present reality is too complex and too disjointed to allow that. There are, for example, widely varying categories of those who are out of place, some who are fleeing for their lives and have inadequate resources to maintain themselves, while others are comfortable and well-educated but simply wish better opportunities elsewhere. Clearly the moral seriousness of the requirements of these various groups differs greatly. Furthermore, the varying nations of the world are situated differently in terms of material resources and vulnerability to social disruption. This too must enter consideration. However, there is room for a good deal more international cooperation than exists at present and for the development of more orderly procedures for coping with people who are out of place. The material cost is quite small and the threat to jealously guarded national sovereignty quite manageable.

INTERNATIONAL DISTRIBUTIVE JUSTICE

People are well aware that there are enormous disparities of wealth and well-being in the world. Nonetheless received opinion has been that nations are entitled to the resources they possess and have no significant moral obligation to share that wealth with others. It is, in Hare's terminology, another of the common intuitive beliefs of the international arena. This assumption has been challenged in the past decade both by representatives of poor nations and in sophisticated works of political philosophy.[25]

A striking feature of arguments about international distributive justice is that they tend to be straightforward applications of common beliefs about domestic apportionment of wealth. The existence of international boundaries is presumed to make relatively little difference or is ignored altogether. Thus, arguments supporting the right of wealthy nations to retain their resources tend to be versions of the usual *laissez-faire* claims about the entitlement of the wealthy to keep what they have gained or the rights of those who happen to possess great resources to exploit them. Poor nations, it is sometimes claimed, fall into their poverty, as do poor individuals, as the result of ineptitude, lack of effort or simple bad luck. Whatever the cause, the argument remains that there is no injustice if the rich retain their wealth and the poor remain destitute.

Arguments in favor of international redistribution of wealth are also drawn from analyses of domestic conditions. Some claim that redistribution is required since wealthy nations, as the result of imperialism or economic exploitation, have made their gains by bleeding the poor. Others claim that redistribution is necessary on the straightforward basis of need.[26] All persons require the basic necessities of life, and those who have more than they need are morally obliged to give their surplus to those who are deficient. Yet others formulate a conception of international distributive justice based on what persons in an idealized position of international choice would want for themselves. They argue from this foundation that it is reasonable to presume that people would choose a far greater equality in distribution of resources than presently exists.[27]

While it is by no means obvious that these extrapolations of domestic distributive justice to the international arena are mistaken, neither should they be accepted without question. At the very least, it would seem that international boundaries must make an important practical difference in issues of the distribution of wealth and resources. Any efforts at redistribution must, for example, enjoy the acquiescence of national governments and, frequently, be carried out by means of their agency. Further, the fact that nations are often essentially independent economic units, as well as politically autonomous, may make a significant difference in the ways in which wealth should be apportioned.

Issues of international distribution are clearly entwined with those of emigration and immigration. Commonly the impulse to leave one's homeland is prompted by economic deprivation or the hope of better material prospects elsewhere. Much of the resistance to open borders found among those in wealthy nations is prompted by the fear that their own economic well-being will be diluted by a flood of aliens or the view that others have no entitlement to share in whatever benefits may be enjoyed by participating in the economic system which they have created. Further, it is plausible to assume that dropping all barriers to international population flow will result in greater equality of material wealth for individual persons, and this is sometimes avowed to be an important attraction of such an arrangement.

The two sets of issues obviously diverge, however. There are other ways to redistribute national wealth than by population flow, and individuals are often prompted to emigrate for reasons other than economic. The most fundamental point of divergence is that the primary focus of concern in matters of population flow is individuals rather than nations. If there is a strong moral entitlement to free movement across national borders, it is held by persons rather than states. In fact, such freedom can legitimately be thought to pose a significant threat to nation-states. Free movement across national borders dilutes governmental power by, for example, allowing individuals to escape onerous or undesirable governmental activity. Such movement can also imperil national and political culture by disrupting the homogeneity of populations or circumventing their mechanisms for the transmission and inculcation of culture. The arguments about international distributive justice mentioned earlier, though, alternate between a focus on persons and a focus on nations. Redistributivist arguments based on need, to consider one instance, focus on individual persons, while those grounded on claims of colonial exploitation focus on nations. Positions supporting the status quo normally take nations as the fundamental units in these matters.

These differences expose what is perhaps the most fundamental issue of international distributive justice. The question is whether justice mandates that individuals hold ultimate claim to the resources of the world or whether nation-states do. If nation-states as such are holders of entitlement to resources, donors will satisfy their obligations when resources are delivered to the nation in question. (It is worth noting that the assumption of the discussions of the Law of the Sea Treaty and the North-South arguments is that nations are indeed the holders of these entitlements.) If persons rather than nations bear the claims to the world's resources, however, donors may feel that their obligations are not satisfied until goods are delivered into the hands of needy people. They may believe, further, that they are sometimes required to override the sovereignty of governments to carry out these obligations. Clearly, the flow of discussion will differ if persons rather than nations are the focus of analysis.

A closely related question adds further complexity. It is not clear who is obligated to distribute resources to those entitled to them. It is possible, for example, that nations as such have no moral claim to the resources of the world but that they are nonetheless obligated to ensure that human needs are met. Or it may be the case that individual persons are the ultimate bearers of obligation in these matters, and governments serve only as their representatives.

The moral perspective developed early in the present work is that only the needs and desires of individual persons are of fundamental importance. Nation-states are morally significant but only in so far as they are entwined with the welfare of individuals. As claimed in Chapter 1, whatever freedom of action, rationality or morally significant vulnerability to harm nations may possess derives from the capacities of the individual persons that comprise them and make them operate. There is a sense in which national governments can be considered moral agents, with the obligations other moral agents have, but they are not moral patients – that is, entities whose welfare is of moral concern *per se*. Considerations of entitlement to resources or claims to wealth and goods therefore only have moral bite when linked to individual needs. Nation-states in and of themselves have no claim to them.

Nonetheless, the idea that states themselves are holders of significant moral entitlements to resources is an enduring and persuasive one which cannot be dismissed easily. Because of this, it is worth examining the factors that have contributed to its longevity. It is probable that one such factor is the common conflation, mentioned in an earlier chapter, of government, national culture and the mass of people living within it. 'National defense', for example, can only be justified where what is being violently defended is people, not simply governments or cultures. Where 'nation' refers to 'people', it is highly important, but this is simply because the welfare of great masses of people is highly important. It is true that competent, or at least decent, government can have enormous benefit for the welfare of persons. Certainly, inept or cruel government can have the opposite effect. 'Government' and 'people', in other words, are clearly distinguishable. Governments are of moral concern only because of their relation to individual persons.

A second factor contributing to the illusion of their moral prominence is that governments have established, and continue to manipulate, the systems of international and domestic law in order to retain *legal* priority in the distribution and entitlement to resources. It should be apparent, though, that *de facto* legal claims need not amount to moral entitlement. The current structure of international law need not be accepted without question. It is clear, however, that there must be rules governing the possession and use of resources and that these must have some measure of stability. Human beings and human institutions simply could not function if goods and the practices governing them were changed capriciously. There are good practical reasons, in other words, for placing great weight on these practices – and the practical concerns merge with the moral once it is recognized that this stability is a basic condition of human well-being. But, once more, if the ultimate moral justification for these legal structures is to be found in human welfare, it is apparent that there will also be occasions when human welfare will override them. Furthermore, it may be the case that explicit attention to the moral basis of practices governing the distribution of material resources will reveal that global concern for human welfare requires that they be modified.

A third factor is that whatever agreements are made concerning the redistribution of the world's riches will have to be accepted and implemented by the governments of nation-states. This is a simple fact resulting from the current political structure of the world and the monopoly control over the instruments of physical coercion enjoyed by national governments.[28] In other words, the fact that governments must be the agents of any redistribution, and that governments are closely identified with nations, need not be taken to imply that either governments or nations are the holders of moral entitlement in such matters. The political structure of the world does not conflict with the view that only individuals possess moral entitlement to the means of life.

If the focus is changed from government to national culture, similar considerations apply. It is plausibly claimed that national culture, or the common way of life of a people, must loom larger than the solitary individual. This is in part because ways of life give shape and value to the individual's life by molding choices, expectations and relationships or by engendering valued skills and practices. Clearly human cultures have considerable intrinsic value as well. It is easy to understand that individuals should feel themselves to be of miniscule importance in comparison to their encompassing ways of life and even that they should be willing to sacrifice their own persons on behalf of them. But, again, it is essential to distinguish ways of life from the individuals who are caught up within them. Individuals eager to sacrifice themselves for, say, the Kurd ethnic group may not clearly distinguish between its distinctive language and way of life and the welfare of their kin and friends who are enmeshed within it. Where this distinction is kept firmly in hand, a culture without people, however admirable, is simply a lifeless abstraction existing only in the notebooks of archaeologists or the narrative of scholarly works. People keep it alive and keep it vibrant and are genuinely worthy of self-sacrifice.

The perspective of the present work is that issues of international distributive justice are best met by drawing on the distinction between basic wants and secondary wants worked out earlier. 'Basic wants' refer to the basic necessities of a minimally decent human life. 'Secondary wants' refer to those more individualized and socially conditioned desires which often emerge only when basic needs are secured.

The fundamental contention is that all persons, everywhere, have the strong obligation to do what they can to ensure that the basic wants of every person are met. The existence of national boundaries is, from the most fundamental moral perspective, essentially irrelevant to these responsibilities, since they are owed to persons rather than nation-states. This implies, of course, that where meeting the basic wants of people requires a global redistribution of material resources, those with the ability to contribute are morally obligated to do so. Given the complexities of human life, this broad-gauge obligation can take many forms. Individuals, simply as individuals, have the personal responsibility to contribute what they are able to meet the vital needs of others, without regard to political division.[29]

It is clear, though, that solitary individuals can achieve relatively little in these matters and that the various private and *ad hoc* organizations devoted to international assistance operate under serious limitations. National governments are capable of achieving much more in this regard both because of their greater resources and their more imposing influence. Those both within and outside them, who are in a position to exert pressure to mold government policy, have an obligation to do so – one that is distinct from their duty as private persons.[30] It should be clear from this that, once more, governments will be the moral agents of international redistribution in only a derivative fashion. Governments cannot change themselves. Only individual people can work to change them and their policies. Some people will be better situated than others to effect these changes, and their responsibilities in these matters will be shaped by this fact. Clearly, however, it must be the initiative and vision of individual persons that bring about such alteration. Institutional structure and cultural influence will no doubt shape what can be accomplished and the way in which it may be achieved. It may also be true that institutions will sometimes pose definitive barriers to what persons are able to effect. Nonetheless, persons can operate upon and within them and are often capable of effecting change.

As a practical matter, however, it makes sense to consider states as legally the instruments of change and to consider them the bearers of the moral responsibility which is ultimately possessed by individual persons. It makes good sense, in other words, to work to establish an intuitive morality in which governments are deemed the holders of moral agency in matters of international distribution. This is because governments are able to act and assert themselves on the international arena in a way that individual persons cannot. Further, it is much easier, from a practical standpoint, for those in need to apply to governments than to masses of individual persons. It is easier as well to effect changes through their agency. However, this is only a kind of fiction mandated by the pressure of circumstances, for if individuals cease to think of themselves as having responsibility in these matters or cease to apply pressure for change, governments will do nothing.

On yet another level, those both within and outside governments have the obligation to do what they can to create international institutions and agreements which establish specific responsibility and authority for tending to the basic wants of all human beings, wherever they are found. Once more, the considerations of the previous paragraph will apply. Even on this level individual persons must be the ultimate holders of moral responsibility. They must create institutions with the fiction of agency in order to give themselves the mechanisms for undertaking what they, as individuals, are morally compelled but ill-equipped to undertake. Matters of legality and current political reality probably require that such international institutions be established by representatives of nation-states and with their consent. But, once more, this should not be taken to imply that governments are the ultimate bearers of moral responsibility in these matters. They can only serve as the instruments of the initiative of individuals, since without the activity and concern of well-placed persons, nothing will be done.

The view presented here – that is, the view that persons have no absolute moral entitlement to resources at their command when these are required to maintain the minimal conditions of life for others – will not make any great practical difference to their wealth. It is commonly understood that no huge redistribution of the world's wealth is required to meet the vital needs of people across the globe. It would cost the members of the wealthy nations of the world very little to meet the needs of the destitute.[31] Certainly transfers of this sort would not have any significant impact on the control they enjoy of the resources claimed as their own.

If the practical difference in control of property is small, the theoretical change in the concept of property would be only slightly greater. Only a few radical theorists would claim that the entitlement of individuals to control their property is absolute and can never be outweighed by other factors. States, for example, as a matter of course remove and redistribute private property by means of taxes. Further, it is commonly agreed that property can be taken or even destroyed as necessary in order to preserve human life when confronted with immediate threat. All that is required on the present schema is an expansion of the acknowledged conditions under which personal control of property may be overruled. The claim is merely that the moral entitlement that persons have to control their property is limited to the extent that these resources are required to preserve the lives of others. This view entails, of course, that many instances of what are now considered charity would become moral obligations. It is also true that these strictures would apply to obligations of assistance within nations, as well as those of transnational distribution. In other words, the existence of national borders does not genuinely make any fundamental theoretical difference for questions of distributive justice.

This discussion is further complicated by the fact that nations or governments do not generally directly 'own' the resources within their borders. Individuals or private institutions, at least in non-socialist nations, have legal title to resources and normally exercise day-to-day

control over them. Nations, whether through the agency of government or by means of social mores, regulate the use and transfer of
these resources and, often, make efforts to ensure that wealth is not
removed either outside national boundaries *or* outside the control
of their good offices. Nations only 'have' property in this extended
and derivative sense of being able to control the mechanisms which
regulate its use and of working to keep it within the domain of their
authority.

The issue of international redistribution, in other words, is not
whether nation-states as such are required to give up their property
to assist non-citizens, but rather whether national governments are
morally entitled to use their powers of taxation or regulation of the
ownership and transfer of property to remove resources from their
own domain for the purpose of meeting the vital needs of others.
Even in socialist nations this analysis would not be substantially
different, since governments are not legal owners in these nations
but essentially exercise a more extensive form of the sort of control
undertaken as a matter of course in non-socialist nations.

Seen in this light, the question of the legitimacy of redistribution
can be met on several levels. On one, recall that it has been argued
that nations are morally justified in normally giving priority to the
needs of citizens, on grounds that such arrangements are most likely
to secure them. However, nations are not justified in ignoring the
basic wants of non-citizens or giving greater weight to the secondary
wants of citizens than the basic needs of others. On another level, it
can be noted that citizens themselves have the obligation to assist
meeting the vital needs of all everywhere, and that governments
would only be serving as mechanisms to address that which is their
moral duty in any case. But this does not meet the issue of whether
governments are justified in using their coercive powers to achieve
what citizens should do anyway. Those in positions of influence over
the course of governmental activity are guiding not merely their own
choices and felt obligations but are deciding for all within a nation.
Given the position of this work, it is clear that such coercion would
be justified where significant numbers of lives are at stake. Such
coercion should be viewed with suspicion and should always be used
with caution, but this does not imply that there will never be cases
where it it justified – and the claim is that this is one.

The special obligations which people develop toward one another
as the result of living together or working within a common social or
economic system do not suffice to override their fundamental duty

to meet the basic wants of all. Recall that the utilitarian justification for respecting these special relationships is that they work to ensure that the basic wants of all are satisfied and that they contribute immeasurably to establishing a context for meeting secondary wants as well. The disarray in the international arena resulting from its lack of similar arrangements vividly illustrates their importance. But where basic wants are clearly being met within a system, and those of others who are outside are not, the requirements of these special arrangements must give way before greater need.

A closer look at the ways in which economic systems and the individuals functioning within them come to enjoy wealth – or suffer from its absence – further undermines claims to unrestricted enjoyment of their resources. The wealth of the world is distributed as the result of a combination of a number of factors: luck, personal initiative, social development and the contingencies of history and technology. (On this latter, note the striking impact which world-wide use of internal combustion engines has had on the wealth and influence of several nations of the Middle East, or which the development of modern techniques of agriculture has had on the fortunes of Nauru, which has the good fortune to lie atop large deposits of potash.)[32] In so far as the welfare of particular individuals is concerned, the operation of these factors is largely arbitrary.

Individuals are sometimes able, by means of personal initiative or ingenuity, to improve their lives within their local sphere. This, however, should not be allowed to obscure the fact that the degree and type of success that is available to them through their efforts, however clever or daring they may be, will be fixed by what local conditions allow. The prospects for success of even the most ingenious and ambitious peasant in Bangladesh will be quite different from those of an equally capable counterpart in Appalachia, and the outlook for both will be far removed from what can be sought by an adept operator on Wall Street.

The same sorts of constraints apply to governments or to societies as a whole. The kinds of success that may be enjoyed by the most enlightened and capable government of Bangladesh must diverge greatly from those of an equally far-sighted government in West Virginia, which differs in turn from what can be achieved in New York state. Whatever application such ideas as 'desert' or 'merit' possess must lie within the orbit of operation of these systems. Individuals struggling within them can make a difference for their own lives, but the difference will be shaped and limited by what the systems allow. In some cases the pressures of the system will push most people into poverty and contain only a few options for comfortable or opulent lives. In others, there will be greater opportunity for middle-class standards of life, but also possibilities for dire poverty or great wealth.

Claims and entitlements to resources, in other words, are not founded on moral bedrock. They are created, molded and limited by local conditions. There is nothing universal or absolute about them – even when they result in reward for genuine merit. To say this is not to imply that such claims have no moral weight at all. These conditions define the legitimate expectations and ways of life of the people living within them. When they are overridden, those involved may plausibly believe they have been treated unjustly, since the rules they have accepted and observed in their conduct have been cast aside. It should be obvious that there will be occasions when this overriding will be justified, but such occasions must be of grave – that is, life-threatening – importance.

The discussion thus far has focused on the strength of the entitlement of all persons to have their basic wants secured. Claims of entitlement to resources based on property rights, the obligations of governments to their citizens, or the special ties citizens have to one another, must give way when confronted by the requirement of basic need.

There is a much weaker obligation, in the present view, that secondary wants be satisfied. They have moral pull, of course, simply because on a utilitarian scheme all human desires have moral pull. They are presumed to have lesser weight than basic wants because, as pointed out earlier, it is reasonable to assume that human beings in the usual course will place greater importance on the basic requirements of life. They do not have the same urgency and importance as basic wants. If, for example, requirements for food and water go unmet for a comparatively brief period of time, death soon follows, and it is too late to be of assistance. The desire for, say, education or a satisfying job or a pleasant home, however, can be met next year or the one following if resources for them are not presently available. They are important, and the cost of delay is certainly not negligible, but all is not lost if they are deferred. Furthermore, as noted in Chapter 1, secondary wants are more difficult for others to meet and more difficult to measure. Quite often they are deeply culturally relative. The requirements of stability and the need for firmly established responsibility allow those in positions of responsibility in nations to focus their attention and efforts on the needs of their own citizens. This by no means implies, however, that officials may overlook the requirements of the secondary wants of others or that they have no obligation to assist them.

The obligation on those in comfortable circumstances to address the requirements of the secondary wants of others is clearly less than for basic wants, and is liable to be outweighed by a broader array of factors. It is possible that claims to secondary wants may, given the constraints of empirical circumstance, be overridden by factors of efficiency, stability, incentive, or the special claims and obligations arising from residing within a particular social or economic system. These factors may sometimes work to increase the supply of secondary goods for all, *or* may be necessary to ensure the stability of a continued supply of them. Obviously, however, their moral importance will have limits. Where, for example, there is a clear choice between an increase in the secondary wants of an already comfortable nation and greater prosperity for an impoverished one, impartiality requires that the claims of the latter take precedence. Or if there is a clear choice between a *decrease* in the secondary wants of an opulent society and boosting the fortunes of a destitute nation, then, again, the claims of the latter will take precedence. Furthermore, it will sometimes be possible to nurture the prospects of impoverished nations without significantly affecting the wealth of the comfortable. When this opportunity arises, there is a clear obligation to take advantage of it. Finally, it is feasible for the nations of the world to take steps to create international institutions and arrangements which will improve the prospects of the impoverished – and they have the obligation to do so.

The disarray of the world and the mysteries of economics will often combine to ensure that the above choices are rarely available in clear-cut fashion. However, there are occasions when they will be, and there are a number of steps that can be taken to meet the obligations which those whose needs are abundantly filled have regarding those who are destitute. There are clear cases, as in negotiations over the Law of the Sea Treaty, where agreements can be made in an orderly way which will greatly assist the impoverished while literally taking nothing away from the wealthy.[33] In other cases, as has been the policy of the United States among others, tariff rates and rules governing transfer of technology can be easily adjusted to assist those who are comparatively worse off without creating any more than minimal hardship for prosperous nations.[34] Furthermore, the requirements of others will clearly be of sufficient weight in relation to the prosperity of some to require that direct transfers of wealth be made, whether through foreign aid programs or by means of the good offices of such institutions as the International Monetary Fund. There is clearly a great deal that can be done by comfortable nations at only minimal cost to themselves, and the argument of the present work is that taking this responsibility is a moral obligation rather than a morally optional act of charity.

It is not, however, an implication of this account that there must be a precisely equal distribution of material goods across the globe. Strict equality is always there as a value to be overridden, but it *may* be overridden by other factors. Where ways of life, patterns of effort, values and systems of behavior differ so greatly, and where the continued provision of secondary goods depends on the operation of an entire cultural and political infrastructure, strict equality of the distribution of material goods may be both irrelevant and nearly impossible to achieve.

International conditions become important once more when the mechanics of how this wealth is to be distributed are examined. While obligations to give aid lie directly with human individuals, deference to reality requires that any well-organized and adequately effective program of world-wide assistance be organized and operated by governments, as the agents of these single persons. Only governments have the coercive power, authority and organizational ability to gather necessary resources and distribute them as needed. In this matter, as in other areas of international relations, governments must currently be the effective agents of activity. From the perspective of those who are in *need*, the reality of the international context is that such transfers must take place through the auspices of their own governments rather than provided directly to individuals themselves. The obligation on the members of the world community is to ensure that assistance goes where it is required – to those people who are in need. Private individuals are unlikely to possess the means to cope effectively with alien governments, to ensure that assistance reaches needy persons. Again, only other national governments are likely to have this influence. For this reason they will have to play a role. The difficulties that private aid groups have in attempting to cope with local governments while helping the destitute are lucidly examined and vividly exemplified in William Shawcross's book on Cambodia, *The Quality of Mercy: Cambodia, Holocaust, and Modern Conscience*.[35]

A second problem is that the suffering of people is often due to social practice, governmental ineptitude, or bias within the local economy. Thus the poor within poor nations are often likely to be kept in destitution by structural features of their own nation-state. By itself this makes little difference to the obligation of the well-off to be of assistance in meeting basic wants. What is important, though, is that these structures are likely to ensure that basic needs are met in only minimal and haphazard fashion, and will fail to achieve permanently a minimally decent human existence for the poor. Furthermore, the systemic nature of these ills implies that in actual cases it will often be difficult to separate cleanly problems of providing basic wants from those of meeting secondary wants. Measures more ambitious than simply meeting crises of the moment must address whole systems that are as likely to fail in both areas as be deficient in only one. These structural problems cannot, moreover, be ignored, even where the problems themselves are complex and the solutions difficult and elusive. Where human life and well-being are at stake and governments are unwilling or unable to make changes, their sovereignty is subject to being overridden. These issues thus reconnect with the questions of intervention discussed in Chapter 3. Intervention of this sort is not as drastic or as unusual as may appear at first. The International Monetary Fund, for example, already employs the standard method of imposing demands for reform of policy and practice on nations who seek assistance from it. And often these regimens are quite severe.[36] The broader issues discussed here differ in part from those faced by the IMF in that it waits for nations to apply to it for assistance. The necessity of supplying the basic wants of persons may sometimes mean that donors will not have the moral option of sitting back to wait for official requests for their aid. They may sometimes be required to take the initiative and apply pressure to nations not actively seeking assistance or which seek assistance on terms that will only further enrich the privileged and leave the destitute no better off than they were.

As a way of fleshing out these abstract discussions, it may be illuminating to examine the case of Bolivia. It is a nation without catastrophic and spectacular threats to human life, as there are in Ethiopia or Bangladesh.[37] It is nonetheless a nation of grinding poverty with little hope of improvement. While there can be little doubt that there is much suffering and death in Bolivia as the result of its conditions, these are the result of the deep-rooted poverty of the system as a whole rather than transient and spectacular events, such as flood, famine or warfare. Because its problems are less easily pinned down and solutions certainly less clearly apparent than elsewhere, Bolivia is a richer and ultimately more edifying example than other, more newsworthy, instances of need.

Part of Bolivia's difficulty is that any long-term improvements for its people must result from structural changes in the nation itself and the addition of fixed institutions, such as hospitals, schools and government.[38] The difficult questions include those of who will decide how such institutions will be established and how to continue to meet their financial needs. Lack of governmental expertise and planning is certainly part of the problem. If so, are others justified in exercising coercion to force change? But if this *is* justified, what is the best way of doing so? Options include threats, financial manipulation and peer pressure. Bolivia's economy is already receiving assistance from the International Monetary Fund, which has given aid subject to demanding stipulations.[39] It is plausible to ask whether these strictures are justified or whether the IMF is authorized to make them.

Further questions involve issues of which nations are obligated to be of assistance and what forms their assistance should take. Are nations obligated in accordance with their wealth or ability to pay? Are they obligated by the extent to which they have trade relations with Bolivia or have benefited in some way, at Bolivia's expense, from association with it?

It does not appear helpful to cast the issues in terms of past exploitation. The relation between past benefit and present need is too tenuous and too difficult to measure.[40] In any case, the nation that has engaged in the greatest exploitation in South America, Spain, is in difficult circumstances itself and certainly in little position to make amends. A more fruitful tack is to argue simply that those nations who are able to be of benefit should be required to do so. However, financial aid is not the only, or perhaps even the most basic, need in this case. What is necessary in the long term is planning and expertise, at all levels, which can only be provided by people and not merely by money. From the abstract moral perspective, all nations have an obligation to help in so far as they can to meet the immediate vital needs of the Bolivian people. However, long-term structural changes will require carefully conceived programs which are perhaps best supplied by those with closest and most enduring ties to Bolivia, such as the Organization of American States. Furthermore, it may be legitimate to put various sorts of pressure on the Bolivian government to help meet these needs because of the exceptional suffering of its people. One of the themes of this work is that sovereignty is not sacrosanct. Where human life is at stake the prerogatives of sovereignty may clearly be overridden. In addition, there are various ways of applying pressure which need not be seen as coercive and which need not be seen as in the service of the coercer.

The question of feasibility remains. Various elements of the organization required for addressing problems of this sort already exist, including the International Monetary Fund, the American Peace Corps, and the quiet and long-term aid programs of the Scandanavian nations. What is still required is merely the political will to address them in prosperous and fully developed nations. National leaders have the moral obligation to build bases of domestic political support for such programs. They have this obligation both as individuals and as persons well-situated within powerful and wealthy nations whose resources can make a difference. National governments only have these obligations in the oblique fashion of representatives and agents of those whom they rule. Yet there are individuals within them who are well situated to change the course of their policy and make them responsive to need. Certainly, national heads of state fall into this category. Jimmy Carter clearly recognized it as his responsibility when President of the United States. Building this enthusiasm and awareness was performed brilliantly by President John Kennedy in the United States twenty-five years ago when he established the Peace Corps and built broad enthusiasm for it. The last American President, Ronald Reagan, was no Kennedy, but he was an adept salesman and could easily have built substantial domestic support for programs of this sort, had he choosen to do so. The same kind of human concern is there waiting to be tapped in other corners of the world, and indeed has been by Reagan's antagonists the Cubans.[41]

In the concluding chapter the questions of why national leaders are apt to ignore their responsibilities in these areas and how such obstacles may be met by those of good intentions will be examined in greater detail.

In sum, citizens are correct in believing that they do have special ties and responsibilities to one another which they do not share with aliens. They are correct, in addition, in believing that they have claims to the material and cultural resources within their nation. And they are correct in believing that these claims and entitlements have moral weight. They are mistaken, however, in so far as they share the commonly held opinions that these entitlements are absolute and that they have no obligations to concern themselves with the needs of non-citizens. Particularly where the fundamental requirements of human life and well-being are at stake, they have the strong obligation to relinquish their resources for the benefit of others. Even where secondary wants are at issue, people do have some requirements to concern themselves with the deficiencies of others, though these issues are less pressing and more complex and problem-ridden than are basic human wants. National boundaries, in other words, make no moral difference in any fundamental sense. Nations, as such, have no overwhelming claim to the earth's resources or to maintain their own viability. National borders matter only in the practical and derivative sense that they are likely to set the stage for people to establish various obligations and entitlements which do carry some moral weight.

Ironically, the strong sense of national identification, which appears in common-sense fashion to create strong ties among individuals, has no moral weight in and of itself. It may be useful in nurturing a sense of responsibility in individuals and perhaps providing part of the motivation necessary for people to overcome their usual inertia when action is required. But it is also clear that national identification has often caused a great deal of harm and often gets in the way of coping with the problems of the world. Emotionally, it may be both greatly satisfying and important. Morally, it has derivative importance at most.

Conclusion: Present and Future Prospects

It is a commonplace that the relations of nation-states are amoral at best. It is less commonplace to note that national leaders nevertheless cloak their deeds in the language of high moral purpose. If hypocrisy is the tribute vice pays to virtue, it is worth asking why leaders think the tribute needs to be paid and why there is so little prospect of word passing into deed.

This work has been devoted to discovering what morality requires of national leaders and how its demands on them differ from the requirements of personal morality. While their moral failings are well-known and often tragic, it seems unlikely that national leaders are inherently more wicked than ordinary mortals. It is possible that politics attracts a certain type of person, one possessing a taste for power and the willingness to be ruthless in attaining and keeping it. Of course, it is likely that this picture is far too simple, but even if it is not, power-hungry individuals are found in all walks of life. The circumstances of leadership serve to magnify the consequences of personal failings and insensitivity. Vacillation and ambiguity, which may be minor flaws when found in a clerk, bus driver, or college instructor, become much more serious when displayed by governmental leaders. The zany brutality, which may have been a relatively minor flaw in Idi Amin the Ugandan sergeant, became much more serious when he gained control of a nation.

It is well to recognize that the actions and decisions of national leaders are often not as callous as they may appear to observers. It is easy to overestimate the extent of immorality of governments. This is so for several reasons. For one, heads of government are often forced to make difficult choices, sometimes among a variety of evils. Israel, at the time of writing, is edging toward closer relations with the Soviet Union, in spite of grave differences over the emigration of Soviet Jews and Russian support of Israel's enemies. It has been roundly excoriated for this effort by the noted dissident, and recent emigrant, Anatoly Shcharansky.[1] Israeli leaders have reason to believe that improved relations with the Soviet Union will serve to decrease Israeli isolation in the world and may be of assistance in mitigating its bitter conflicts with its neighbors, and so they are dealing with the Devil. It is easy to view this as the normal amorality of nations. But it may also be seen as the understandable response of a nation that is in a difficult position and is attempting to achieve an added measure of security for itself in the world. Part of the difficulty, of course, is that the benefits of Israel's course are uncertain and difficult to foresee. It is possible that no benefit will result. So it is paying a cost – dealing with what it views as an unsavory character – in return for a remote and uncertain benefit. But if the result is increased security for the lives and well-being of Israeli citizens, the cost will have been worth paying, morally. What initially seems an amoral venture is revealed to be a morally comprehensible, though risky and difficult, choice.

On a larger scale, President Harry Truman of the United States was forced to decide whether to use the newly developed atomic bomb against Japan in hopes of ending the war sooner and saving, quite possibly, millions of lives. Given the world's horror of the use of atomic weaponry in war, it is easy in many quarters to believe that Truman's choice was the gravest sort of immorality. But it is important to make the distinction between acts which are morally wrong and those which are immoral. Truman's choice may be criticized in a number of ways, and it is possible that it was the wrong one. However, making the wrong choice under the pressure of time and circumstance does not amount to immorality, the conscious disregard of moral scruple. It is one thing to debate the correctness of Truman's choice, but quite another to claim that he acted totally without regard for moral scruple.

The difficulties of Israeli leaders and of Harry Truman serve to reveal a second element of the inflated perception of national immorality. Decisions of governmental response must often be made in highly fluid situations where accurate information is difficult to gain but where events will not await calm and reasoned deliberation. In such cases leaders must act, but their action must often be a jump into a void of uncertainty and ambiguity, with possibly disastrous results. Ronald Reagan has been criticized for the invasion of Grenada in October of 1983. It has been called a cowboy's adventure and the imperial arrogance of a great power. But the regime in Grenada certainly was bloodthirsty and unstable, and there is little doubt that the local populace welcomed the incursion. Reagan's decision may have been an over-reaction, but it may also have saved a good deal of human suffering and turmoil in a small corner of the world. If it had been possible to remove Idi Amin by similar means, and with equivalent cost, at an early stage in his career as ruler of Uganda, few would presently deny the value of such a venture. But *at the time* it would have been difficult to know how Amin would turn out or to guess the extent of his brutality. So, *at the time* a decision would have been a risky and controversial one, and would eternally lack the benefit of hindsight for proof of whether it was justified or not.

There remains another cause for the often inflated perception of national immorality. It arises from a misunderstanding common among the so-called realists, those who claim that no international morality is feasible. Their mistake is to presume that, since particular moral standards must often be overridden in international affairs, no morality can govern decisions of national policy. This is false. Very often when particular moral standards are set aside by governmental leaders, those governing honesty or taking human life for example, the standards are overridden by a more fundamental guide, that of the principle of utility. So it is not the case that morality has been cast aside. Rather, the pressures of a situation require that some standards give way to other, more fundamental ones. George Kennan, for example, claims that nations must always seek to preserve their own security.[2] Surely he cannot mean that there is some law of nature requiring that nations always seek security, for he must be well aware that nations often act recklessly. So his claim is not about inexorable nature but about standards of rational conduct, and the claim requires reasoned justification. If Kennan were to provide a justification for his assertion, it is not unlikely that he would frame his defense in terms of the lives and well-being of the citizens of the nations in question – a moral claim, in other words.

National leaders, then, are not so immoral as is sometimes fashionable to believe. This result gives grounds for optimism, for it implies that the task at hand is not that of somehow foisting morality on essentially immoral agents, though some, of course, *are* immoral. It is rather the project of extending the range of moral sensitivity and responsibility of national leaders. That is, national leaders commonly feel morally responsible only for their own citizens and do not place great importance on the human rights, material welfare and moral claims of those in other nations. The problem is to acknowledge these broader obligations and make them effective features of national policy. If this task is to succeed, it is essential to understand clearly which sorts of constraints and opportunities can be found in the circumstances of institutional leaders. Only then will it be possible to determine whether such a broadening of moral responsibility is feasible and discover how it may come about.

The importance of the circumstances which frame individual action, the interaction between human situation and acts of will, have not been much discussed by philosophers. For example, moralists commonly insist that human beings are free, which is to say that they are able to control their actions rationally. If this were not possible, morality would be impossible. They may further insist that there are no temptations so strong that humans are unable to resist them. But it is a feature of human life that there are many temptations insistent enough that few will in fact resist them. Some circumstances are much more conducive to sane and responsible action than others, and some people are much better situated to initiate such action than others. A morality which is for all people, and not only for saints and heroes, must take these factors into account.

An effective morality – one likely to make a difference in the world of live human beings – should include reference to those circumstances and pressures which encourage most persons to act responsibly. This does not imply that humans lack freedom. They always retain the ability to respond to given circumstances in a variety of ways. It does mean that differing circumstances allow differing arrays of response and that as a matter of fact conditions will press individuals to act in one way rather than others. Some actions in some circumstances will be performed only by individuals of great determination and integrity. Others will likely press almost all persons of a given time and culture to respond in the same way. To note this is not to deny human freedom but is simply to take account of the real conditions under which humans must act, and clear the way for insight into how to make genuine moral sensitivity and responsibility not only feasible but commonplace.

With this perspective it is natural to examine the general features of the international arena which serve to inhibit moral responsibility and seek ways in which they might be transformed or mitigated. Two examples are instructive. One is the serious attempt of US President Jimmy Carter to establish the concern for human rights as a keystone of his foreign policy, an attempt which did not meet with notable success.[3] His is an instance of a politically powerful individual making the earnest decision to conduct a morally sensitive foreign policy, yet failing. It is possible that his efforts could not have succeeded, and that the efforts of anyone else in his office would be similarly doomed. However, consider nations such as Sweden, which have quietly made various moral concerns centerpieces of their foreign policy and, in fact, devote significant portions of their wealth to assisting those in other parts of the world.[4]

The example of Sweden suffices to demonstrate that a morally sensitive foreign policy is possible on the international level. What it does not do is demonstrate either that such sensitivity is possible for other nations, such as the United States, or that concerns of this sort are likely to become the norm in international relations. Clearly Sweden is an exception to the usual rule of international conduct. A number of factors are available as possible explanations for this general lack of moral enthusiasm. Some, in fact, have been discussed earlier in this work.

Politicans, for one thing, often claim that it is part of their moral duty as leaders to look after the interests of their nation and that they would be remiss in this duty if they allowed other factors to have weight. As earlier discussions have shown, this is an argument which deserves to be considered seriously, even if it is often used in self-serving fashion. The earlier examination, however, also shows that this duty does not morally justify always placing highest priority on national interest, and certainly does not preclude accepting general responsibilities to humanity as a whole. It does, however, explain the psychological reluctance of even well-intentioned leaders to place burdens on the people of their nation. A parent, for example, may feel she has no right to ask her family to make sacrifices which she would feel justified in making by herself alone. This reluctance is sometimes fully understandable, but it has moral weight only in cases where moral action is morally optional or where great sacrifices are likely to be required of the agent. Neither of these conditions apply in the great majority of instances requiring moral concern on the international scene.

A second intrusive factor is the matter of security. Leaders often feel that long- or short-term national security interests conflict with the moral claims of those in other nations. Jimmy Carter's policies came to grief in part because of the Philippines and South Korea, where concern for human rights appeared to conflict with American security requirements – and with American commitments to other nations in East Asia. No leader can afford to ignore matters of security, since they are matters, ultimately, of the lives and well-being of their own people. Of course, as claimed in Chapter 2, there is some question of what counts as a genuine problem of security and what does not. Governments sometimes treat the remotest threats to the lives and well-being of their people as matters justifying extreme measures in response. In such cases, ignoring moral responsibilities to others is unjustified, but where there is likely to be a direct and serious threat to a nation, extreme measures – and exclusive concern for the welfare of one's own citizens – may be justified. The difficulty is that there are many cases in between, where a small threat left unchecked today may develop into a major problem in the future. When these difficult cases arise, it is understandable that even sensitive leaders will be uncertain and choose to err, if that is the danger, on the side of the welfare of their own citizens.

An easily overlooked, but often crucial, factor is that there is usually no strong domestic constituency which supports international moral responsibility or which has a significant stake in supporting moral issues in the international arena. Any political leader, even in authoritarian nations, is under insistent pressure to satisfy the demands of various constituencies. Dealing with these must of necessity rank high on the list of priorities of those wishing to remain in office. In the nature of things, moral concerns extending beyond national borders will rank low, particularly under present conditions where leaders are not expected to be responsive to international moral concerns and there are few protocols governing morally responsible policy even where sensitivity exists. It would require an unusually determined and persuasive leader to risk taking the initiative in such conditions.

A related problem arises from an important difference between the ethics of personal relations and the ethics of international relations. On the personal level, a moral wrong will usually be committed against specifiable individuals whose hurt can be seen and felt. On the international level, moral wrongs will harm individuals whom the agent may never see and whose pain may never be felt. Because of this, the consequences of wrongdoing will often be much easier to live with, for the agent, than on the personal level. Politicians, accustomed to responding to pressure, will see little reason to act when no pressure is being brought to bear.

The rhetoric of international morality is presently so abstract and vague that political leaders can emphatically endorse it without committing themselves to anything very definite. Widely diverse rulers, for example, can pledge allegiance to human rights, or the human right to life, without shouldering any specific obligation. The world has not yet built a fund of experience in applying these general principles to particular cases, so there is no commonly

accepted standard of what precise actions constitute a violation of
the right of freedom of speech or exactly which military maneuvers
constitute aggression. Where the atmosphere of moral practice is so
very thin, vague gestures are easy to make and the link to concrete
action is tenuous.

It is possible that the combined weight of the factors of national
interest, security concerns, lack of domestic constituency, and the
ethereal character of international moral scruples presently make
significant concern for morals infeasible for most nations. Sweden
remains a distinct exception, so it is worth turning to this particular
case to see what factors have made broad international moral
sensitivity viable there, as a step towards seeking progress in
other nations. Or, if the case of Sweden proves so eccentric as to
be impossible to duplicate elsewhere, that too is worth knowing.[5]
The lack of theoretical or moral barriers to an international moral
sensitivity claimed elsewhere in this work would then pale in the
face of substantial practical difficulty. At first glance many of the
factors discovered to contribute to the Swedish moral sensitivity are
unique and unlikely to be easily replicated. The issue then becomes
whether these are the crucial elements in the Swedish instance or
whether there are others, more readily transferred, which may suffice
as catalysts for change.

To begin with, Sweden is small in size and militarily weak.
Centuries have passed since it was a significant force in Europe,
though it has exerted disproportionate influence in its own remote
corner. This remoteness has also had its role to play in removing
it from the conflicts and hazards of more centrally located nations.
Poland, for example, would find it difficult to escape immersion in
world turmoil, however great an effort it made. Yet Sweden is near
enough to the battlegrounds and great powers of the world that it
can appreciate the benefits of remaining aloof from the struggles
of others. As a result, it has developed a tradition of neutrality
extending from the beginning of the nineteenth century.[6]

Its history and location thus conspire to frame a certain turn of
mind. It is prevented from having aspirations to power itself and has
no need of allying itself to other powers for protection.[7] It cannot
afford the luxury of burying itself in the affairs of far-off nations or
worrying about extending the web of security concerns far beyond its
own borders. Thus it does not view itself in competition or in conflict
with distant nations and has little to seek from the rest of the world in
military terms. It is not situated to view the world in Hobbesian terms

of unrelenting war. In so far as the Hobbesian perspective has been a formidable barrier to the feasibility of international ethics, Sweden is not affected. Lack of aspiration to power also means that Swedish leaders will see fewer occasions to override humanitarian concerns in the service of other, more profitable goals. But these factors are only negative; they illustrate that certain barriers to international moral responsibility are not present in Sweden. They do not give an explanation of why the sensitivity developed there. After all, other nations, such as Iceland, Brazil, Australia and New Zealand share similar isolation and freedom from geo-political struggle. Some, like New Zealand, are professed neutrals, yet have not been active in developing a positive international morality to the degree that Sweden has.

A possible factor is that Sweden has been dominated by socialist governments for a number of years, long enough to ensure that socialist governmental institutions will remain even when other parties are in office.[8] This factor contributes several elements to the Swedish outlook. For one thing it has added a sense of solidarity with other socialist governments and something of the internationalist outlook common to socialist groups. This internationalism has included the notions that there is a solidarity of people crossing international boundaries, that unjustice and human suffering across the world are not to be ignored but should be matters of active concern, and that one socialist group should be actively involved with socialist movements in other nations.[9] The sense of being part of a distinct movement has sparked a sense of kinship and identification with socialists in other nations.[10] What is essential, however, is that the entire socialist movement is founded on a moral vision of the wrongness of human suffering *along with* the strongly felt responsibility to do something about it.

There is, of course, another facet to socialism, namely its less than total reverence for the institution of property. Socialists have fought against the idea that people are entitled to keep whatever they have gained, no matter how much they possess or how much others may need it.[11] A central core of socialist doctrine is that material goods should go where they are most needed. This implies, one would expect, that there should be less reluctance in socialist nations to part with national wealth for the sake of greater need elsewhere. Once again, however, dozens of nations in the world profess adherence to socialist principles and institutions, yet few are known for international moral activism.

There is something unique to Sweden, however. For some years it has enjoyed a general standard of living which is among the highest in the world.[12] Yet its socialist ethos has determined that while there are few really poor in Sweden there are also few really wealthy individuals. There are clear limits to the amount of wealth each individual is able to accumulate, together with the secure sense that there are limits below which one cannot fall.[13] Thus, two more barriers to international moral sensitivity are dissolved. Swedes do not have the excuse that there are starving and struggling persons at home who have a claim to assistance before resources are sent abroad to help others. Limits on personal wealth also mean that one has little hope of real gain, say, in hopes of lowered taxes by pressing for reductions in foreign aid.

The above, though, are for the most part shared with other nations and do not disclose the causal mechanism which triggered Swedish policy. This causal influence is found quite easily, in the handful of prominent and energetic Swedish citizens who not only helped provide the theoretical foundations of internationalism but have worked vigorously over the years to put them into practice. This group includes the Myrdals, Gunnar and Alva, who were closely associated with the United Nations from the beginning and spoke and wrote widely on its behalf and on behalf of greater international moral sensitivity. Dag Hammarskjöld, of course, must be included. He was possibly the most successful President of the United Nations and remains a guiding presence even in death. Tage F. Erlander, the Social Democrat Swedish Prime Minister for over twenty years, remained a staunch supporter of the United Nations and of internationalism throughout his tenure. The group must also include the late Olaf Palme, Erlander's successor, who held office almost continuously from 1968 until his recent death. The influence of such a group in a small, insular nation is much greater than in a larger, more diverse nation such as the United States. Their aura was heightened by the pride which isolated Swedes took in the international stature these persons enjoyed.

Their influence lay in cementing Swedish relations with the United Nations, a strong interest in world peace and nuclear disarmament, and, what is most unusual, an identification with the Third World and its concerns.[14]

In practical terms Palme was best situated among members of this group to implant such concerns in Swedish policy. He gained notoriety even before becoming Prime Minister, while still

Minister of Education under Tage Erlander, for his vigorous, even virulent, criticism of the United States' involvement in Vietnam. He had several distinct advantages in his endeavors. He enjoyed a lengthy period in office, a total of nearly twenty years, long enough to press for programs, tinker with them till they worked, and nurture public support for them. It helped that Palme was an entrenched party leader, able to count on his party's support, and an individual of some presence, enjoying domestic popularity and international renown. But it certainly helped that the climate of Swedish opinion was favorable to his efforts. The Swedes supported his position on Vietnam, for example. Common opinion apparently even moved ahead of him and the Social Democrats in the mid-1970s when the goal of contributing 1 per cent of Sweden's gross national product to foreign assistance was debated – and eventually became policy.[15]

Palme's experience contrasts sharply and instructively with the efforts of US President Jimmy Carter to achieve similar, though in some ways more modest, goals. It is this contrast that must be examined to see what of the Swedish effort can be usefully exported. Save for the honest conviction that the net of moral sensitivity should be cast more widely, Carter in many ways was not everything that Palme was. Carter's tenure was brief, a single term of four years. For the greater portion of this time he enjoyed broad support neither within his own political party nor among the electorate at large. Worse, he was not skilled at maneuvering his programs through the labyrinthine branches of government. He is widely considered to have been an ineffectual and narrowly moralistic leader. He had none of the skills and weight of Palme in organizing support for his programs or piloting them through the branches of government. His brief stay in office gave him little time to build support for his programs, refine them, or learn how to make them work. But even if Carter had enjoyed the broad popularity or persuasive manner of a John F. Kennedy – or Ronald Reagan – he would still have faced formidable, possibly fatal, obstacles in the way of his ambitions.[16]

The situation and climate of opinion of the United States is nearly the mirror opposite of that of Sweden. It is a major power, locked in protracted conflict with the Soviet Union. There is a strong, perhaps irresistible, tendency to view all international issues through the prism of this one issue.[17] Further, the conflict is often thought to be a mortal one, with the ultimate outcome being the destruction of one, or both, the contending powers. A result of this struggle is to give credence to the Hobbesian view that international conditions do not allow effective morality, on grounds that struggle to the death with a vicious and imperialistic enemy makes moral restraint suicidal. Thus, within the United States there is an influential body of opinion holding that moral constraints cannot apply on the international level. All is viewed in terms of the struggle with the Soviet Union. Even where moral constraints are recognized to be applicable, it is thought justifiable to overrule them for the sake of the larger conflict.

Though the United States is far stronger in military terms than Sweden, it sees itself as locked in bitter struggle and *feels* more threatened. Perceptions of security are difficult to control rationally. It is likely that however large an arsenal the United States builds, it will never feel secure with what it has. Its position as a great world power makes it a looming target of irritation and jealousy. It cannot attain the anonymity and lack of resentment or scrutiny that Sweden enjoys. Because Sweden cannot hope for overwhelming military power and complete security from external threat, it is not tempted to seek them. The United States' loftier position, however, makes these temptations much more difficult to avoid. Then, too, its pre-eminent stature has resulted in its becoming entangled in the security of other nations of the world, so that it cannot rest content with defending its own borders but busies itself with the security of others – often, it should be noted, at their specific request and to their apparent advantage.[18]

Nuclear weaponry also plays its role in fostering a mentality of beleagured wariness. Nuclear weapons are sufficiently powerful to destroy any nation in the space of a few hours. Even a single, well-placed charge is capable of generating enormous human suffering. In such circumstances a false move, or a brief lapse of attention or a mechanical glitch could, literally, be fatal for the nation as a whole. In the face of a threat of that magnitude, suspicion, a desire to stand firm and a reluctance to forgo any advantage are strongly re-enforced. Sweden, happily, is not the direct object of nuclear threat and would have little hope of effective response if it were.[19] For this reason, it does not have to contend with such a possiblilty and need not become obsessed with it.

The United States, in addition, most emphatically does not share the Swedish socialist ethos. It is proudly and militantly capitalist. While there are certainly other capitalist nations in the world, they do not share the close sense of identity and messianic purpose of socialist nations. Capitalism, unlike socialism, is not founded on a sense of moral outrage over poverty and injustice. There is none of the crusading zeal on behalf of the underprivileged that lies at the core of socialist doctrines. Of course, capitalism has a strong moral foundation, but it is focused on the sturdy prerogatives of the self-reliant individual, and not on the plight of those unable to secure the necessities of life. Many doctrinaire capitalists view the lot of the poor as bad luck, regrettable but not such as to generate socially enforceable programs of assistance.[20] While there may be a private obligation of charity for such persons, there can be no public requirement of justice that they be assisted or that there be a redistribution of wealth for their benefit. Naturally this perspective is not congenial to programs of massive international assistance. Such assistance as is granted is usually best marketed when couched in terms of the battle against the Marxist spectre. Even in the matter of tyrannical government or gross violations of human rights, the perspective of this sturdy individualism is that such abuses are best met by the afflicted people themselves, and that outside intervention would constitute a violation of their autonomy.[21]

A further complication, of course, is that there are undisputably poor people within the United States. There are people without food and shelter who are nearly as impoverished as any in the world. When the issue of international assistance is raised, one inevitable response is that whatever resources are available should first go to the impoverished at home, that it is immoral to assist outsiders before those near at hand receive attention.

These are all formidable barriers to the development of inter-national moral sensitivity. The question is whether they are in-superable or whether they can be altered to allow such sensitivity to develop. The essential fact is that many of the obstacles are *attitudes* developed in response to certain conditions. The factual conditions are that the United States is a major power, that it is engaged in bitter rivalry with the Soviet Union, that nuclear weaponry contributes an edge of insecurity to this confrontation, and that the United States remains as securely capitalist as any nation in the world. All these are subject to evolution, for better or for worse. The United States has become a welfare state over the years, and its capitalism is presently less orthodox than in years past, though this too may alter. The arms race and confrontation with the Russians is subject to variations in intensity. Furthermore, the United States, like Russia, is gradually losing its overwhelming pre-eminence in the world. Only the latter trend is likely to be irreversible.

Whatever may develop, these attitudes need not remain unaltered. A more sophisticated appreciation of security requirements, for example, would not result in framing all events and conflicts, anywhere in the world, strictly in terms of the hostility between the United States and Russia. America's stature as a great power has nurtured a positive sense of responsibility for what occurs elsewhere that may be, and sometimes has been, channeled into a sense of moral concern and activism. Indeed, there is a messianic, moralistic vein of American consciousness, dating from the American Revolution, that has been tapped by such leaders as Woodrow Wilson, Franklin Roosevelt, John Kennedy and, briefly, by Jimmy Carter as well. The idea, dating back to the revolutionary era, is that the United States has an obligation to set a moral example for the rest of the world and to aid in the battle against repression elsewhere.[22] This messianic tone was reinforced by American experience during the world wars, whence it emerged with the sense of being a savior of the world and a guarantor of freedom and decency. The rest of the world has been less than overwhelmed by this idea, but it has remained an underground current, occasionally rising to the surface of American consciousness.

It need not be extraordinarily difficult for a forceful and imaginative leader to touch this sensitivity and shape it into broad support for moral responsibility. As previous discussions have shown, the material cost will not be great and the risk to national security quite small.[23] In fact, demonstrated concern for the welfare of those in other nations and impartial concern for human rights is likely to increase security. It is a policy which a sufficiently persuasive leader in the United States would not find ruled out by circumstance.[24] It has been done before, by Woodrow Wilson and by John Kennedy. But such a plan, to be effectual, would have to draw on a broad base of well-crafted support.

Short of absolute dictators, who are unlikely to be attracted by such ideas in any case, even the most forceful leader cannot simply decide to alter policies and then expect a government to change course instantly. Other segments of governments, as well as the public at large, must be cultivated. The leader seeking change must *first* look to domestic politics. Furthermore, such plans would have to be carefully devised to counter problems such as those that arise when concern for human rights appears to collide with requirements of security or the perceived threat of Marxism. Indeed, it is unlikely that moral sensitivity would prevail in all instances of conflicts of this sort. Imperfect moral sensitivity is better than none at all, and there is always the hope that the range of effective moral sensitivity will eventually spread beyond issues of easy agreement.[25] There is no guarantee that such sensitivity will finally prevail, but that does not imply that it is infeasible and that it must fail.

Even in the best case, where an effectual leader is able to build substantial support for moral sensitivity, there are other needs. Presidents of the United States are only in office a few years, and they are not able to carry out policies single-handedly. These policies require institutional support within government to make them viable and to preserve their effect. Furthermore, even in the absence of a well-intentioned leader, it is possible that installing such an apparatus would suffice to ignite moral fervor. Members of the United States Congress have tried this approach in the past few years.[26] Their efforts involve several elements. A first step is to establish mechanisms to create governmental awareness of, and attention to, human rights abuses and monitor the effects on them of US foreign policy. To this end, there is legislation requiring the State Department to monitor human rights in nations receiving aid from the United States and to make periodic reports to the Houses of Congress. To keep the State Department honest, other private and independent monitoring groups are regularly consulted. A further, also necessary, step is to prepare long-range plans for integrating moral concerns into a broader moral sensitivity. It seems likely that at least part of the reason for the neglect of international moral concerns by governmental leaders is that they simply do not know how to integrate them into their planning. There is no tradition of doing so and no established practice to guide them. A third step is to create a constituency for moral concerns, to establish groups and interests that will actively press for moral responsibility.[27]

With substantive support in the Houses of Congress and the cooperation of government agencies, it is quite possible that the above measures, by themselves, would suffice to alter United States practice. However, it is difficult to imagine what circumstances would cause this enthusiasm to develop. Congressmen are even more sensitive than Presidents, as a group, to varying political pressures. It is more difficult for them to resist such pressures, because they must act collectively and periodically seek re-election. It is more difficult for them to rise above the tasks of responding to the various pressures of their constituents. There is also the problem that they have relatively little influence as individuals. If they had a clear chance of success in changing national policy, more could be motivated to make the attempt.[28] As things stand, a few Congressmen are interested in such issues and are overwhelmed by those who are moved only by the more traditional concerns of anti-communism or American military and economic supremacy. Furthermore, the Congress has only indirect and limited influence on the course of foreign policy, which, after all, is traditionally the special prerogative of the executive branch. Congress can attempt to set limits and guidelines, but it is not structured to take the initiative on policy issues. Thus, while the support of Congress and the legislative machinery which it controls is necessary for a morally sensitive moral foreign policy, they are not sufficient to bring it into existence.

The spontaneous development of broad-based popular support for such policies from the grassroots is another possibility. If such enthusiasm were to emerge, the government would eventually respond. Spontaneous private support in the past has been a factor in shaping foreign policy. Jewish groups have some influence on United States' policy towards Israel, and Arab groups are attempting to learn similar techniques.[29] In more direct fashion, public outcry did seem to affect US policies towards South Africa in the summer of 1985 when President Reagan reversed his long-standing opposition to economic sanctions, though the measures he approved were minimal.[30]

The difficulty with this avenue, as the above examples illustrate, is that such outpourings are likely to be sporadic and episodal – to be sparked by particular events and to support specific outcomes. Where there are no direct and long-term interests, as in the ties binding American Jews and Israel, or American Blacks and South Africa, popular support is unlikely to sustain long-term policy or to respond to less than spectacular events.

The key, then, is a committed President. With such an individual in place, moral sensitivity is possible, though not inevitable. Lacking such, the prospects are much diminished. For any long-term success, efforts would have to be founded on a coherent policy which faced the practical difficulties and conflicts in its way, which was built on a carefully nurtured base of public and Congressional support, and which included the installation of the appropriate governmental machinery.

These attempts, while valuable, remain the efforts of single nations, in general acting independently of one another and without the benefit of an established international moral culture. The remaining question, then, is that of what steps might be taken – and *how* they might be taken – to create a culture of this sort. The existence of such a culture would be signaled not only by a common set of moral precepts and some means of exerting pressure for enforcement, but on conditions where acts of moral sensitivity and responsibility would not require the determined, and solitary, effort of exceptional individuals or nations. That is, such a culture would be signaled by moral sensitivity becoming a matter of course and a matter for all relevant actors. Efforts to establish an international moral culture have been made in the past, by the League of Nations and, most recently, by the United Nations. In the years following the founding of the United Nations, serious thought was given to the problems of establishing such a culture. Distinguished and reflective persons were enlisted to examine the practical and conceptual difficulties. The most visible fruit of this effort was the formulation of the Universal Declaration of Human Rights. It was ratified by the United Nations in 1948, but influential people recognized that a document, by itself, could have little practical effect. They organized commissions to set standards of human rights compliance in various parts of the world, to monitor progress in meeting standards, and to note deficiencies, as well as issue reports and publicize difficulties.[31]

These efforts were thorough, based on careful thought and analysis, and nurtured by a widespread core of good-will on the part of people whose views carried weight in the world. Yet the UN has had little discernible effect. The Universal Declaration has shaped the rhetoric of debate in the United Nations and in international dealings generally. It has had sufficient power occasionally to drive nations to hypocrisy. The latter is a not inconsiderable achievement, but overall the practical effect on the lives and well-being of human individuals has been slight. The commissions, though still functioning, have largely been forgotten and are clearly ineffectual.[32]

The reasons for these failures are not difficult to discern. The nations joining the UN have been loath to give up the prerogatives of their sovereignty. Thus, the UN has little practical means of enforcing sanctions and must depend for its very existence on the continued financial and political support of its members.[33] Then, too, the UN has grown enormously, swelled by small, poor, insecure nations who have little experience in international affairs and little sense of responsibility for them. The UN is thoroughly fragmented into shifting groups and coalitions of nations that are better suited to forestall threats to their interests than to work for constructive results. In light of this, the UN has become hopelessly and likely permanently politicized.[34] In the early years a measure of cohesiveness was possible because of the overwhelming domination of the United States. This domination, regrettable in itself, did sometimes allow effective action. However, the leading role of the US soon dissolved. It is unlikely that either it or any other nation or coalition of nations will achieve similar domination at any time in the foreseeable future.

The conditions of political fragmentation, politicization and jealous guarding or the prerogatives of sovereignty are thus likely to remain unchanged for some time to come. It is difficult to imagine what could happen to cause any significant change in this regard. For these reasons, the United Nations is not apt to become the vehicle of any significant improvement in international moral sensitivity or of the development of an international moral culture. Its chief value remains what it has traditionally been, simply to be available to help implement, as a tool, the beneficial changes or agreements which particular nations have decided by themselves to make. Its value is as a facilitator and enabling device, a mechanism for use by those who have already worked out their differences on their own initiative.

Another possibility remains. A spontaneous upsurge of moral sensitivity on the part of the mass of nations is quite unlikely. However, it is conceivable that a single group of influential nations or a single highly influential nation could exert pressure or set an example which others might, helter skelter, come to follow. If the influence of this mass of nations continued to spread, something like an informal moral culture could develop. Its particular advantage would be that it would allow the development of a moral culture in a gradual and loose-jointed manner, which would not require the overt renunciation of legal sovereignty on the part of particular nation-states. If the practice were to grow slowly, and there were no formal means of enforcement other than peer pressure, nations may gradually come to accept the constraints of a moral culture.

Sweden has not been notably successful in setting an example for others. Its very isolation, weakness and neutrality, the conditions which have helped nurture its moral sensitivity, also prevent it from serving as a significant influence on others. It is improbable that groups of the smaller nations of the world would be able to spark such a change. There is little prospect that they will develop the stability, cohesiveness or sense of responsibility requisite for such an effort.[35] The very large and powerful nations, the superpowers, remain. If either the United States or the USSR were to undertake to develop such sensitivity and put it into practice in an evenhanded manner, the influence on others would be substantial. If sensitivity developed in this way, the result might not be a single, cohesive moral culture. Possibly several would develop, with differing standards and therefore likely to clash or disagree over specific issues.

The odds are that significant numbers of nation-states would remain beyond the reach of any moral culture. While such conditions would not be ideal, they would certainly be vast improvements on the present and would generate some of the features of an international moral culture and nurture its sensitivity. Furthermore their existence may have the effect of preventing or mitigating the very worst abuses. This is not a simple or elegant picture, but it is not beyond the realm of the feasible and could produce substantial benefits. It is worth seeking.

Notes

Chapter 1: Issues and Challenges

1. As an example, note 'Famine Reports Show TV's Power', *New York Times* (22 November 1984).
2. The most pungent statements of the skeptical position are found in the works of H.J. Morgenthau, including: *Politics Among Nations*, 5th edn (New York: Alfred A. Knopf, 1973); *In Defense of National Interest* (New York: Alfred A. Knopf, 1952); and 'The Twilight of International Morality', *Ethics*, 58 (January 1948) 79–99. Hobbes himself, of course, was the original skeptic on these matters. See *Leviathan*, edited by M. Oakeshott (Oxford: Basil Blackwell, 1960) 83. Among contemporaries, George F. Kennan stands out as a vigorous proponent of the view that foreign policy and ethics should be kept separate. A recent, succinct statement of his position is 'Morality and Foreign Policy', *Foreign Affairs*, 64 (Winter 1985/86) 205–18.

    A number of authors provide useful general discussions of these skeptical theories, sometimes called 'realist'. They include: C. Beitz, *Political Theory and International Relations* (Princeton: Princeton University Press, 1979) 15–27; S. Hoffmann, *Duties Beyond Borders* (Syracuse: Syracuse University Press, 1981) 45–55; and M. Walzer, *Just and Unjust Wars* (New York: Basic Books, 1977) 3–20.

    Among recent works, one stands out as being stringently moralistic in the sense of wishing to establish international moral norms without detailed examination of their relation to the context of moral action or of their feasibility. See Beitz in *Political Theory and International Relations* (especially pp. 154–61). It must be noted that Beitz acknowledges this issue but argues that it does not undermine his position.
3. A most useful discussion of the importance of the Hobbesian state of nature for this issue can be found in Beitz, *op. cit.*, 27–50.
4. In the United States, for example, ordinary people, and newspaper editorialists, appear to conflate morality with sexual morality, so that lamentations about declines in moral standards refer to changes in norms of sexual behavior. Professional philosophers do not go that far, but the significant works of Anglo-American philosophy all presume that morality is essentially a matter of relations between individual persons.
5. A considerable body of opinion holds that institutions are not capable of being moral agents. George Kennan claims that governments are not moral agents in 'Morality and Foreign Policy', 205–6. Richard DeGeorge offers a thorough discussion of whether corporations can be moral agents in 'Can Corporations Have Moral Responsibility?', in T.L. Beauchamp and N.E. Bowie (eds), *Ethical Theory and Business*, 2nd edn (Englewood Cliffs: Prentice-Hall, 1979) 57–67.

190

6. Stanley Hoffmann denies any substantive body of international moral principles in *Duties Beyond Borders*, 98–9, as does George Kennan in 'Morality and Foreign Policy', 207–8. J.E. Hare and C.B. Joynt agree with this. See *Ethics and International Affairs* (New York: St. Martin's Press, 1982) 139–40. Charles Beitz clearly assumes that there *are* such norms in *Political Theory and International Relations*, 46–9.
7. Hobbes, *op. cit.*, 83.
8. The most recent and thorough statements of their positions are: R.M. Hare, *Moral Thinking* (Oxford: Clarendon Press, 1981) and R.B. Brandt, *A Theory of the Good and the Right* (Oxford: Clarendon, 1979).
9. See J. Rawls, *A Theory of Justice* (Cambridge: Harvard University Press, 1971); H. Shue, *Basic Rights* (Princeton: Princeton University Press, 1980); D.A.J. Richards, *A Theory of Reasons for Action* (Oxford: Oxford University Press, 1971); C. Beitz, *op. cit.*; R. Dworkin, *Taking Rights Seriously* (Cambridge: Harvard University Press, 1977); and A. Gewirth, *Reason and Morality* (Chicago: University of Chicago Press, 1978).
10. L. Simmons, *The Role of the Aged in Primitive Societies* (New Haven: Yale University Press, 1945) 232–3. See also W.G. Sumner and A.G. Keller, *The Science of Society*, vol. 4 (New Haven: Yale University Press, 1927) 1164.
11. 'Islam Today: The *Koran* as Constitution', *New York Times* (6 September 1974) and 'A Land of Prayer, Public Beheadings . . . and No Movie Houses', *US News*, 74 (7 May, 1973) 87.
12. K.S. Latourette, *The Chinese: Their History and Culture*, 4th edn (New York: Macmillan, 1964) 566.
13. R. Critchfield, 'Science and the Villager', *Foreign Affairs*, 61 (Fall 1982) 14–41.
14. T. Scanlon, 'Contracturalism and Utilitarianism', in A. Sen and B. Williams (eds) *Utilitarianism and Beyond* (Cambridge: Cambridge University Press, 1982) 103.
15. H. Shue, *op. cit.*, 13–34.
16. A. Gewirth, *op. cit.*, 21–42, though he would claim that these are not 'goods' in the sense of Rawls or Shue.
17. J. Rawls, *op. cit.*, 62 and 90–5.
18. *Ibid.*, 161–75.
19. Dworkin, *op. cit.*, 94–100 and 234.
20. See T. Harkin, 'Human Rights and Foreign Aid: Forging an Unbreakable Link', in P.G. Brown and D. MacLean (eds) *Human Rights and US Foreign Policy* (Lexington: Lexington Books, 1979) 15–26.
21. See, for example, 'To The Mounties, Far North Feels Like Hill Street', *New York Times* (27 February 1986) and 'Quebec's Far North: Land of Broken Promise?', *New York Times* (27 August 1985).
22. J.J. Putman, 'Greenland Feels the Winds of Change', *National Geographic*, 148 (September 1975) 366–93.
23. See 'Marshall Plan Again?', *New York Times* (9 January 1984).

24.   The best known of these is, of course, M. Friedman, *Capitalism and Freedom* (Chicago: University of Chicago Press, 1962) 133–6.
25.   A good example of this is the recent efforts of NASA to institute changes which will encourage people to report and publicize lapses in safety and design. See 'New NASA System Aims to Encourage Blowing the Whistle', *New York Times* (June 5, 1987). This, of course, is not equivalent to a program to encourage speaking out against immorality of any and all sorts but does illustrate some of the steps which would have to be taken to encourage greater moral responsibility.
26.   R.B. Brandt, 'Utilitarianism and the Rules of War' *Philosophy and Public Affairs*, 1 (Winter 1972) 145–65.
27.   At the height of the Cold War, for example, preventive war against the Soviet Union was considered, though rejected, by President Eisenhower. John F. Kennedy contemplated a nuclear strike during the Cuban Missile Crisis. 'How Leaders Think the Unthinkable', *New York Times* (2 September 1986).

Chapter 2: Violence in International Relations

1.   'Even in "Peacetime", 40 Wars are Going On', *US News*, 95 (11 July 1983) 44–5.
2.   In the past decade or so a number of scholars have turned to examining questions of the frequency of wars of various types, and their human cost in suffering and death. The quoted figures are taken from F.A. Beer's useful recent study and are offered with appropriate circumspection. See *Peace Against War: The Ecology of International Peace* (San Francisco: W.H. Freeman, 1981) 37–8. Beer notes that the period 1963–4 is the single interlude since the Second World War in which no major wars were underway (p. 34).
3.   There is, however, growing evidence that terrorist attacks previously thought to be the work of shadowy political groups are, in fact, sometimes the covert operations of governments of nation–states. See '12 Months of Terror: The Mideast Connection' (8 April 1986) and 'Loose-Linked Network of Terror: Separate Acts, Ideological Bonds' (28 April 1986), both in the *New York Times*. For a discussion of the ways in which nation-states support and manipulate terrorist groups, see N.C. Livingstone, *The War Against Terrorism* (Lexington: Lexington Books, 1982) 9–29.
4.   An excellent source on these matters is J.G. Gray, *The Warriors* (New York: Harper & Row, 1973) 29–69.
5.   John Somerville has a sensitive and perceptive discussion of this issue in 'Patriotism and War', *Ethics*, 91 (July 1981) 568–78.
6.   For instance, see C.F. Cortese, *Modernization, Threat, and the Power of the Military* (Beverly Hills: Sage Publications, 1976) 7 and 21–2.
7.   'A Quandary For Teheran', *New York Times* (24 July 1987).
8.   F.A. Beer estimates some 50 million deaths resulting from battle in

that conflict but does not attempt to estimate deaths from indirect causes. *Op. cit.*, p. 38.

9. N. Ascherson, 'No Place for Them', *New York Review of Books*, 33 (27 February 1986) 5–8.

10. M. Walzer, *Just and Unjust Wars* (New York: Basic Books, 1977) 51–3.

11. 'Supplementary Material from The New York Times News Service and The Associated Press', *New York Times* (22 August 1978).

12. Theodore Draper presents a useful analysis of the way such vague and universal goals have haunted and befuddled United States policy since the Second World War. See 'American Hubris: From Truman to the Persian Gulf', *New York Review of Books*, 34 (16 July 1987) 40–8.

13. B.M. Blechman is a keen observer of these matters. See 'Global Power Projection – The US Approach', in U. Ra'anan, R.L. Pfaltzgraff, Jr and G. Kemp (eds) *Projection of Power* (Hamden: The Shoe String Press, 1982) 174–86 and B.M. Blechman and S.S. Kaplan, *Force Without War: US Armed Forces as a Political Instrument* (Washington: The Brookings Institution, 1978).

14. For example, the United States has declared that any powerful Soviet MIG fighter planes appearing in Nicaragua would be eliminated by force. 'Is Nicaragua's Revolution Exportable?', *New York Times* (16 March 1986).

15. D. Pipes, 'Fundamentalist Muslims', *Foreign Affairs*, 64 (Summer 1986) 939–59.

16. This point is nicely illustrated by the fact that Reagan Administration officials were reluctant even to inform the US Congress of their plans for response in the event of an Iranian attack on American vessels in the Persian Gulf in the summer of 1987. See 'US and Iraq Plan a Joint Inquiry', *New York Times* (20 May 1987).

17. This point illustrates the folly of attempting to base policy on the present intentions of those in other nations. Some who argue in favor of unilateral disarmament, for example, claim that there is no evidence that the Russians intend to mount an attack on the United States. However, if the United States unilaterally jettisoned its weaponry, new possibilities would exist – and the way would be open for new intentions as well.

18. J.E. Hare and C.B. Joynt make use of a distinction similar to this one. They distinguish between capacity and intention and analyze the interaction between them. *Op. cit.*, 118–19. I believe that 'motives' serves as a useful and distinct addition.

19. In June of 1987 a United States Naval ship, the USS Stark, on patrol in the Persian Gulf, was struck by two missiles fired by an errant Iraqi warplane. The Stark was caught by surprise and severely damaged, with the loss of 37 lives, because, according to its captain, it did not perceive the Iraqi plane as a threat. Following this incident, US ships in the Gulf were placed on what the government called a 'hair-trigger alert'. They became, in other words, hypersensitive to possible threat. 'A Shouted Alarm, A Firey Blast', *Time* (1 June 1987); 'US Navy Defense Is on Hair Trigger on Escort in Gulf', *New York Times* (17 June 1987); and 'Rough Seas and New Names', *Time* (29 June 1987) 13.

20. 'US Says Iraqis Use Poison Gas; Shultz and Baghdad Official Meet', *New York Times* (26 March 1985); 'US Makes Direct Charge', *New York Times* (27 March 1985) and 'The Broken Treaty', *New York Times* (28 March 1985).

21. See 'How Assad Has Won', by S. McLeod, *New York Review of Books*, 33 (8 May 1986) 26 and 31–4.

22. The classic study of these difficulties is M.W. Boggs, *Attempts to Define and Limit 'Aggressive' Armament in Diplomacy and Strategy* (Columbia: University of Missouri Press, 1941).

23. Robert Oakely, for example, while a prominent member of the Reagan Administration and active in its anti-terrorist efforts, notes the decline in numbers of attacks in the summer of 1986 but does *not* attribute this result to the raid on Tripoli. 'International Terrorism', *Foreign Affairs*, 65 (1986) and 616–20.

24. Draper, *op. cit.*

25. In a recent instance the United States maneuvered spy ships in Soviet territorial waters, to test Russian defenses, it was claimed. This, of course, was viewed by the Soviets as a hostile gesture, or so they claimed. Nothing further has come from the incident, however. '2 US Ships Enter Soviet Waters Off Crimea to Gather Intelligence' and 'Soviet Lodges Protest', *New York Times* (19 March 1986).

26. Empirical studies show that signalling to friendly allies is most likely to be effective when the signal is sent to support a course of action already decided upon, but for which resolve is lacking. B.M. Blechman and S.S. Kaplan, 'US Military Forces as a Political Instrument', in C.W. Kegley, Jr and E.R. Whittkopf (eds) *Perspectives on American Foreign Policy* (New York: St. Martin's Press, 1983) 74.

27. The build-up of threats, counter-threats and hostile gestures is detailed in a series of *Newsweek* reports. See 'Kaddafi's Crusade' (7 April 1986) 20–4; 'Targeting A "Mad Dog"', (21 April 1986) 20–5 and 'Getting Rid of Kaddafi' (28 April) 18–25 of vol. 107.

28. Livingstone, *op. cit.*, 177–9.

29. Livingstone, for example, defines terrorism in this way: 'the word *terrorism* has come to mean acts of violence designed to influence political behavior through a process of intimidation' (*ibid.*, 2). But he then almost immediately notes that the term is widely used to cover instances where intimidation is not a primary goal, and he himself uses the term to refer to cases where intimidation is not a significant consideration (p. 4).

30. Again, Livingstone notes the connection between terrorism and political aims (*ibid.*, 4), while A.D. Sofaer analyzes the conceptual and practical difficulties involved in distinguishing common criminal activity from the violence of political groups. See 'Terrorism and the Law', *Foreign Affairs*, 64 (Summer 1986) 901–22.

31. The great majority of terrorist groups (86 per cent) have fewer than 50 members, according to Livingstone (*ibid.*, 37–8).

32. A now famous chart in *Newsweek* shows that many more Americans die in their bathtubs (150 in 1984) than in international terrorist attacks (25 in 1985) – 'How Safe?', 107 (2 June 1986) 7. The inclusion of deaths

of Europeans and citizens of the Middle East would push the toll much higher, but it would still very probably be less than the number of Americans who died from choking on food (3,100 in 1984) and certainly less than the number killed in automobile accidents (43,500 in 1984).

33. There is increasing evidence that Syria is the ultimate agent of many acts of terror, but it has worked hard to keep its connection secret and has thus far escaped the wrath of the United States and Western Europe. Libya's involvement is much easier to trace, and it has thus been the target of great enmity, not to mention bombing raids by the United States. See 'Loose-Linked Network of Terror: Separate Acts, Ideological Bonds', *New York Times*, *op. cit.*

34. However, no less an authority than Thomas C. Schelling believes that informal agreements can be extremely useful and important under certain conditions. See 'What Went Wrong With Arms Control?', *Foreign Affairs*, 64 (Winter 1985/86) 224.

35. For example, see *World Armaments and Disarmament: Stockholm International Peace Research Institute Yearbook, 1981* (London: Taylor & Francis, 1981) xvii, 15, and 16.

36. The arrest of an American newsman, Nicholas Daniloff, by the Soviet Union in the late summer of 1986 on charges of spying was viewed as a hostile gesture by the United States, with the potential of upsetting plans for talks on nuclear weapons control. At least one commentator considered the possibility that this may have been the intention of the act, desired by those in the Soviet government who wished to forestall such discussions. Ronald Steel, 'Why the Daniloff Arrest?', in an Op-Ed column in the *New York Times* (12 September, 1986).

37. Thomas C. Schelling holds views in agreement with this. Op. cit., 225–9.

38. Boggs, *op. cit.*

39. See footnote 32.

40. Livingstone, *op. cit.*, 97–124 and R.H. Kupperman and D. M. Trent, *Terrorism: Threat, Reality, Response* (Stanford: Hoover Institution Press, 1979) 48–74.

41. For a quick sketch of the fortunes of various American terrorist groups, see B.K. Johnpoll, 'Perspectives on Political Terrorism in the United States', in Y. Alexander (ed.) *International Terrorism: National, Regional, and Global Perspectives* (New York: Praeger, 1976) 30–45.

42. J.P. Bennett and T.L. Saaty, 'Terrorism: Patterns for Negotiation; A Case Study Using Heirarchies and Holarchies', 244–84, and R.H. Kupperman, R.H. Wilcox and H.A. Smith, 'Crisis Management: Some Opportunities', 224–43, both in Kupperman and Trent, *op. cit.*

43. Livingstone, for example, has evidence that members of the German Red Army Faction were demoralized by the success of bold German anti-terrorist actions, *op. cit.*, 179–82.

44. These issues are lucidly discussed by the current Legal Adviser for the Department of State of the United States, Abraham D. Sofaer. See Sofaer, *op. cit.*, 901–22.

45. Sofaer presents a useful sketch of the development of the tradition of

providing political asylum in the United States (*op. cit.*, 906–10), and specifically examines the recent treaty with Great Britain concerning the extradition of IRA suspects (p. 910). See also 'Pact With Britain on Extraditions Backed By Senate', *New York Times* (18 July 1986).

46. In a single issue of the *New York Times* there were reports of a Kurd attack on the Iranian embassy in Paris and of violence involving Basques near the border with Spain in north-eastern France. '1 Killed, 8 Hurt in Paris Explosion' and 'Suddenly Basques Find Haven Full of Hazards' (9 September 1986).

47. Sofaer makes comments relevant to this suggestion (*op. cit.*, 906).

48. See footnote 45.

49. See Sofaer, *op. cit.*, even though, as one commentator usefully points out that Mid-East terrorist groups wreak far more havoc on one another, and on non-combatant Middle Easterners, than on Western Europeans. See Saul Bakhash, 'Reign of Terror', *New York Review of Books*, 33 (14 August 1986) 13.

50. Refer to footnote 3 of this chapter, as well as Saul Bakhash, *op. cit.*, 12–4.

Chapter 3: Sovereignty

1. The island nation of Kiribati, for example, has a population of 58,000 in a territory of 264 square miles while Liechtenstein has a population of 25,000 in an area of 61 square miles. *The Hammond Almanac* (Maplewood: Hammond Almanac Inc., 1981) 603 and 612.

2. T. Buergenthal, 'Domestic Jurisdiction, Intervention, and Human Rights: The International Law Perspective', in P.G. Brown and D. MacLean (eds) *Human Rights and US Foreign Policy* (Lexington: Lexington Books, 1979) 111–20.

3. It is extremely difficult, given the years of turmoil and present isolation, to establish precise estimates of either the population of Cambodia or the numbers killed Recent estimates are that one to one and a half million Cambodians died as the result of the policies of the Khmer Rouge. 'Controversy Over Toll', *New York Times* (13 March 1987). The American CIA gave a rough estimate of a population of 5 million in 1980. *The Hammond Almanac, op. cit.*, 540.

4. No less a figure than Senator George McGovern urged in 1978 that an international force be created to intervene in Cambodia to attempt to halt the gruesome activity of the Khmer Rouge. His efforts had little effect both because of a distaste for further adventures in South-east Asia and daunting practical difficulties of mounting and deploying such a force. 'Supplementary Material from The New York Times News Services and The Associated Press', *New York Times* (22 August 1978).

   The Vietnamese invasion in 1978 inescapably polarized the great powers, with Russia supporting the Vietnamese and their Lon Nol government, while the United States, wishing to maintain its good relations with China, saw fit to endorse the Khmer Rouge. Most recently there has been a movement to charge the Pol Pot regime with the crime of genocide under the auspices of the United Nations. 'Campaign Seeks Genocide Trial of Khmer Rouge' (13 March 1987) and 'Cambodia's Unpunished Genocide' (21 May 1987), both in the *New York Times*. It would cost the nations of the world little to reaffirm their declared opposition to genocide by supporting this effort, and a concrete demonstration of serious effort to enforce the ban on genocide would be worth a great deal. It would take some courage on the part of political leaders and some determined effort to set aside politics as usual in order to join together to support their lofty rhetoric with concrete action, but there is no reason to believe it should be impossible for them to do so.

5. In the summer of 1986 turmoil in South Africa reached a crescendo. In response, Western European nations and the United States began to consider seriously applying economic sanctions in the effort to force peaceful change and perhaps avert violent and bloody revolution. In September the nations of Western Europe agreed to sanctions which were both weak and received without enthusiasm by the business community. 'Western European Nations Impose Weakened Sanctions on Pretoria' and 'Europe's Industry Cool to Sanctions', both in the *New York Times* (17 September 1986). This was followed some days later by votes in the US Congress to override President Reagan's veto in order to impose sanctions of its own. 'Africa Issue: Not Gone by Any Means', *New York Times* (10 October 1986). Near the end of October major multinational corporations began an exodus from South Africa. 'IBM to Pull Out From South Africa As Problems Grow' (22 October 1986) and 'Why GM Decided to Quit South Africa' (30 October 1986), both in the *New York Times*. It was later argued that these actions were largely cosmetic, that corporations had simply transferred control of their operations to local subsidiaries and had not ceased to function in South Africa. 'Slash Ties, Apartheid Foes Urge', *New York Times* (9 February 1987). This was followed later in the year by the demand of the Reverend Leon Sullivan, author of the Sullivan Principles governing proper conduct of corporations in South Africa, that corporations completely withdraw on grounds that quiet pressure had proven ineffective and that the South African government appeared determined to preserve the status quo. 'Sullivan Asks End of Business Links With South Africa', *New York Times* (4 June 1987).

    By the summer of 1987 the world had its attention focused on the war in the Persian Gulf, the international debt crisis and the antics of Lieutenant-Colonel Oliver North, William Casey and Admiral John Poindexter of Ronald Reagan's National Security Council. It had largely forgotten about South Africa. Sadly, it will probably require an outbreak of mass violence to regain its attention.

6. 'Suddenly Basques Find Haven Full of Hazards', *New York Times* (9 September 1986).

7. Studies of the United Nations' efforts in these areas show that its successes have been patchy at best. See P.R. Baehr and L. Gordenker,

The United Nations: Reality and Ideal (New York, Praeger, 1984); J.F. Green, *The United Nations and Human Rights* (Washington: The Brookings Institution, 1956) and T. Zuijdwijk, *Petitioning the United Nations: A Study in Human Rights* (New York: St. Martin's, 1982). More recently the UN Secretariat has responded to budgetary difficulties by cutting disproportionate shares of its funding for the UN's own Human Rights Center. Secretary General Javier Perez de Cuellar has been less than enthusiastic in his support of human rights issues. 'West Seeks Budget Reprieve for UN Rights Effort', *New York Times* (9 June 1987).

8.   A. James, *Sovereign Statehood* (London, Boston and Sydney: Allen & Unwin, 1986) 152.

9.   Jimmy Carter stated the point nicely in his commencement speech at Notre Dame in 1977 when discussing US relations with China:

> It's important that we make progress toward normalizing relations with China. We see the American and Chinese relationship as a central element in our global policy, and China as a key force for global peace. We wish to cooperate closely with the creative Chinese people on the problems that confront all mankind, and we hope to find a formula which can bridge some of the difficulties that still separate us.

President Jimmy Carter, 'Commencement Address at the University of Notre Dame', in D.P. Kommers and G.D. Loescher (eds) *Human Rights and American Foreign Policy* (Notre Dame: University of Notre Dame Press, 1979) 307.

10. This point is urged with great vigor by D. Luban in 'Just War and Human Rights', *Philosophy & Public Affairs*, 9 (Winter 1980) 160–81. See also: C. Beitz, *Political Theory and International Relations* (Princeton: Princeton University Press, 1979) 79 n.; and M. Walzer, *Just and Unjust Wars* (New York: Basic Books, 1977) 98–9.

11. Michael Walzer is the most prominent advocate of this view. See *op. cit.*, 53–5.

12. Luban, *op. cit.*

13. One scholar who possibly shares this view is Gerald Doppelt, 'Walzer's Theory of Morality in International Relations', *Philosophy and Public Affairs*, 8 (Fall 1978) 3–27 and 'Statism Without Foundations', *Philosophy and Public Affairs, 9, (Summer 1980) 398–404.

14. As R. Bendix notes, 'In the past, one ruler stood at the summit of the social heirarchy. Rulers possessed supreme status, great wealth, and commanding authority' (p. 21). He states as well that, 'The *principle* of hereditary monarchy was challenged only some two centuries ago' (p. 4). *Kings or People* (Berkeley: University of California Press, 1978). Bendix provides a thorough discussion of the usual arguments in favor of the legitimacy of the idea of hereditary monarchy and of the transition to new views of legitimacy. See also: J. N. Figgis, *The Divine Right of Kings*, 2nd edn (Cambridge: Cambridge University Press, 1922).

15. I. Buruma, 'Marcos and Morality', *The New York Review of Books*, 34 (13 August 1987) 24–7.

16. J. Locke, *The Second Treatise of Government*, edited by T.P. Peardon (Indianapolis and New York: Bobbs-Merrill Co., 1952). See p. 105 for a nice juxtaposition of these two elements.

17. Gary Wills, however, has recently argued that Thomas Jefferson was more profoundly influenced by the Scottish Philosopher James Wilson. *Inventing America: Jefferson's Declaration of Independence* (Garden City: Doubleday, 1978) 248–55. His views on this matter, however, have received a careful and skeptical response from Edmund S. Morgan, 'The Heart of Jefferson', *The New York Review of Books*, 25 (17 August 1978) 38–40.

18. E.O. Reischauer, *Japan: The Story of a Nation*, revised edition (New York: Alfred A. Knopf, 1974) 216–19.

19. Socrates' arguments on this matter are nicely laid out and examined by N.E. Bowie and R.L. Simon, *The Individual and the Political Order* (Englewood Cliffs: Prentice-Hall, 1977) 234–7.

20. The legal scholars John Austin and John Chipman Gray make this claim. See 'John Austin: A Positivist Conception of Law', 35–6 and 'John Chipman Gray: A Realist Conception of Law', 44–5 in J. Feinberg and H. Gross (eds) *Philosophy of Law*, 2nd edn (Belmont: Wadsworth Publishing Co., 1980).

21. The turmoil and shifts of personnel and policy which followed the success of the Sandinista revolution are outlined in detail by Shirley Christian, *Nicaragua: Revolution in the Family* (New York: Random House, 1985) 98–112.

22. One recent study concludes:

> At one time westerners were concerned with freedom and fearful of the state. But in the latter half of the twentieth century they have become so enamored of government they have, for the most part, ceased even to perceive freedom and government as antipodes.

B. Ginsberg, *The Captive Public* (New York: Basic Books, 1986) 230–1. Ginsberg's thesis is supported by a Gallup Poll of 1977–8, which shows that three-quarters of the adults interviewed had at least some confidence in Congress and the Supreme Court, a higher percentage of approval than they gave to large business concerns (about two-thirds). The Gallup Opinion Index, *Religion in America 1977–78* (Princeton: American Institute of Public Opinion).

23. Merrill Jensen points out that there was less than unanimous support for independence in 1776, and it was not altogether clear that all colonies would support the Declaration of Independence. *The Founding of a Nation* (New York: Oxford University Press, 1968) 667–704. Robert Middlekauff notes that of the population of 2,500,000 at the time of the Revolution (p. 32), only 200,000 men actually served in the Continental Army or the various militias (p. 547), while 500,000 colonists remained loyal to Great Britian throughout the war (pp. 549–50). *The Glorious Cause* (New York and Oxford: Oxford University Press, 1982). Another scholar states, 'The Revolution was in some respects a civil war – protracted hostilities between irreconcilably antagonistic segments of society within the same country', and notes that approximately 19,000

colonists served actively in some 42 loyalist provincial corps. R.M. Calhoun, *The Loyalists in Revolutionary America 1760–1781* (New York: Harcourt Brace Jovanovich, 1973) 502.

24. This analysis owes much to Charles Beitz's useful examination and criticism. *Op. cit.*, 97–105.

25. Again, Beitz provides careful elaboration and criticism of this intuition, *ibid.* The core idea is also examined by M. Walzer, *op. cit.*, 53–63.

26. In part this realization is the basis of the view that it is necessary to introduce bills of rights into the constitutions of nations – to delimit the sphere which must be protected from majority interference. This idea has played a central role in the constitutional philosophy of Judge Robert Bork, among others. 'Neutral Principles and Some First Amendment Problems', *Indiana Law Journal*, 47 (Fall 1971) 1–37 or 'Styles in Constitutional Theory', *South Texas Law Journal*, 26 (1985) 383–95. The argument of the present work, however, is that it may not be sufficient to have restraints on majority will *within* a constitutional structure; but may be necessary to restrain majority will in the very choice of government itself.

27. Beitz himself wishes to replace popular will with justice as the fundamental criterion of legitimacy. However, he uncharacteristically waffles when faced with a clear conflict between the two, and says it may in some cases be proper for popular will to take precedence over justice. *Op. cit.*, 102–4. David Luban clearly believes that justice should take precedence. Luban, *op. cit.*

28. H. Shue, *Basic Rights: Subsistence, Affluence, and US Foreign Policy* (Princeton: Princeton University Press, 1980).

29. Shue, *op. cit.*, ix.

30. Among the more balanced treatments of the CIA's activities include R.L. Borosage and J. Marks (eds) *The CIA File* (New York: Grossman Pub., 1976). Philip Agee presents a useful day-to-day description of the CIA's activities in *Inside the Company: CIA Diary* (New York: Stonehill Pub., 1975).

31. R.K. Ramazani, *Revolutionary Iran* (Baltimore and London: The Johns Hopkins University Press, 1986) 74–6; and C.M. Helms, *Iraq* (Washington: The Brookings Institution, 1984) 185–94.

32. A. Sampson, *Sovereign State: The Secret History of ITT* (London: Hodder & Stoughton, 1973) and R. Sobel, *ITT* (New York: Truman Nalley Books-Times Books, 1982) 302–35 and 349.

33. J. Contreras and J. Whitmore, 'Can Anyone Save Haiti?', *Newsweek*, 108 (25 August 1986) 47.

34. 'Haiti's Justice is Ramshackle and in Need of Money', *New York Times* (20 September 1986).

35. Both the Philippines and Mexico have begun to recognize the importance of these problems and to attempt to do something to address them, but the practices are so deeply entrenched that only fitful progress has been made. See 'In Mexico, the Graft Loosens Its Grip', *New York Times* (17 April 1987) and 'Aquino's Moral Tone: Is Anybody Listening?', *New York Times* (30 October 1986).

36. John King Fairbank, for example, has forcefully argued that Mao

and the government he established can only be fully understood by placing them in the context of the ancient patterns of Chinese history. 'Numero Uno', *The New York Review of Books*, 22 (1 May 1975) 18–20. Aileen Kelly discusses some of the continuities between Tsarist Russia and Marxist Russia in 'Russia's Old New Right', *The New York Review of Books*, 30 (17 February 1983) 34–7.

37. No less an observer than the redoubtable conservative Edmund Burke has noted this – and then claimed that this does not provide a good ground for wishing to tinker with governments. He avowed:

> The errors and defects of old establishments are visible and palpable. It calls for little ability to point them out . . . To make everything the reverse of what they have seen is quite as easy as to destroy. No difficulties occur in what has never been tried.
> At once to preserve and to reform is quite another thing.

E. Burke, *Reflections on the Revolution in France*, edited by T.H.D. Mahoney (Indianapolis: Bobbs-Merrill, 1955) 196.

38. K. Rogal with R. Moreau, 'The Youngest Martyrs', *Newsweek*, 101 (21 March 1983) 51.

39. As one commentator describes the most notorious of the oposition parties:

> Mujahedin-e Khalq members and sympathisers were predominantly young, male and female, and came from traditional middle class homes: merchants, shopkeepers, clerics, and artisans. They were drawn to the party because it offered modern, egalitarian interpretations of Islam – something quite apart from the medieval interpretations current among traditional ulema. They wanted to create an Islamic society which was forward-looking, democratic and equalitarian. (p. 189)

The Tudeh Party, the foremost Marxist party of Iran, he says,

> drew its strength from modern middle classes [sic] and industrial workers. Its stress on modernism and progress in the socio-cultural field had a popular appeal for women and young people. (p. 200)

D. Hiro, *Iran Under the Ayatollahs* (London, Boston and Henley: Routledge & Kegan Paul, 1985).

40. A fine description of the very different attitude and perspective to law and its relation to ordinary citizens can be found in Harold J. Berman's *Justice in the USSR* (New York: Vintage Books, 1963).

41. See, for example, S. Bialer, *The Soviet Paradox* (New York: Alfred A. Knopf, 1986) 15–6 and M.S. Shatz, *Soviet Dissent in Historical Perspective* (Cambridge: Cambridge University Press, 1980) 157–8.

42. 'Philippine Defense Chief Is Stirring Anxiety', *New York Times* (11 September 1986); 'Defense Chief Says He May Quit Manila Cabinet', *New York Times* (19 October 1986); 'Aquino Meets With Her Angry Defense Minister', *New York Times* (21 October 1986) and 'Philippine Defense Chief Faults Aquino', *New York Times* (26 October 1986).

43. 'US Sends a Warning to Manila Defense Minister', *New York Times* (30 October, 1986) and 'US Voices Praise for Aquino Action', *New York Times* (24 November 1986).
44. 'Aquino Said to Win in a Key Plebiscite on a Constitution', *New York Times* (3 February 1987).
45. Beitz, once more, works out a helpful analysis of what counts as intervention, *op. cit.*, 71–5.
46. John Somerville presents an outraged analysis of the connection between military activity and the reflexive urge to participate, in 'Patriotism and War', *Ethics*, 91 (July 1981) 568–78.
47. Many of those struggling against oppression throughout the world applauded Jimmy Carter for simply taking a stand in favor of human rights, and felt that his advocacy genuinely assisted their efforts. As Gaddis Smith notes:

    But the victims [of human rights violations] who survived and had enough freedom to speak out applauded the American policy and believed that conditions would have been far worse had the United States remained silent. (p. 55)

    Morality, Reason and Power (New York: Hill and Wang, 1986). See also S. Goode, *The Foreign Policy Debate* (New York: Franklin Watts, 1984) 30–2.
48. R.B. Cullen, 'Soviet Jewry', *Foreign Affairs*, 65 (Winter 1986/87) 252–66.
49. Aristotle, *Politics*, translated by E. Barker (New York: Oxford University Press, 1962) 1.
50. As the Ayatollah Khomeini himself avowed in an interview in 1980, Islam contains the 'desire to abolish nationality and unite all mankind in a single community, under the aegis of a state indifferent to the matter of race and color'. R. Khomeini, *Islam and Revolution*, translated by H. Algar (Berkeley: Mizan Press, 1981) 332. An American commentator notes:

    The nation [of Iran] is now the nation of Islam and recognizes no distinctions between Iranian and non-Iranian . . . By Islam, the republic means Khomeini's militant and austere version, an ideology that admits of no national boundaries or sovereignty. (p. 138)

    J.W. Limbert, *Iran* (Boulder: Westview Press, 1987). See also, Ramazani, *op. cit.*, 19–23.
51. B. Knei-Paz, *The Social and Political Thought of Leon Trotsky* (Oxford: Oxford University Press, 1978) 337–66.
52. Once more Beitz has worthwhile discussions of this issue, *op. cit.*, 105–15.
53 See footnote 6.

Chapter 4: National Boundaries

1. Alan James notes:

    > The hundred and seventy or so states which engage in inter-national relations have several characteristics in common. Perhaps the most fundamental is that all are territorially based. Each of them represents a physical sector of the land mass of the globe.

    Sovereign Statehood (London, Boston and Sydney: Allen & Unwin, 1986) 13.

2. As James puts it:

    > over the last hundred years the advance in technology together with an increased formalization of international relations has resulted in almost every square kilometre of the earth's surface being allocated to one sovereign state or another, with virtually all frontiers being tidily delineated and clearly demarcated. Thus to all intents and purposes it is possible to say that, jurisdictionally speaking, there is never any doubt about where one stands, and that one always stands on the domain of a single sovereign state.

    Ibid., 31.

3. See James again, 31–4.
4. The connection between land, power and the intrigues of sovereign states is one of the themes of Lewis J. Perelman's 'Speculations on the Transition to Sustainable Energy', *Ethics*, 90 (April 1980) 392–416.
5. This point is vividly illustrated by the enormous contrast between Haiti and the Dominican Republic. They are neighbors, sharing a moderately small island in the Caribbean. The Dominican Repub-lic, however, is both politically stable and modestly prosperous, in stark contrast to impoverished and embattled Haiti. 'Haitian Crisis Worries Neighboring Dominicans', *New York Times* (3 December 1987).
6. In an article entitled '"I Feel a Lot Poorer Today"', *Time* put the matter this way:

    > Though only one in five US households invests directly in the stock market, its gyrations can hurt everyone. People who had never bought stock in their lives were struggling to figure out what the wild ride on Wall Street meant to them, their jobs, their families and their security . . . But the market's health does have an enormous impact on consumer confidence and thus on economic growth. The mechanism is as much psychological as it is financial.

    Vol. 130 (2 November 1987) 37.

7. On various occasions relief convoys have been ambushed and burned, refugees attacked and relief workers have been ordered to leave contested areas. Furthermore, these abuses occur in addition to other irregularities in handling relief supplies as well as bureaucratic

impediments to their distribution. *New York Times*: 'Ethiopian Policies Blamed in Famine' (21 May 1986); 'Ethiopian Guerrillas Raid Convoy, Halting Drought Aid' (27 October 1987); 'Ethiopia's Wars Foil Aid to Hungry' (3 December 1987) and 'Ethiopia, Pressing War on Rebels, Bars Aid Workers in Drought Area' (7 April 1988).

8. Thus, the *World Press Review* quotes the *Asahi Shimbun* of Tokyo: 'America has lost moral ground' (p. 14) and the *Globe and Mail* of Toronto: 'America has yielded to an atavastic impulse to wield its power for the purpose of reordering the world in its own image and to its own liking' (p. 17); both from vol. 30 (December 1983). In each of these statements in the foreign press, there is a clear identification of the actions of the Reagan Administration with the United States as a whole.

9. Russell noted with dismay:

> The prospect [of war] filled me with horror, but what filled me with even more horror was the fact that the anticipation of carnage was delightful to something like ninety per cent of the population . . . I had supposed until that time that it was quite common for parents to love their children, but the war persuaded me it is a rare exception. I had supposed that most people like money better than almost anything else, but I discovered that they liked destruction even better.

The Autobiography of Bertrand Russell, vol. II (London: Allen and Unwin, 1968) 17.

10. Anna Quindlen, a columnist for the *New York Times*, described the bonding effect of World Series Fever in the following way:

> Playoff games produce real community. I monitored the final National League playoff game in stages: first with an entire office full of people clustered around a television in midtown Manhatten; then in the cab with the radio; next in a commuter bus in which two people were listening to Walkman radios and reporting to all assembled. . . , and then to a street being patrolled by a man in a white Pinto who kept leaning out and yelling, "Top of the 16th and still tied". I made it home to watch the last inning with my husband.

'Life in the 30's', *New York Times* (22 October 1986).

11. Hegel claims: 'War has the higher significance that by its agency, as I have remarked elsewhere, "the ethical health of peoples is preserved"'; and:

> In peace civil life continually expands; all its departments wall themselves in, and in the long run men stagnate. Their idiosyncracies become continually more fixed and ossified. But for health the unity of the body is required, and if its parts harden into exclusiveness, that is death.

Philosophy of Right, translated by T.M. Knox (Oxford: Oxford University, 1949) 210–11.

12. Following the Los Angeles Olympics of 1984 *Time* observed:

> some delirious need to wave American flags has surfaced, fanning a passion previously associated with burning them. The sentimental tears and cheers of the pre-Olympic torch run turned into unembarrassed howls and shrieks last week for US medalists taking a transcontinental victory lap.

'One Last US Victory Lap', 124 (27 August 1984) 38.

13. 'A Third of Afghans Have Fled', *New York Times* (20 May 1987).

14. 'Afghans Away from Home: Rugs, Guns and Fear', *New York Times* (10 April 1987).

15. 'Mexico's New Type of Emigrant: Well-to-Do, Skilled, Disillusioned', *New York Times* (21 October 1986).

16. These 'guest workers' have been the topic of considerable controversy and soul searching in the past few years. See 'Europe Turns Its Back on Migrant Workers', *US News*, 87 (29 October 1979) 74–7; P. Gupte, 'Germany's Guest Workers', *New York Times Magazine* (19 August 1984) 88–91; and G. Apitzsch and N. Dittmar, 'Integration or Repatriation?', *UNESCO Courier*, 38 (September 1985) 18–20.

17. *New York Times*: 'Prison Portrayed by Shcharansky' (14 February 1986); '9 Years Later, Shcharansky Seems the Same' (16 February, 1986); 'Shcharansky Skeptical on Soviet Rights Policy' (17 February 1986); 'Shcharansky Urges Public Pressure on Soviet' (10 May 1986); and 'Israelis Still See Future for Talks with Soviet' (25 August 1986).

18. The Soviet Union still has no unrestricted right of emigration. Guidelines issued in the fall of 1986 state that permission to emigrate *may* be given in cases where close family members who reside abroad invite Soviet citizens to join them. The government retains the prerogative of deciding how to interpret these guidelines and also lists nine categories of reasons for denying emigration. 'Soviet Union Lists Formal New Rules on Who May Leave', *New York Times* (8 November 1986).

19. These arguments show intriguing similarity to those advanced by Socrates in the 'Crito'. See, for example, 'Crito', translated by H. Tredennick in *The Complete Dialogues of Plato*, edited by E. Hamilton and H. Cairns (Princeton: Princeton University, 1961) 28–39. R.E. Allen has a probing analysis of Socrates' views in *Socrates and Legal Obligation* (Minneapolis: University of Minnesota, 1980) 65–113.

20. According to 'Slow Pace Seen for Revamping Security Clearances' in the *New York Times* of 28 July 1986, the number of those with security clearances is 3.5 million.

21. West Berlin, for one, has made significant efforts to integrate its migrant population, which in 1979 amounted to 10 per cent of the total. 'West Berlin Seeks Better Future for Its Foreigners', *New York Times* (5 October 1979).

22. R. Carroll and others, 'The Debris of Our War', *Newsweek*, 91 (17 April 1978) 70–3.

23.   B. Krishner, 'Japan: Boat People Stay Away', *Newsweek*, 94 (3 Sep-
      tember 1979) 46, and 'The Icelanders Want Only to be Left Alone',
      New York Times (15 December 1979).
24.   According to the *New York Times*, 700,000 Koreans presently live
      in Japan. 'They Call Japan Home, but Are Hardly at Home' (1
      February 1988). See also, R.H. Mitchell, *The Korean Minority in
      Japan* (Berkeley and Los Angeles: University of California, 1967)
      and E.O. Reischauer, *Japan: The Story of a Nation*, revised edition
      (New York, Knopf, 1974).
25.   W. Brandt *et al.*, *North-South* (Cambridge: MIT Press, 1980);
      A. Fishlow, et al., *Rich and Poor Nations in the Global Economy*
      (New York: McGraw-Hill, 1978); B.P. Menon, *Bridges Across the
      South* (New York: Pergamon, 1980); B. D. Nossiter, *The Global
      Struggle for More* (New York: Harper & Row, 1987); J.W. Sewell
      et al., *The United States and World Development: Agenda 1980* (New
      York: Prager, 1980) and J.W. Sewell *et al.*, *The United States and
      World Development: 1977* (New York and London: Praeger, 1977).
26.   See, for example, H. Shue, *Basic Rights: Subsistence, Affluence, and
      US Foreign Policy* (Princeton: Princeton University Press, 1980) 13–64.
27.   C.R. Beitz, *Political Theory and International Relations* (Princeton:
      Princeton University Press, 1979) 129–36.
28.   A good example of this is the Law of the Sea Treaty, in which
      an agreement concerning exploitation of wealth on the sea bed
      has been negotiated. Provisions of the treaty include payments to
      poorer nations which do not have the means to mine ocean floors.
      The treaty has, of course, been negotiated by representatives of
      national governments. E.L. Richardson, 'Seabed Mining and the
      Law of the Sea', *Department of State Bulletin*, 80 (October 1980)
      60–4. Unfortunately, the final acceptance of the treaty was stalled
      by the then new Reagan Administration and is yet to be completed
      and ratified. 'President Replaces Top US Diplomats at Law of Sea
      Talks', *New York Times* (9 March 1981).
29.   This view is elaborated in striking fashion by Peter Singer in
      his article 'Famine, Affluence and Morality', *Philosophy & Public
      Affairs*, 1 (Spring 1972) 229–43.
30.   Malham Wakin has discovered an illuminating example of this view
      in the response of one US Senator to an incident during the US
      involvement in Vietnam:

           His [Senator Hughes of Iowa] remarks were made in the context of
           Senate hearings regarding the nominations for promotion of general
           officers, two of whom were air force officers who had previously
           been in General John D. LaVelle's chain of command in Southeast
           Asia during the period that General Lavelle was accused of ordering
           falsfied reports of bombing strikes which violated the written rules
           of agreement. Senator Hughes opposed the promotion of these two
           officers on the grounds that they should have questioned General
           Lavelle's orders but did not.

      M. M Wakin, 'The Ethics of Leadership', in M.M. Wakin (ed.)

War, Morality, and the Military Profession (Boulder: Westview, 1979)
207. The example shows how, in the military context, those who are
in position to be responsible may be thought to have the obligation
to use their situation to try to make a difference.

31. There is an international understanding that nations should seek the
goal of giving 0.7 per cent of their gross national product in foreign
assistance, a goal few have reached. Even this modest effort could
make a considerable difference for those in underdeveloped portions of
the world. A. Arnesen, 'Perspective of Norwegian Development Aid
in the 1980's' in *Poverty and Aid*, edited by J.R. Parkensen (Oxford:
Basil Blackwell, 1983) 127.

32. Nauru, a small island in the Western Pacific near the equator, is
entirely unremarkable except for its potash deposits. Their mining
and export resulted in a per capita income of $21,400 in 1987, one of
the highest in the world. Unfortunately, it is expected that these riches
will be exhausted sometime in the next decade. *World Almanac, 1988*
(New York: Pharos, 1987) 702. See also R. Trumbull, 'The World's
Richest Little Isle', *New York Times Magazine* (7 March 1982) 25ff.

33. See footnote 28.

34. S. Weintraub, *Trade Preferences for Less-Developed Countries* (New
York, Washington and London: Praeger, 1966); and H. Shutt, *The
Myth of Free Trade* (Oxford and London: Basil Blackwell, 1985).

35. W. Shawcross, *The Quality of Mercy: Cambodia, Holocaust, and
Modern Conscience* (New York: Simon & Schuster, 1984).

36. What has come to be called 'Fund conditionality' is a central theme
of the essays in *The Political Morality of The International Monetary
Fund*, edited by R.J. Myers (New Brunswick and Oxford: Transaction
Books, 1987). See in particular L. Taylor's 'IMF Conditionality:
Incomplete Theory, Policy, Malpractice', 33–45; H. B. Schechter's
'IMF Conditionality and The International Economy: A US Labor
Perspective', 47–63; and D. Gale Johnson's 'IMF Conditionality and
Agriculture in the Developing Countries', 127–40.

37. Certainly its problems are large enough, however. They include
vicious and persistent political instability allied with a flourishing
cocaine trade which threatens to rule the entire nation, as well as a
crushing international debt. Recent and thorough studies of Bolivia's
problems include: J. Dunkerley, *Rebellion in the Veins* (London:
Verso, 1984) and H.S. Klein, *Bolivia: The Evolution of a Multi-Ethnic
Society* (New York and Oxford: Oxford University Press, 1982).

38. Its problems are stated vividly by Thomas S. Goslin in the *Christian
Century*. He notes that despite its vast mineral wealth,

> the country is plagued by high rates of infant mortality and of
> illiteracy. Its schools are inadequate. The government is too poor
> to provide social services or decent medical care.

'Bolivia: A Nation in Crisis', 102 (6–13 February 1985) 18. It is clear
from Goslin and others that Bolivia's problems are ultimately social
and will be successfully met only through social transformation and
not simply the infusion of money.

39. See Economic Commission for Latin America and The Caribbean, *Debt, Adjustment, and Renegotiation in Latin America* (Boulder: Lynne Rienner, 1986) for an extended analysis of Bolivia's debt and its sometimes contentious relations with the IMF.

40. The problems of coping with past exploitation are both theoretical and practical. The people who were directly harmed are often long dead and may be impossible to identify in any case. The same applies to their exploiters. Further, the descendants of those exploited may presently be in more fortunate circumstances than the descendants of the exploiters, and the former need not have endured any suffering in *their* lifetime, while the latter may not personally be guilty of any wrongdoing. It will also be difficult to determine just how much damage was done and what form recompense should take. It is not clear, for example, what should be due the urban descendants of peasant farmers who were removed from their land many years ago. In addition, if the details of past ethnic history were sufficiently known, they would probably reveal that the continued population shifts of the human species have left few identifiable human groups who have not been *both* exploiters and exploited at some time or another.

    None of the above implies that there are no circumstances where it may be appropriate to demand recompense for past exploitation. The conclusion is only that it cannot be applied in wholesale fashion.

41. As one commentator puts it,

    > the means employed by the Cubans in their self-imposed internationalist mission range over the whole scale of imaginable common endeavors: from literacy and health campaigns, technological assistance in project building, security training and ideological indoctrination, to military involvement and active fighting with dissident national factions and foreign nations.

    A. Jorge, 'How Exportable Is The Cuban Model?', in B. B. Levine (ed.) *The New Cuban Presence in The Caribbean* (Boulder: Westview, 1983) 229. He also quotes the figure of 5,000 Cuban advisers in Nicaragua, evenly divided between military experts and teachers or medical personnel (p. 219). The point is that Cuba is relying much less on transfers of funds and material resources, of which it is in short supply in any case, and more on people.

Conclusion: Present and Future Prospects

1. 'Israelis Still See Future For Talks With Soviet', *New York Times* (25 August 1986).

2. G. Kennan, 'Morality and Foreign Policy', *Foreign Affairs*, 64 (Winter 1985/86) 206.

3. A number of studies of the fate of Carter's attempt have appeared in the past few years, including: G. Smith, *Morality, Reason, and Power: American Diplomacy in the Carter Years* (New York: Hill and Wang, 1986); J. Muravchik, *The Uncertain Crusade: Jimmy Carter*

and the Dilemmas of Human Rights Policy (Lanham: Hamilton Press, 1986); and C. Bell, *President Carter and Foreign Policy: The Costs of Virtue* (Canberra: The Australian National University, 1980). For a partially dissenting view, see T. Jacoby, 'Did Carter Fail on Human Rights?', *Washington Monthly*, 18 (June 1986) 51–5. Jacoby argues that while Carter's plans certainly failed in execution, with the possible exception of some nations in Latin America, he nonetheless *implanted* the ideal of a morally sensitive policy. Jacoby believes, for example, that President Reagan willy-nilly followed Carter's course, as in Haiti and the Philippines, but with much greater deftness of execution.

4.   According to one author:

> Some countries – the Netherlands, Sweden and Norway – give at least 1 per cent of their GNP [for development aid], while the USA gives 0.27 percent, Canada 0.42 percent, Great Britain 0.34 percent, Japan 0.32 percent and the USSR 0.04 percent. The average for western countries is 0.35 percent. This is in spite of an international understanding that aid should reach 0.7 percent of GNP.

A. Arneson, 'Perspective of Norwegian Development Aid in the 1980's', in *Poverty and Aid*, edited by J.R. Parkensen (Oxford: Basil Blackwell, 1983) 127.

5.   Long ago, Joseph Schumpeter made the claim that Sweden's institutions and perspectives are so deeply rooted in its particular social context as to be impossible to duplicate elsewhere. See *Capitalism, Socialism and Democracy* (London: Allen and Unwin, 1943) 325. But the theme of Swedish uniqueness is common and finds voice in a variety of authors, as for example M.W. Childs (who may well have originated the theme), *Sweden: The Middle Way* (New Haven: Yale University Press, 1937) and *Sweden: The Middle Way on Trial* (New Haven: Yale University Press, 1980), or T.J. Anton, *Administered Politics: Elite Political Culture in Sweden* (The Hague: Martinus Nijhoff, 1980).

6.   Sweden's tradition of neutrality dates to policies of the Swedish King Charles XIV John (formerly Napoleon's marshal, Jean-Baptiste Bernadotte) initiated in the early part of the nineteenth century. See A. Roberts, *Nations in Arms: The Theory and Practice of Territorial Defense* (New York: Praeger, 1976) 62–83, for a sketch of the conditions which have allowed and nurtured Swedish neutrality over the years. Marquis Childs offers a useful description of Sweden's often precarious efforts to remain neutral during the Second World War in *Sweden: The Middle Way on Trial, op. cit.*, 120–32.

7.   One strand of Sweden's tradition of neutrality involves avoiding foreign alliances, see Childs, *ibid.*, 129–35.

8.   The Social Democrats have been a major force in Swedish politics for the better part of this century and have enjoyed nearly continuous control of the government since the Second World War, Childs, *ibid.*, 15–42 and 70–80. Commentators hasten to note that the Social

Democrats of Sweden are not socialists in the usual sense, for 97 per cent of Swedish businesses remain in private hands and compete with one another and with foreign corporations in the best capitalist fashion. Social Democrats have, however, established an elaborate system of social welfare which provides life-long security for most Swedes. This combination of thoroughgoing socialist welfare and capitalist business practice is what led Marquis Childs to coin the phrase 'the middle way' over a half century ago, when the Social Democrats' programs were being put into place. This hybrid has proven endlessly fascinating to commentators, much more so than Sweden's distinctive foreign policies. For a comparatively recent description of Swedish economic conditions and a useful bibliography, see R. L. Heilbroner, 'The Swedish Promise', *New York Review of Books*, 27 (4 December 1980) 33–6.

9.   Olaf Palme avowed:

> The third aspect [of Democratic Socialism] is internationalism. I have the firm conviction that any nation's external policy is an extension of its internal policy.

Quoted in 'Palme', *New Yorker*, 52 (10 January 1977) 23.

10.   Palme maintained close contacts with the Socialist International and was elected its Vice-President in December 1976; *ibid.*, 22. In addition, he often collaborated with Social Democrats of other nations, in particular with Willi Brandt of West Germany and Felipe Gonzalez of Spain. See J. Kapstein, 'Palme's Master Plan for Sweden is Alive and Well', *Business Week*, no. 2937 (17 March 1986) 67.

11.   See M. Childs, *The Middle Way on Trial*, *op. cit.*, 48–55 for a description of Sweden's tax structure – and the outbursts of discontent it has occasioned.

12.   A decade ago its standard of living and per capita income were generally agreed to be the highest in the world. A few years later, its per capita income was surpassed by that of a number of oil-producing nations. Recently, economic strains may have undermined its pre-eminence in living standards as well. See 'Swedes Flourishing, Feel Guilty About Their Wealth and Debate Their Obligations', *New York Times* (26 December 1974) and A. Roberts, *op. cit.*, 67.

13.   See Childs, *Sweden: The Middle Way on Trial*, *op. cit.*, 43–50 and Heilbroner, *op. cit.*

14.   In fact the Swedish Parliament (the Riksdag) endorsed a policy of solidarity with the Third World in 1962. H.M. Selim, *Development Assistance Policies and the Performance of Aid Agencies* (London: Macmillan, 1983) 12.

15.   'Swedes Flourishing, Feel Guilty About Their Wealth and Debate Their Obligations', *op. cit.* Swedish programs of international assistance did not begin in significant fashion until 1962. By 1967, however, the Riksdag adopted the goal of increasing assistance in increments, with the goal of reaching 1 per cent of its gross national product by 1975. By the early 1970s, though, the Social Democratic leadership began to shy away from this goal, and national debate ensued over

whether it should be retained. See M. Radetzki, *Aid and Development: A Handbook for Small Donors* (New York: Praeger, 1973) 126–8. The debate was finally resolved with the conclusion that the goal be retained. See footnote 4.

16. See footnote 3 for a listing of recent assessments of the Carter Administration.

17. As commentators point out, Carter himself entered office convinced that world affairs should not be viewed in narrow terms of a massive conflict between the United States and the Soviet Union, yet ended his term excoriating Russian chicanery in good Cold War fashion. Perhaps the transition was made inevitable by the fact that the most tenacious of his advisers was Zbigniew Brzezinski – the doughtiest of cold warriors. See 'Carter's Record', *New Republic*, 183 (4 October 1980) 11.

18. One of the great controversies of Carter's term of office arose in response to his decision to withdraw US troops from South Korea. There was vigorous opposition not only within the United States but in the nations of the Far East, Japan and South Korea, who viewed the presence of American military forces as a counter to Soviet influence and a sign of US commitment in the area. See G. Smith, *op. cit.*, 103–5.

19. As Adam Roberts points out, Sweden's planned response to a major attack is simply to increase the marginal costs of victory for a major opponent, not to attempt to annihilate its forces or achieve conclusive victory. See Roberts, op. cit., 91–4.

20. Certain extreme proponents, such as Ayn Rand, argue that it is a mistake to give any assistance at all to the underprivileged. See *The Virtue of Selfishness* (New York: New American Library, 1964) vii–x.

21. For example, Ronald Reagan, while resisting Congressional pressure for sanctions against South Africa, argued that such efforts would be a violation of autonomy. In his speech of 22 July 1986, he insisted:

> We Americans stand ready to help, but whether South Africa emerges democratic and free or takes a course leading to a downward spiral of poverty and repression will finally be their choice, not ours.

He also claimed, 'We and our allies cannot dictate to the government of a sovereign nation – nor should we try'. 'Transcript of Talk by Reagan on South Africa and Apartheid', *New York Times* (23 July 1986).

22. S. Goode, *The Foreign Policy Debate* (New York: Franklin Watts, 1984) 49–59 provides a useful quick sketch of this consciousness.

23. As Arne Arnesen points out, the accepted international goal is that nations devote 0.7 per cent of their GNP to international assistance, a goal few have achieved. Arnesen, *op. cit.*, 127.

24. Carter's human rights efforts were popular with the American public in the early years of his administration. S. Karnow, 'Carter and Human Rights', *Saturday Review* (2 April 1977) 6 and 'Carter Spins the World', *Time*, 110 (8 August 1977) 8.

25. Tara Jacoby points out that American support of democratic resistance

to the dictators of Haiti and the Philippines was quite popular, even though it was not forthcoming until the Reagan Administration was assured that the popular movements would be successful. Jacoby *op. cit.*, 51.

26. For a sampling of the thinking of two of the Congressmen who have been active in this field, see D.M. Frazer, 'Congress's Role in the Making of International Human Rights Policy', in D.P. Kommers and G.D. Loescher (eds) *Human Rights and Foreign Policy* (Notre Dame: University of Notre Dame Press, 1979) 247–54 and T. Harkin, 'Humanitarian Rights and Foreign Aid: Forging an Unbreakable Link', in P.G. Brown and D. MacLean (eds) *Human Rights and US Foreign Policy* (Lexington: Lexington Books, 1979) 15–26.

27. The American Peace Corps, for example, has created a group of people who have had intensive first-hand experience of the conditions and difficulties of those in underdeveloped nations. According to its first director, Sargent Shriver, large numbers of former volunteers have gone to work for the State Department, CARE, and Catholic Relief Services, among others. An influential and energetic body of people with this sort of immersion could well make a difference in national policy and interests. 'Peace Corps at 25 a Proven Success', *New York Times* (20 September 1986).

28. Members of Congress displayed interest in issues of human rights well before Jimmy Carter's election to the Presidency. Legislation supporting various human rights concerns began appearing in 1973. This interest reached its peak with Carter's election in 1976, but the mood of the nation and of members of government had clearly changed by 1980. Ronald Reagan assumed office with the intention of muting the effect of human rights concerns on United States policy. His intent was reflected both in his rhetoric and in his appointments to office. It is clear that interest in such matters has been dampened during his term in office. This is part of what led Gaddis Smith to the conclusion that Carter's success in 1976 was essentially a fluke, that a unique combination of factors propelled him into office, and that his declared concern for peace and the nurture of human rights fitted the national mood of the day, but of that day only. Smith, *op. cit.*, 27–33 and 241–7. Mark L. Schneider outlines Congressional activity on behalf of human rights in the Carter era and earlier in 'A New Administration's New Policy: The Rise to Power of Human Rights', in P. G. Brown and D. MacLean, *op. cit.*, 3–13.

29. See 'For Pro-Israel Lobby, the Stiffest Test Yet', *US News*, 91 (14 September 1981) 36; 'Fred of Arabia to the Rescue', *Newsweek*, 98 (2 November 1981) 42; 'The Petro Dollar Connection', *New Republic* 186 (19 May 1982) 11–6 and 'The Making of a Foreign Agent: Dutton of Arabia', *New Republic*, 186 (16 June 1982) 18–23. The *New Republic* series was written by S. Emerson.

30. See 'Reagan's Abrupt Reversal', *Time*, 126 (16 September 1985) 42–4.

31. Useful general treatments of the founding of the United Nations, with discussion of how efforts were made to foresee problems and avoid mistakes of the past include T.M. Franck, *Nation Against Nation*

(New York: Oxford University Press, 1985) 1–44, and H. V. Evatt, *The United Nations* (Cambridge: Harvard University Press, 1948) 3–45. Specific treatments of the attempt to cope with issues of human rights include P.R. Baehr and L. Gordenker, *The United Nations: Reality and Ideal* (New York: Praeger, 1984) 99–117 and the particularly thorough treatment by J.F. Green, *The United Nations and Human Rights* (Washington: The Brookings Institution, 1956).

32. For a discussion of some aspects of current UN efforts to promote human rights, difficulties, and proposals for change, presented by the Special Assistant to the Assistant Secretary-General for Human Rights of the United Nations, see B.G. Ramcharan, 'New Avenues for the Promotion and Protection of Human Rights: Advisory Services and Technical Assistance', *Human Rights Internet Reporter*, 10 (May–August 1985) 550 60. There has been concern recently that changes in policy of UN commissions have caused reports to be watered down. P. Alston, 'Remedying U.N. Pussy-Footing on Human Rights', *Human Rights Internet Reporter*, 11 (June 1986) 7–8.

The difficulties in the way of UN efforts on behalf of human rights – including outrageous hypocrisy – resulting from its dependence on the support and finances of member nations are examined by S. Hazzard, 'UNhelpful', *New Republic*, 182 (12 April 1980) 10–13.

The difficulties and politics which lie in the way of gaining solid information on human rights abuses is chronicled by S.D. Bailey, 'UN Fact-Finding and Human Rights Complaints', *International Affairs*, 148 (April 1972) 250–66. Also see T.J.M. Zuijdwijk, *Petitioning the United Nations: A Study in Human Rights* (New York: St. Martin's Press, 1982) for a detailed study of the machinery and limitations of the UN in dealing with complaints of human rights abuses.

33. The UN is financed entirely by voluntary payment of dues by its members and cannot, in accordance with the provisions of its charter, borrow to pay its debts. In late summer of 1986, the United States caused great concern by threatening to withhold its dues, which amount to 25 per cent of the overall UN budget. The ostensible reason for this threat was dissatisfaction with UN management and financial practices, but the larger cause is the frustration of many in the United States over the perceived anti-American bias of many decisions of the UN. See 'UN Chief Says US Cuts in Payments Are Crippling', *New York Times* (12 September 1986). The consequences of this disarray for human rights programs are discussed in a recent issue of the *Human Rights Internet Reporter*. See 'The UN Arrears Crisis: Its Implications for Human Rights', 11 (June 1986) 6–7.

34. The fortieth anniversary of the founding of the United Nations was the occasion for a number of chronicles of its difficulties. See 'The UN's Midlife Crisis', *Time*, 126 (28 October 1985) 38–40 and 'The UN's Mid-Life Crisis', *Newsweek*, 106 (28 October 1985) 52, and notice the lack of inspiration in titles.

35. The principal forum of these nations is the Nonaligned Movement, founded in 1961. The 101 members of this group include both Iraq and Iran, recently engaged in bitter war; India and Pakistan, who have

fought in the past and continue to be mutually suspicious and hostile; Egypt and Libya, whose checkered relations are a major facet of the tangle of antipathy in the Middle East, Argentina and Cuba, polar opposites of politics in Latin America; and, in addition to Cuba, nations such as North Korea, Vietnam, Cambodia, Afghanistan and Ethiopia, whose nonaligned status is suspect. At a recent, typically dramatic, meeting, Muammar el-Qaddafi loudly proclaimed that the group was ineffectual and threatened to withdraw. The group was able to agree to press economic sanctions against South Africa, yet recognized that such actions could have little effect without the support of the advanced industrialized nations, who are the major trading partners of South Africa. See '101 Members of Nonaligned Movement' (4 September 1986); 'Leader of Liberia Backs Washington' (6 September 1986) and 'Third-World Group Faults US on Libya' (8 September 1986), all in the *New York Times*.

Bibliography

Books

Aiken, W. and LaFollett, H. (eds), *World Hunger and Moral Obligation* (Englewood Cliffs: Prentice-Hall, 1977).

Alexander, Y. (ed.), *International Terrorism: National, Regional, and Global Perspectives* (New York: Praeger, 1976).

Anscombe, G.E.M., *Ethics, Religion, and Politics*, vol. 3 (Minneapolis: University of Minnesota Press, 1981).

Anton, T.J., *Administered Politics. Elite Political Culture in Sweden* (The Hague: Martinus Nijhoff, 1980).

Baehr, P.R. and Gordenker, L., *The United Nations: Reality and Ideal* (New York: Praeger, 1984).

Barry, B., *Selected Essays of Brian Barry*, 2 vols (Totowa: Rowman & Littlefield, 1986).

Beer, F.A., *Peace Against War: The Ecology of International Peace* (San Francisco: W. H. Freeman, 1981).

Beitz, C.R., *Political Theory and International Relations* (Princeton: Princeton University Press, 1979).

Beitz, C.R., Cohen, M., Scanlon, T. and Simmons, A.J., *International Ethics* (Princeton: Princeton University Press, 1985).

Bell, C., *President Carter and Foreign Policy: The Costs of Virtue* (Canberra: The Australian National University, 1980).

Blake, N. and Pole, K., *Dangers of Deterrence* (London and Boston: Routledge & Kegan Paul, 1984).

Blake, N. and Pole, K., *Objections to Nuclear Defence* (London and Boston: Routledge & Kegan Paul, 1984).

Blechman, B.M. and Kaplan, S.S., *Force Without War: U. S. Armed Forces as a Political Instrument* (Washington: Brookings Institution, 1978).

Boggs, M.W., *Attempts to Define and Limit 'Aggressive' Armament in Diplomacy and Strategy* (Columbia: University of Missouri Press, 1941).

Boserup, A., *War Without Weapons: Non-violence in National Defense* (New York: Schocken, 1974).

Brandt, R.B., *A Theory of the Good and the Right* (Oxford: Clarendon Press, 1979).

Brown, H., *Thinking About National Security* (Boulder: Westview Press, 1983).

Brown, P.G. and Shue, H. (eds), *The Border That Joins* (Totowa: Rowman & Littlefield, 1983).

Brown, P.G. and Shue, H. (eds), *Boundaries* (Totowa: Rowman & Littlefield, 1981.

Brown, P.G. and Maclean, D. (eds), *Human Rights and U.S. Foreign Policy* (Lexington: Lexington Books, 1979).

Brown, P.G. and Shue, H. (eds), *Food Policy: The Responsibility of the United States in Life and Death Choices* (New York: The Free Press, 1977).

215

Buergenthal, T. (ed.), *Human Rights, International Law and the Helsinki Accords* (New York: Universe Books, 1977).

Carlton, D. and Schaert, C. (eds), *Contemporary Terror: Studies in Sub-State Violence* (New York: St. Martin's, 1981).

Childs, M.W., *Sweden: The Middle Way* (New Haven: Yale University Press, 1937).

Childs, M.W., *Sweden: The Middle Way on Trial* (New Haven: Yale University Press, 1980).

Christoph, B., *Third-World Conflict and International Security* (Hamden: Archon Books, 1982).

Clausewitz, C. von, *On War*, edited by A. Rapoport (Baltimore: Penguin Books, 1972).

Cortese, C.F., *Modernization, Threat, and the Power of the Military* (Beverly Hills: Sage Publications, 1976).

Crenshaw, M. (ed.), *Terrorism, Legitimacy, and Power* (Middletown: Wesleyan University Press, 1983).

Dworkin, R., *Taking Rights Seriously* (Cambridge: Harvard University Press, 1977).

Fain, H., *Normative Politics and the Community of Nations* (Philadelphia: Temple University Press, 1987).

Falk, R., *Human Rights and State Sovereignty* (New York: Holmes & Meier, 1981).

Falk, R., *The Promise of World Order* (Philadelphia: Temple University Press, 1987).

Falk, R.A., Kolko, G. and Lifton, R.J. (eds), *Crimes of War* (New York: Random House, 1971).

Fotion, N. and Elfstrom, G., *Military Ethics* (Boston, London and Henley: Routledge & Kegan Paul, 1986).

Franck, T.M., *Nation Against Nation* (New York: Oxford University Press, 1985).

French, P.A. (ed.), *Individual and Collective Responsibility* (Cambridge: Schenkman Publishing Co., 1972).

Friedman, M., *Capitalism and Freedom* (Chicago: University of Chicago Press, 1962).

Gewirth, A., *Reason and Morality* (Chicago: University of Chicago Press, 1978).

Goode, S., *The Foreign Policy Debate* (New York: Franklin Watts, 1984).

Goode, S., *Guerrilla Warfare and Terrorism* (New York and London: Franklin Watts, 1977).

Gray, J.G., *The Warriors* (New York: Harper & Row, 1973).

Graubard, S.R. (ed.), *The State* (New York: Norton, 1981).

Green, J.F., *The United Nations and Human Rights* (Washington: The Brookings Institution, 1956).

Hampshire, S. (ed.) *Public and Private Morality* (Cambridge: Cambridge University Press, 1978).

Hare, J.E. and Joynt, C.B., *Ethics and International Affairs* (New York: St. Martin's Press, 1982).

Hare, R.M., *Freedom and Reason* (Oxford: Oxford University Press, 1965).

Hare, R.M., *Moral Thinking* (Oxford: Clarendon Press, 1981).

Heclo, H. and Madsen, H., *Policy and Politics in Sweden* (Philadelphia: Temple University Press, 1986).

Held, V., Morgenbesser, S. and Nagel, T. (eds), *Philosophy, Morality, and International Affairs* (New York: Oxford University Press, 1974).

Hesburgh, T.M. and Halle, L.J., *Foreign Policy and Morality, Framework for a Moral Audit* (New York: Council on Religion and International Affairs, 1979).

Hobbes, T., *Leviathan*, edited by Michael Oakeshott (Oxford: Basil Blackwell, 1960).

Hoffmann, S., *Dead Ends: American Foreign Policy in the New Cold War* (Cambridge: Ballinger Publishers, 1983).

Hoffmann, S., *Duties Beyond Borders* (Syracuse: Syracuse University Press, 1981).

Hoffmann, S., *Gulliver's Troubles, or the Setting of American Foreign Policy* (New York: McGraw-Hill, 1968).

Horowitz, I.L., *Beyond Empire & Revolution: Militarization and Consolidation in the Third World* (New York: Oxford University Press, 1982).

Independent Commission on Disarmament and Security Issues (The Palme Commission), *Common Security: A Blueprint for Survival* (New York: Simon and Schuster, 1982).

James, A., *Sovereign Statehood* (London, Boston and Sydney: Allen & Unwin, 1986).

Jordan, A.A. and Taylor, W.J., *American National Security: Policy and Process* (Baltimore: Johns Hopkins Press, 1981).

Keegan, J., *The Face of Battle* (New York: Viking Press, 1976).

Kipnis, K. and Meyers, D.T. (eds), *Political Realism and International Morality* (Boulder: Westview Press, 1987).

Kommers, D.B. and Loescher, G.D., *Human Rights and Foreign Policy* (Notre Dame: University of Notre Dame Press, 1979).

Kupperman, R.H. and Trent, D.M., *Terrorism: Threat, Reality, Response* (Stanford: Hoover Institution Press, 1979).

Latourette, K.S., *The Chinese: Their History and Culture*, 4th ed. (New York: Macmillan Co., 1964).

Leyton-Brown, D. (ed.), *The Utility of International Economic Sanctions* (New York: St. Martin's, 1987).

Lillich, R.B. and Newman, F. (eds), *International Human Rights: Problems of Law and Policy* (Boston: Little, Brown and Co., 1979).

Livingstone, N.C., *Fighting Back* (Lexington: Lexington Books, 1986).

Livingstone, N.C., *The War Against Terrorism* (Lexington: Lexington Books, 1982).

Luper-Foy, S. (ed.), *Problems of International Justice* (Bolder: Westview Press, 1988).

MacIntyre, A., *After Virtue* (Notre Dame: University of Notre Dame Press, 1981).

MacLean, D. (ed.), *The Security Gamble* (Totowa: Rowman & Littlefield, 1984).

May, L., *The Morality of Groups* (Notre Dame: University of Notre Dame Press, 1987).

Morgenthau, H.J., *In Defense of National Interest* (New York: Alfred A. Knopf, 1952).

Morgenthau, H.J., *Politics Among Nations*, 5th ed. (New York: Alfred A. Knopf, 1973).

Muravchik, J., *The Uncertain Crusade: Jimmy Carter and the Dilemmas of Human Rights Policy* (Lanham: Hamilton Press, 1986).

Murphy, J.F., *Punishing International Terrorists* (Totowa: Rowman & Littlefield, 1985).

Murphy, J.F., *The United Nations and the Control of International Violence* (Totowa: Allanheld Osmun, 1983).

Paskins, B. and Dockrill, M., *The Ethics of War* (Minneapolis: Minnesota University Press, 1979).

Ra'anan, U., Pfaltzgraff, R.L. Jr. and Kemp, G. (eds), *Projection of Power* (Hamden: Shoe String Press, 1982).

Radetzki, M., *Aid and Development: A Handbook for Small Donors* (New York: Praeger, 1973).

Ramsey, P., *The Just War: Force and Political Responsibility* (New York: Scribners, 1968).

Rand, A., *The Virtue of Selfishness* (New York: New American Library, 1964).

Rawls, J., *A Theory of Justice* (Cambridge: Harvard University Press, 1971).

Richards, D.A.J., *A Theory of Reasons for Action* (Oxford: Oxford University Press, 1971).

Roberts, A., *Nations in Arms: The Theory and Practice of Territorial Defense* (New York: Praeger, 1976).

Robinson, N., *Universal Declaration of Human Rights: Its Origins, Significance and Interpretation, (1950)*.

Rosenbaum, A.S. (ed.), *The Philosophy of Human Rights: International Perspectives* (Westport: Greenwood Press, 1980).

Schelling, T.C., *Arms and Influence* (New Haven: Yale University Press, 1966).

Schumpeter, J., *Capitalism, Socialism, and Democracy* (London: Allen and Unwin, 1943).

Selim, H.M., *Development Assistance Policies and the Performance of Aid Agencies* (London: Macmillan, 1983).

Shawcross, W., *The Quality of Mercy: Cambodia, Holocaust, and Modern Conscience* (New York: Simon and Schuster, 1984).

Shue, H., *Basic Rights: Subsistence, Affluence, and U.S. Foreign Policy* (Princeton: Princeton University Press, 1980).

Simmons, L., *The Role of the Aged in Primitive Societies* (New Haven: Yale University Press, 1945).

Smith, G., *Morality, Reason, and Power: American Diplomacy in the Carter Years* (New York: Hill and Wang, 1986).

Smith, S., *et al.* (eds), *Foreign Policy Implementation* (London, Boston and Sydney: Allen & Unwin, 1985).

Sumner, W.G. and Keller, A.G., *The Science of Society*, 4 vols. (New Haven: Yale University Press, 1927).

Thompson, K.W., *Foreign Assistance* (Notre Dame: University of Notre Dame Press, 1988).

Thompson, K.W. (ed.), *Moral Dimensions of American Foreign Policy* (New Brunswick: Transaction Books, 1984).
Thompson, K.W., *Morality and Foreign Policy* (Baton Rouge: Louisiana State University Press, 1980).
Thompson, K.W., *Understanding World Politics* (Notre Dame: University of Notre Dame Press, 1987).
Tolley, H., Jr., *The U. N. Commission on Human Rights* (Boulder and London: Westview Press, 1987).
U.N. Educational, Scientific and Cultural Organization, *Human Rights, Comments and Interpretations: A Symposium* (1949).
VanDeVeer, D., *Paternalistic Intervention* (Princeton: Princeton University Press, 1986).
Vasak, K. (ed.), *The International Dimension of Human Rights*, 2 vols. (Westport: Greenwood Press, 1982).
Vincent, R.J., *Human Rights and International Relations* (Cambridge: Cambridge University Press, 1986).
Waldock, H. (ed.), *The Law of Nations* (Oxford: Oxford University Press, 1963).
Wakin, M.M. (ed.), *War, Morality and the Military Profession* (Boulder: Westview Press, 1979).
Walzer, M., *Just and Unjust Wars* (New York: Basic Books, 1977).
Wasserstrom, R.A., *Philosophy and Social Issues* (Notre Dame: University of Notre Dame Press, 1980).
Wasserstrom, R.A. (ed.), *War and Morality* (Belmont: Wadsworth Press, 1970).
Williams, H., *Kant's Political Philosophy* (New York: St. Martin's Press, 1982).
World Armaments and Disarmament: Stockholm International Peace Research Institute Yearbook, 1981 (London: Taylor & Francis, 1981).
Zuijdwijk, T., *Petitioning the United Nations: A Study in Human Rights* (New York: St. Martin's, 1982).

Articles

Aiken, W., 'Realpolitick, Morality, and International Affairs', *Humanities in Society*, 5 (Winter/Spring 1982) 95–108.
Alston, P., 'Remedying UN Pussy-Footing on Human Rights', *Human Rights Internet Reporter*, 11 (June 1986) 7–8.
Arnesen, A. 'Perspective of Norwegian Development Aid in the 1980's', in J.R. Parkensen (ed.), *Poverty and Aid* (Oxford: Basil Blackwell, 1983) 125–38.
Axinn, S., 'The Law of Land Warfare as Minimal Government', *Personalist*, 59 (October 1978) 374–85.
Bailey, S.D., 'UN Fact-Finding and Human Rights Complaints', *International Affairs*, 148 (April 1972) 250–66.
Bakhash, S., 'Reign of Terror', *New York Review of Books*, 33 (14 August, 1986) 13 *et seq*.

Barry, B., 'Do Countries Have Moral Obligations? The Case of World Poverty', Tanner Lecture, Harvard University (October 1980).

Barry, B., 'Do Neighbors Make Good Fences? Political Theory and the Territorial Imperative', *Political Theory*, 9 (August 1981) 293–302.

Barry, R., 'Just War Theory and the Problem of Reconciliation', *New Scholasticism*, 54 (Spring 1980) 129–52.

Bay, C., 'On Needs and Rights Beyond Liberalism: A Rejoinder to Flathman', *Political Theory*, 8 (August 1980) 331–4.

Bay, C., 'Peace and Critical Political Knowldege as Rights', *Political Theory*, 8 (August 1980) 293–318.

Bay, C., 'A Human Rights Approach to Transnational Ethics', *Universal Human Rights*, 1 (January–March 1979) 19–42.

Beitz, C.R., 'Bounded Morality: Justice and the State in World Politics', *International Organizations*, 33 (Summer 1979) 405–24.

Beitz, C.R., 'Cosmopolitan Ideals and National Sentiment', *Journal of Philosophy*, 80 (October 1983) 591–9.

Beitz, C.R., 'Economic Rights and Distributive Justice in Developing Societies', *World Politics*, 33 (April 1981) 321– 46.

Beitz, C.R., 'International Distributive Justice', in J.R. Pennock and J.W. Chapman (eds), *Ethics, Economics and the Law* (New York: New York University Press, 1982) 275–302.

Beitz, C.R., 'Justice and International Relations', in G. H. Blocker (ed.), *John Rawls' Theory of Justice* (Athens: Ohio University Press, 1980) 211–38.

Beitz, C.R., 'Nonintervention and Communal Integrity', *Philosophy & Public Affairs*, 9 (Summer 1980) 385–91.

Bell, C., 'From Carter to Reagan', *Foreign Affairs*, 63 (1985) 490–510.

Bender, F.L., 'World Hunger, Human Rights and the Right to Revolution', *Social Praxis*, 8 (1981) 5–30.

Beneman, G.D., 'The High Technological Society and Human Rights', *Philosophy & Social Action*, 5 (July–September–December 1979) 17–32.

Bennett, J.C., 'Morality and Foreign Policy', in W.M. Finnin, Jr. (ed.), *The Morality of Scarcity* (Baton Rouge: Louisiana State University Press, 1979) 81–96.

Beran, H., 'What Is the Basis of Political Authority?', *Monist*, 66 (October 1983) 487–99.

Beres, L.R., 'Human Rights and World Order: The United States Imperative', *Humanities in Society*, 5 (Winter/Spring 1982) 109–36.

Berleant, A., 'Multinationals, Local Practice, and the Problem of Ethical Consistency', *Journal of Business Ethics*, 1 (August 1982) 185–93.

Blechman, B.M. and Kaplan, S.S., 'U.S. Military Forces as a Political Instrument' in C.W. Kegley, Jr. and E.R. Whittkopf (eds), *Perspectives on American Foreign Policy* (New York: St. Martin's Press, 1983) 62–78.

Boxill, B., 'Theories of Justice and the United Nations Declaration on the Establishment of a New International Economic Order', *Teaching Philosophy*, 8 (April 1985) 129–36.

Brown, L., 'Intentions in the Conduct of a Just War', in C. Diamond (ed.), *Intention and Intentionality* (Ithaca: Cornell University Press, 1979) 133–45.

Brandt, R., 'Utilitarianism and the Rules of War', *Philosophy & Public Affairs*, 1 (Winter 1972) 145–65.

Bruening, W., 'World Peace and Moral Obligation', *Journal of Social Philosophy*, 12 (May 1981) 11–19.

Clough, M., 'Beyond Constructive Engagement', *Foreign Policy*, 61 (Winter 1985/86) 3–24.

Coady, C.A.J., 'The Leaders and the Led', *Inquiry*, 23 (September 1980) 275–9.

Cohen, M., 'Moral Skepticism and International Relations', *Philosophy & Public Affairs*, 13 (Fall 1984) 299–346.

Cotto, S., 'Legitimacy: A Mirage?', *Diogenes*, 134 (Summer 1986) 96–105.

Critchfield, R., 'Science and the Villager', *Foreign Affairs*, 61 (Fall 1982) 14–41.

Cutler, L.N., 'The Right to Intervene', *Foreign Affairs*, 64 (Fall 1985) 96–112.

DeGeorge, R., 'Can Corporations Have Moral Responsibility?', in T.L. Beauchamp and N.E. Bowie (eds), *Ethical Theory and Business*, 2nd ed. (Englewood Cliffs: Prentice-Hall, 1979) 57–67.

DeMarco, J.P., 'International Application of the Theory of Justice', *Pacific Philosophical Quarterly*, 62 (October 1981) 393–402.

Dombrowski, D.A., 'What Does "War Is Hell" Mean?', *International Journal of Applied Philosophy*, 1 (Fall 1983) 19–24.

Doppelt, G., 'Statism Without Foundations', *Philosophy & Public Affairs*, 9 (Summer 1980) 398–404.

Doppelt, G., 'Walzer's Theory of Morality in International Relations', *Philosophy & Public Affairs*, 8 (Fall 1978) 3–26.

Dubick, J.M., 'Human Rights, Command Responsibility, and Walzer's Just War Theory', *Philosophy & Public Affairs*, 11 (Fall 1982) 354–71.

Dubick, J.M., 'Social Expectations, Moral Obligations, and Command Responsibility', *International Journal of Applied Philosophy*, 2 (Spring 1984) 39–48.

Dyck, A.J., 'Assessing the Population Debate', *Monist*, 60 (January 1977) 29–46.

Elfstrom, G., 'On Dilemmas of Intervention', *Ethics*, 93 (Summer 1983) 709–25.

Ellsberg, D., 'Risk, Ambiguity and Rational Choice', *Quarterly Journal of Economics*, 75 (1961) 643–9.

Falk, R., 'Comparative Protection of Human Rights in Capitalist and Socialist Third World Countries', *Universal Human Rights*, 1 (April–June 1979) 3–29.

Falk, R., 'Nuclear Power and the End of Democracy', *Praxis International*, 2 (April 1982) 1–11.

Felder, D.W., 'Command Theory and International Law', *Philosophical Forum* (Dekalb), 15 (May 1977) 299–306.

Freedman, L., 'The War of the Falkland Islands', *Foreign Affairs*, 61 (Fall 1982) 196–210.

Freund, N., 'Nonviolent National Defense', *Journal of Social Philosophy*, 13 (May 1982) 12–17.

Friedman, M., 'The Social Responsibility of Business is to Increase Its

Profits', in W.M. Hoffmann and J.M. Moore (eds), *Business Ethics* (New York: McGraw-Hill Book Company, 1984) 126–31.

Fullinwider, R.K., 'The New Patriotism', *QQ – Report from the Center for Philosophy & Public Policy*, 5 (Spring 1985) 9–11.

Genovesi, V.J., 'Just War Doctrine: A Warrant for Resistance', *Thomist*, 45 (October 1981) 503–40.

Gilbert, A., 'Moral Realism, Individuality, and Justice in War', *Political Theory*, 14 (February 1986) 105–35.

Glazier, M., 'Ten Whistleblowers And How They Fared', *Hastings Center Report*, 13 (December 1983) 33–41.

Glossop, R.J., 'Hume and the Future of Society of Nations', *Hume Studies*, 10 (April 1984) 46–58.

Glossop, R., 'War, Peace and Justice', *Journal of Social Philosophy*, 11 (January 1980) 9–11.

Goodin, R.E., 'The Development-Rights Trade-Off: Some Unwarranted Economic and Political Assumptions', *Universal Human Rights*, 1 (April–June 1979) 31–42.

Goodpaster, K.E., 'The Concept of Corporate Responsibility', in T. Regan (ed.), *Just Business: New Introductory Essays in Business Ethics* (New York: Random House, 1984) 292–322.

Hare, R.M., 'Liberty, Equality, and Fraternity in South Africa?', *South African Journal of Philosophy*, 5 (August 1986) 69–74.

Hare, R.M., 'Philosophy and Practice: Some Issues About War and Peace', *Philosophy*, 18 (1984 Supplement) 1–16.

Hazzard, S., 'UNhelpful', *New Republic*, 182 (April 12, 1980) 10–13.

Heilbroner, R.L., 'The Swedish Promise', *New York Review of Books*, 27 (December 4, 1980) 33–6.

Held, V., 'Philosophy and International Problems', *Teaching Philosophy*, 8 (April 1985) 121–8.

Henkin, L., 'International Human Rights as "Rights"', in J. R. Pennock (ed.), *Human Rights* (New York: New York University Press, 1981) 257–80.

Hewlett, S.A., 'Coping With Illegal Aliens', *Foreign Affairs*, 60 (Winter 1981/82) 358–78.

Hindrey, R., 'Applying Comparative Ethics to Multinational Corporations', in J. Gaffney (ed.), *Essays in Morality and Ethics* (New York: Paulist Press, 1980) 85–105.

Hoffmann, S., 'States and the Morality of War', *Political Theory*, 9 (May 1981) 149–72.

Hormats, R., 'The World Economy Under Stress', *Foreign Affairs*, 64 (1986) 455–78.

Jacoby, T., 'Did Carter Fail on Human Rights?', *Washington Monthly*, 18 (June 1986) 51–5.

Johnson, C., 'Who Is Aristotle's Citizen?', *Phronesis*, 29 (1984) 73–90.

Johnson, M.G., 'Historical Perspectives on Human Rights and U.S. Foreign Policy', *Universal Human Rights*, 2 (July–September 1980) 1–8.

Jong, Y.Y., 'Nationalism into Global Familism', *Philosophical Forum* (Dekalb), 16 (May 1980) 239–51.

Karnow, S., 'Carter and Human Rights', *Saturday Review* (April 12, 1977) 6.

Kelsen, H., 'Collective and Individual Responsibility in International Law with Particular Regard to the Punishment of War Criminals', *California Law Review*, 31 (1953).

Kennan, G.F., 'Morality and Foreign Policy', *Foreign Affairs*, 64 (Winter 1985/86) 205–18.

Kennedy, E., 'The Politics of Toleration In Late Weimar: Hermann Heller's Analysis of Fascism and Political Culture', *History of Political Thought*, 5 (Spring 1984) 109–28.

Laber, J. and Rubin, B., 'A Dying Nation', *New York Review of Books* (January 17, 1985) 3–4.

Lackey, D., 'A Modern Theory of Just War', *Ethics*, 92 (April 1982) 533–46.

Lackey, D.P., 'Missles and Morals: A Utilitarian Look at Nuclear Deterrence', *Philosophy & Public Affairs*, 11 (Summer 1982) 189–231.

Levinson, S., 'Responsibility for Crimes of War', *Philosophy & Public Affairs*, 2 (1973) 244–73.

Lippman, M., 'The Protection of Universal Human Rights: The Problem of Torture', *Universal Human Rights*, 1 (October–December 1979) 25–55.

Luban, D., 'Just War and Human Rights', *Philosophy & Public Affairs*, 9 (Winter 1980) 160–81.

Luban, D., 'The Romance of the Nation-State', *Philosophy & Public Affairs*, 9 (Summer 1980) 392–7.

Mann, J.A., 'Ethics and the Problem of World Hunger', *Listening*, 16 (Winter 1982) 67–76.

Mavrodes, G.I., 'Conventions and the Morality of War', *Philosophy & Public Affairs*, 4 (Winter 1975) 117–31.

McLeod, S., 'How Assad Has Won', *New York Review of Books*, 33 (May 8, 1986) 26 & 31–34.

McKinsey, M., 'Obligations to the Starving', *Nous*, 15 (September 1981) 309–24.

Meyers, D.T., 'Human Rights in Pre-affluent Societies', *Philosophical Quarterly*, 31 (April 1981) 139–44.

Miles, T.R., 'On the Limits to the Use of Force', *Religious Studies*, 20 (March 1984) 113–20.

Molnar, T., 'On Legitimacy', *Diogenes*, 134 (Summer 1986) 60–77.

Morgenthau, H.J., 'The Twilight of International Morality', *Ethics*, 58 (January 1948) 79–99.

Mulholland, L.A., 'Kant on War and International Justice', *Kantstudien*, 78 (1987) 25–41.

Mushkat,M., 'Human Capital Losses Resulting From War as a Policy Analysis', *International Journal of Applied Philosophy*, 2 (Spring 1984) 49–60.

Naor, J., 'A New Approach to Multinational Social Responsibility', *Journal of Business Ethics*, 1 (August 1982) 219–25.

Narveson, J., 'Pacifism: A Philosophical Analysis', *Ethics*, 75 (1965) 259–71.

Nayar, M.G.K., 'Human Rights and Economic Development: The Legal Foundations', *Universal Human Rights*, 2 (July–September 1980) 55–81.

Niebanck, R.J., 'Transnational Capital and the Illusion of Independence', in G.W. Forell (ed.), *Corporation Ethics* (Philadelphia: Fortress Press, 1980) 26–30.

O'Neil, P., 'Rawls, The Right of Emigration, And the Muted Promise of the Original Position', *Southern Journal of Philosophy*, 20 (Winter 1982) 489–502.

Pangle, T.L., 'A Note on the Theoretical Foundation of the Just War Doctrine', *Thomist*, 43 (July 1979) 464–73.

Park, H.S., 'Human Rights and Modernization: A Dialectical Relationship?', *Universal Human Rights*, 2 (January–March 1980) 85–92.

Pipes, D., 'Fundamentalist Muslims', *Foreign Affairs*, 64 (Summer 1986) 939–59.

Portness, L., 'Philosophy & International Affairs', in M. Bradie (ed.), *The Applied Turn in Contemporary Philosophy* (Bowling Green: Bowling Green University, 1983) 97–110.

Ramcharan, B.G., 'New Avenues for the Promotion and Protection of Human Rights: Advisory Services and Technical Assistance', *Human Rights Internet Reporter*, 10 (May–August 1985) 550–60.

Regan, T., 'A Defense of Pacifism', *Canadian Journal of Philosophy*, 2 (1972) 73–86.

Richards, D.A.J., 'Rights, Resistance and the Demands of Self-respect', *Emory Law Journal*, 32 (1983) 405–35.

Ryan, C.C., 'Self-Defense, Pacifism, and the Possibility of Killing', *Ethics*, 93 (April 1983) 508–24.

Sandel, M.J., 'The Procedural Republic and the Unencumbered Self', *Political Theory*, 12 (February 1984) 81–96.

Scanlon, T., 'Contracturalism and Utilitarianism', in A. Sen and B, Williams (eds), *Utilitarianism and Beyond* (Cambridge: Cambridge University Press, 1982) 103–28.

Schelling, T.C., 'What Went Wrong With Arms Control?', *Foreign Affairs*, 64 (Winter 1985/86) 218–33.

Segal, J., 'Income and Development', *QQ – Report from the Center for Philosophy and Public Policy*, 5 (Fall 1985) 9–12.

Shue, H., 'The Burdens of Justice', *Journal of Philosophy*, 80 (October 1983) 600–7.

Shue, H., 'Exporting Hazards', *Ethics*, 91 (July 1981) 579– 606.

Shue, H., 'Foundations for a Balanced U.S. Policy on Human Rights: The Significance of Subsistence Rights', *Center for Philosophy and Public Policy Working Paper HRFP-1* (College Park: Center for Philosophy and Public Policy, 1977).

Shue, H., 'The Geography of Justice: Beitz's Critique of Skepticism and Statism', *Ethics*, 92 (July 1982) 710–19.

Simon, R.L., 'Global Justice and the Authority of States', *Monist*, 66 (October 1983) 556–72.

Simpson, J.R., 'Ethics and Multinational Corporations vis-a-vis Developing Nations', *Journal of Business Ethics*, 1 (August 1982) 227–37.

Simpson, J.R., 'Humanism and Hunger', *Humanist*, 40 (March–April 1980) 41–4.

Simpson, P., 'Just War Theory and the IRA', *Journal of Applied Philosophy*, 3 (March 1986) 73–88.

Singer, P., 'Famine, Affluence, and Morality', *Philosophy & Public Affairs*, 2 (Spring 1972) 229–43.

Smyser, W.R., 'Refugees: A Never-Ending Story', *Foreign Affairs*, 64 (Fall 1985) 154–68.
Sofaer, A.D., 'Terrorism and the Law', *Foreign Affairs*, 64 (Summer 1986) 901–22.
Solarz, S.J., 'When To Intervene', *Foreign Policy*, 63 (Summer 1986) 20–39.
Somerville, J., 'Patriotism and War', *Ethics*, 91 (July 1981) 568–78.
'Terrorism', *QQ – Report from the Center for Philosophy and Public Policy*, 7 (Fall 1987) 1–5.
Thee, M., 'Militarism and Militarization in Contemporary International Relations', in A. Eide and M. Thee (eds), *Problems of Contemporary Militarism* (New York: St. Martin's Press, 1980) 15–35.
Thompson, D., 'Ascribing Responsibility to Advisers in Government', *Ethics*, 93 (April 1983) 546–60.
Thompson, J.J., 'Self-defense and Human Rights', *The Lindley Lectures* (Lawrence: University of Kansas Press, 1976).
Thompson, K.W., 'Science, Morality, and Transnationalism', *Interpretation*, 9 (September 1981) 415–26.
Ungar, S.J. and Vale, P., 'South Africa: Why Constructive Engagement Failed', *Foreign Affairs*, 64 (Winter 1985–86) 234–58.
Urquhart, B., 'International Peace and Security', *Foreign Affairs*, 60 (Fall 1981) 1–16.
Vance, C.R., 'The Human Rights Imperative', *Foreign Policy*, 63 (Summer 1986) 3–19.
VanWyk, J.H., 'Comments on "The Just War"', *Philosophical Papers*, 7 (May 1978) 15–24.
Walzer, M., 'The Moral Standing of States: A Response to Four Critics', *Philosophy & Public Affairs*, 9 (Spring 1980) 209–29.
Walzer, M., 'Response to Lackey', *Ethics*, 92 (April 1982) 547–8.
Wicclair, M.R., 'Rawls and the Principle of Non-intervention', in G.H. Blocker (ed.), *John Rawls' Theory of Social Justice* (Athens: Ohio University Press, 1980) 289–308.
Zacher, L., 'Remarks on Nationalism, Patriotism and Globalism', *Philosophical Forum* (Dekalb), 16 (May 1980) 253–65.

Index